CONTINENT, COAST, OCEAN

Established in 1972, the **Institute of the Malay World and Civilization**, also known by its Malay acronym **ATMA**, of Universiti Kebangsaan Malaysia (UKM), is the only full-fledged academic research institute in Malaysia that concentrates on the study of the "Malay World", the vast maritime-riverine complex of Southeast Asian Studies. The research activities are conducted through an application of the three major academic orientations, namely, disciplinary (sociology, economics, history, etc.), thematic (development studies, communication studies, gender studies, etc.) and area studies (Malay studies, Chinese studies, European studies, etc.)

Research is the Institute's core activity around which other activities are built and generated, organized around five major areas of interest related to the Malay World, namely, (i) theory construction, (ii) language, (iii) literature, (iv) culture, and (v) education. For each area, a senior scholar is designated as the lead scholar-cum-coordinator for all research and related-activities, including securing research funds. ATMA has since 1983 published its journal, *SARI*, which is now available online. In 1999, ATMA constructed a portal on Malay World Studies accessible at www.malaycivilization.com.

The **Institute of Southeast Asian Studies (ISEAS)** was established as an autonomous organization in 1968. It is a regional research centre dedicated to the study of socio-political, security and economic trends and developments in Southeast Asia and its wider geostrategic and economic environment.

The Institute's research programmes are the Regional Economic Studies (RES, including ASEAN and APEC), Regional Strategic and Political Studies (RSPS), and Regional Social and Cultural Studies (RSCS).

ISEAS Publishing, an established academic press, has issued more than 2,000 books and journals. It is the largest scholarly publisher of research about Southeast Asia from within the region. ISEAS Publishing works with many other academic and trade publishers and distributors to disseminate important research and analyses from and about Southeast Asia to the rest of the world.

CONTINENT, COAST, OCEAN

Dynamics of Regionalism in Eastern Asia

EDITED BY

OOI KEE BENG
DING CHOO MING

INSTITUTE OF THE MALAY WORLD AND CIVILIZATION
Malaysia

INSTITUTE OF SOUTHEAST ASIAN STUDIES
Singapore

First published in Singapore in 2007 by
Institute of Southeast Asian Studies (ISEAS)
30 Heng Mui Keng Terrace
Pasir Panjang
Singapore 119614

E-mail: publish@iseas.edu.sg
Website: <http://bookshop.iseas.edu.sg>

jointly with
Institute of the Malay World and Civilization (ATMA)
Universiti Kebangsaan Malaysia
43600 Bangi
Selangor Darul Ehsan, Malaysia
E-mail: pghatma@pkrisc.cc.ukm.my

The responsibility for facts and opinions in this publication rests exclusively with the authors and their interpretations do not necessarily reflect the views or the policy of the publisher or its supporters.

ISEAS Library Cataloguing-in-Publication Data

Continent, coast, ocean : dynamics of regionalism in Eastern Asia / edited by Ooi Kee Beng and Ding Choo Ming.
   1.   Regionalism—East Asia.
   2.   Asian cooperation.
   3.   East Asia—Foreign relations.
   4.   East Asia—Economic integration.
   I.   Ooi Kee Beng, 1955–
   II.   Ding Choo Ming.
   II.   Title: Regionalism in Eastern Asia
DS33.3 C76   2007

ISBN 978-981-230-447-6 (soft cover)
ISBN 978-981-230-448-3 (hard cover)
ISBN 978-981-230-455-1 (PDF)

Typeset by Superskill Graphics Pte Ltd
Printed in Singapore by

CONTENTS

PART THREE: INTER-REGIONALISM AND REGIONALISM

PART FOUR: NEW KNOWLEDGE, NEW PROBLEMS,
NEW SOLUTIONS

FOREWORD

Shamsul A.B.

The Institute of the Malay World and Civilization (ATMA), Universiti Kebangsaan Malaysia, had since April 2000 been holding a series of international conferences involving more than 100 scholars from Southeast Asia and the rest of the world on the theme "The construction of knowledge about the Malay world by Others". They amount to an effort to understand in a systematic manner the Malay world as an analytical abstraction, a body of knowledge, and, more importantly, as a region that had actually mattered greatly to the rest of the world for more than a thousand years. In other words, ATMA has been developing from its own perspective a notion of "regionalism" that is arguably quite different from those articulated by scholars in the fields of international politics and economics. ATMA's notion of regionalism is informed by the broad sweep of socio-historical analysis introduced by *The Annales School* in France, with the late Fernand Braudel as its main contributor.

It must be mentioned that the terms "Others" used in the said ATMA conferences refers to mainly non-English speakers and writers. This angle has been chosen because scholars and researchers in the Malay world, especially in Malaysia, have traditionally been too dependent on English sources when they construct/reconstruct and write/rewrite our history and have had very little input from Indian, Chinese, Arab, Portuguese, Spanish, Dutch, Japanese, French, German, and Nordic sources. Therefore, the series of conferences provides us with a golden opportunity to learn at first hand what others, especially non-English speakers, outside the Malay world have to say about the region and its civilizations in the reports, records and writings of travellers, missionaries, sailors, merchants, scientists, scholars, administrators, and the like who visited or stayed in the Malay world.

The overall result has been an exhilarating one for ATMA, to say the least.

We held two conferences involving the Chinese contribution, with participants both from the People's Republic of China (PRC) and the expansive global Chinese diaspora: first, on "Chinese scholarship and the Malay world", held in mid-September 2002 (published as *Chinese Studies of the Malay World*) and, second, on "Building on Our Past and Investing in Our Future: An International Seminar on Multidisciplinary Discourse" held on 16–17 February 2004.

This book is the product of the second conference, which was a pioneering attempt by ATMA to deal with matters beyond the field of Malay world studies but not unrelated to it. It was also a chance to bring together scholars not only from the field of Malay world studies but also international politics and economics to brainstorm on whether the notion of regionalism could be expanded beyond the current interests of political analysts and economic advisers.

I think this we managed to do very well. The chapters in this book are a record of our endeavour, and in the end, it is the reader who must decide on the level of success achieved.

Professor Shamsul A.B.
Director, ATMA,
Universiti Kebangsaan Malaysia

Bangi, 10 January 2007

THE CONTRIBUTORS

Arujunan Narayanan is a Lecturer attached to the Programme of Strategic and International Relations, Department of Political Science, Universiti Kebangsaan Malaysia. He received his Ph.D. from the Law Department, University of Wales, Aberystwyth (UK) in 2000. His research interests include military history, war crimes, human rights, international law as well as ethics and morality. His major publications include "Japanese War Crimes and Allied War Crime Trials in Borneo during World War II" (2003), and "Japanese Atrocities and British War Crimes Trials in Malacca after World War II" in *Strategy: Journal of Strategic Studies and International Relations* (2003).

Chen Yu-Hsi is a Professor at the Department of Religious Studies. Fu Guang University, Taiwan. His research interests include political economy, international political economy, psychology of religion.

Ding Choo Ming is Senior Research Fellow at the Institute of the Malay World and Civilization, Universiti Kebangsaan Malaysia. Besides extensively publishing articles on information retrieval, Malay literature and Malay manuscripts in journals, he has written many books including *Raja Aisyah Sulaiman: Pengarang Ulung Wanita Melayu* (2000) and *Kajian Manuskrip Melayu: Masalah, Kritikan dan Cadangan* (2003). He is also a key member of the term developing the portal on Malay World Studies available at <www.malaycivilization.com> and <www.atma.ukm.my>.

Hsu Chieh-Lin is a Professor at the Department of Political Science, Fu Guang University, Taiwan. His research interests are Japanese Politics and Policy, Sino-Japanese Relationship, Modern Political History of Taiwan.

K. S. Nathan is Senior Fellow at the Institute of Southeast Asian Studies, Singapore. He obtained his Ph.D. in International Relations from Claremont Graduate University in California, USA in 1975. His teaching, research and publications concern big power relations in the Asian-Pacific region, ASEAN regionalism, and Malaysian politics, security and foreign policy. His publications include *India and ASEAN: the Growing Partnership for the 21st Century* (2000), *The European Union, United States and ASEAN: Challenges and Prospects for Cooperative Engagement in the 21st Century* (2002).

Khoo Kay Kim is Professor Emeritus, Department of History, Faculty of Arts and Social Science, University of Malaya. His research interests are in Malaysian history and politics. To date, he has published 15 books including *Seeking Alternative Perspectives of Southeast Asia* and the *Malay-Muslim Community of Singapore (1819–1965)*.

Klaus C. Hsu is Professor at the Department of Political Science, Fu Guang University, His research interests include comparative politics, public administration and policy, and European governments. His books include *Political Relationship between Taiwan and European Countries* (1980); *The Vocational Schooling of the Secondary Level II of the Federal Republic of Germany* (1981); *Vocational Training Law of the Republic of Austria* (1991, translated from the German), and *The Governments and Politics of European Countries* (1997).

Mohamad Abu Bakar is Professor at the Department of International and Strategic Studies, Faculty of Art and Social Studies, University of Malaya. He lectures and researches on contemporary Islam, Malaysian foreign policy, Malay politics and the philosophy of history. Some of his writings have been translated into Indonesian, Japanese, Spanish and Tagalog. His works on Islam include a book in Malay, *Penghayatan Sebuah Ideal* (1987), and his articles include "Islam, Civil and Society and Ethnic Relations in Malaysia" in *Islam and Civil Society in Southeast Asia*, edited by Nakamura et al. Singapore: ISEAS, 2001, "Contemporary Islam Challenges of Continuity", to appear in *Asian Islam in the 21st Century*, edited by John Esposito.

Narayanan Ganesan, is Professor of Southeast Asian Politics at the Hiroshima Peace Institute, Hiroshima City University, Japan. He lectures and researches on peace and security as well as contemporary politics and foreign policy in Southeast Asia. He earned his Ph.D. from Northern Illinois University. In

2002, he was appointed to the international network and panel of assessors for grant applications in the Global Security and Cooperation Program of the Social Science Research Council in New York.

Ooi Kee Beng is a Fellow at Singapore's Institute of Southeast Asian Studies (ISEAS), where he coordinates its Malaysia Study Programme. His Ph.D. is in Sinology, received from Stockholm University. His books include *The Reluctant Politician: Tun Dr Ismail and His Time* (2006), *Chinese Strategists: Beyond Sun Zi's Art of War* (2006), *Era of Transition — Malaysia after Mahathir* (2006); *The State and its* Changdao: *Sufficient Discursive Commonality in Nation Renewal, with Malaysia as Case Study* (2001).

Shamsul A. B. is Professor of Social Anthropology and currently Director of the Institute of the Malay World and Civilization and Director of the Institute of Occidental Studies, Universiti Kebangsaan Malaysia. He researches, lectures and writes intensively on politics, culture and economic development, with an empirical focus on Southeast Asia. His best-known book is *From British to Bumiputera Role* (1996), a phenomenology of class relations in a Malay rural community.

Sun Yi-ching, Assistant Professor of Political Science, is also the Director of Survey Research Center, Fu Guang University, Taiwan. He received his Ph.D. degree from University of Texas at Austin, specializing in International Relations, Comparative Politics, and Research Methodology. His current research focuses on international conflict, American foreign policy, and sampling methods. He edited two books on the topic of the interaction between information technology and politics, published in 2004 and 2006.

Tham Siew Yean obtained her Ph.D. from University of Rochester, USA, specializing in international trade. She is Professor in International Trade at the Institute of Malaysia and International Studies (IKMAS), Universiti Kebangsaan Malaysia. She has researched and written extensively on issues pertaining to foreign direct investment, productivity, trade competitiveness, regional trade and regional groupings, from the Malaysian perspective. She also served as consultant for agencies such as ESCAP in the United Nations, Asian Development Bank and the National Productivity Corporation in Malaysia, and was a member of the Joint Study Team for the ASEAN-China Free Trade Area and the Malaysia-Japan Closer Economic Partnership.

INTRODUCTION

Ooi Kee Beng and Ding Choo Ming

HISTORICAL CONDITIONS OF REGIONALISM IN EASTERN ASIA

Research on East and Southeast Asia generally follows the common practice of focusing on nation states. Where this proves unsatisfactory (and this happens increasingly often), scholars resort to frameworks such as regional studies or "area studies" as alternatives, or phrase issues that are relevant to geographic regions beyond national boundaries. Where East Asia is concerned, national borders have remained more useful as boundaries for academic disciplines than they have been where Southeast Asia is concerned.[1]

The geo-political "leftover" that is Southeast Asia consists of a political and cultural plethora beyond what one would expect, given its relatively small land surface. The predominantly maritime nature of human contacts in the region, especially in the south, is the main reason for this. Southeast Asian studies, therefore, is a regional discipline by nature, where the region's national policies must necessarily consider inter-cultural dynamics throughout maritime Asia from India to Japan. In fact, "culture" as understood in Southeast Asia assumes inter-cultural dynamics and hybridity to a larger extent than in continental regions such as East Asia.

Historical traditions in East Asia, influenced as strongly as they were by the bureaucratic class, have generally been about domestic order and barbarian invasions. This prolonged prejudice has allowed the history and reality of inter-state trade and communication through the ages to be overshadowed by central perspectives. However, wide-ranging extra-political factors were always significant, and exerted an influence that cannot be denied. In the case of China, the centre of its culture and its economy had been moving steadily southwards throughout the centuries under pressure from northern peoples pushing across porous boundaries. The inter-cultural exchanges involved and how they have in fact impacted on Chinese civilization and politics are not widely known. This southward movement was to an extent slowed in the fourteenth century by the usurping third monarch of the Ming Dynasty (1368–1644), the Yongle Emperor (reign period 1403–24), when he moved the imperial capital, which had shown a tendency to shift eastwards and southwards since the Tang Dynasty (618–907), if not already during the Later Han (25–220), to his own power base in Beijing, one of the traditional capitals of non-Chinese dynasties in the north, including the Yuan Mongols. While the Yongle Emperor exercised extraordinary authority and curiosity throughout his realm and beyond — sending seven gigantic naval expeditions under Admiral Zheng He (1371–1435) to the southern seas all the way to eastern Africa — the emperors who came after him were more defensive and perhaps more realistic, and pursued policies that in contrast introverted the Ming. This move northward and inward did not, however, change the fact that the cultural and economic focus continued its historical movement southwards into richer, gentler and safer lands.

When the Manchus invaded the empire in 1644, Ming loyalists fled south, making the presence of Chinese culture all the more obvious in warmer climes. Taiwan was wrested in the process from the Dutch in 1661 by Koxinga (Zheng Chenggong, or Guoxingye, "the guardian of the royal surname") and his followers, only to be lost to the unstoppable northerners. The Manchurian Qing Dynasty enthroned itself in Beijing, and seeing the need to exercise control through the orthodoxy of Song Confucianism, they turned expressly conservative in their worldview, re-orientating the empire northwards and territorially creating the largest version of the Chinese Empire ever known. Nevertheless, contacts between coastal China and lands across the South China Sea continued unabatedly, as borne out by the reports of eighteenth century Chinese traveller-scholars such as Cheng Xunwo, Wang Dahai and Chen Hongzhao.

Merchants as a rule were not in the habit of recording their secrets and their various activities for posterity. Nevertheless, the strong presence of East Asian emissary and trading vessels, and of Chinese colonies throughout Southeast Asia, is undisputed and boasts a long history, gaining mention in a large number of contemporary documents.[2] It is this huge maritime world stretching from Japan to Indonesia, with its pre-modern and modern history of lingual, cultural and genetic hybridity, and of trade, migration, colonialism, invasion, piracy, conquest and warfare, that form the backdrop for the subjects discussed in this present book.

The coming of the British and other Europeans brought a new military and economic reality to the Pacific Ocean, which the Manchu regime could not deny in the long run. Beijing's loss of effective control, in quick succession, over Hong Kong, the treaty ports and coastline, and then northernmost Vietnam and Tibet, caught its strategists and policy-makers wrong-footed. A series of catastrophic revolts throughout the nineteenth century in large areas of southern and eastern China left most of the economy in ruins, and subjected the population to great suffering.

The entry of the Japanese into international colonialism through the first Sino-Japanese War of 1894–95 earned these once isolationistic neighbours control over Taiwan, Liuqiu (Ryukyu), Korea, Shandong Province, and then Manchuria itself by 1931.

As Japan declared war on China in 1937, and on the allied European powers in 1941, the military impetus for synthesizing the modern history of East and Southeast Asia switched from European to Japanese hands. Japan's merciless war against China, and its occupation of European colonies in the region left deep wounds whose scabs still easily peel off to renew bleeding at the slightest touch. These open sores pose a stubborn hindrance to warm relations between governments and peoples throughout the region.

The fall of Imperial Japan in 1945 started a staggered regaining of most of what had been Qing territory by the central Chinese government. Interestingly, the Chinese capital moved north again to Beijing after the communists took power in 1949, from the Kuomintang's peace-time capital of Nanjing, and its war-time capital of Chongqing. This marked a paradoxical return to the afore-mentioned pre-1840 continental orientation in ideology, despite the globalistic pretensions of Marxist thought. The Kuomintang government, in turn, moved out to sea, so to speak, and found refuge for itself and China's imperial treasures on the newly retrieved Japanese colony of Taiwan.

The destruction of Japanese colonial ambitions turned out to be the death knell of European colonialism as well. Jealously guarded colonial turfs turned into nation states all throughout East and Southeast Asia, some through peaceful means as in British Malaya, and others through decimating conflicts as in Vietnam. Of all the territories in East and Southeast Asia, only Thailand and inland China emerged from the colonial era without experiencing direct external control.

With the withdrawal of foreign troops from the region, excepting American troops at special bases, eastern Asia would have been free to quickly forge new patterns of international relations if it were not for the extremism of the Cold War that lasted for forty years. It was only with the crumbling of the Berlin Wall in 1989 and the demise of the Soviet Union thereafter that the frozen international relations within eastern Asia could start to thaw.

Over the following sixteen years, improvements in economics and in political ties were staggering. Deng Xiaoping's reforms in China proved a great success in the creation of wealth within China, and in the warming of relations in the region as a whole. The rebuilding of old and troubled relationships was, however, strongly configured by the disparate agendas of the many new national regimes. Trading and security trends were moving inexorably towards regionalism, encouraging nation states to conflate national goals with regional growth.

In Southeast Asia, the Association of Southeast Asian Nations (ASEAN) — founded on 8 August 1967 by Indonesia, Malaysia, the Philippines, Singapore, Thailand — increased in relevance as it expanded to include all the states west of India and south of China, presently excepting only the freshly formed East Timor. It promises to provide these countries with sufficient clout in the future in negotiations with the giants to the north and the west. Be it ASEAN+1 or ASEAN+1+1, ASEAN+3 or ASEAN+3+3 — the last of which is what the East Asian Summit held in Kuala Lumpur in December 2005 amounted to — the regional strategic tendency is quite clear.

For diplomatic and other reasons, China, despite its rising strength, has allowed ASEAN to retain the initiative. Nevertheless, since it perceives its interests to be best served by the continuous improvement of trading ties with resource-rich neighbours in the region, it is difficult for it to hide its impatience.

China's growth has largely been in the coastal areas, and the importance of this for the further development of regional economic integration will be hard to under-estimate. However, just when global international relations never looked better — leading even to populist books being published about the end of ideological differences and thus of history itself — grievances that had long been denied airtime, political consideration and academic acknowledgement burst onto TV monitors with a vengeance on 11 September 2001, as hijacked passenger planes attacked New York and Washington. History was resurrected from the dead, as a virulent form of terrorism appeared on the scene. The attacks led to highly controversial responses from the United States, and the moral support it enjoyed after 9/11 was quickly dissipated as its military was sent in retaliation to invade poverty-stricken Muslim countries.

In eastern Asia, terrorism and Islamic extremism threw a spanner into the machinery of proud economies still recovering from the financial crisis of 1997–98. The Bali, the Jakarta J.W. Marriott Hotel and Jakarta Australian Embassy bombings followed, leaving governments dazed. Not only did these lead to calls for action against terrorist suspects, security cooperation between nations was also encouraged, such as the agreement between Indonesia, Malaysia and Singapore to coordinate patrols along the Straits of Malacca. The need for mutual defence has further heightened awareness among politicians that regional issues are as important as domestic squabbles. Hatchets will have to be buried and extenuating circumstances in historical wars will have to be re-circulated for improving intra-regional relations.

The *tsunami* disaster that struck on 26 December 2004 left 300,000 individuals dead all along the Indian Ocean coastline. It was now even more evident to governments and world organizations that jealously guarded national borders could be a big hindrance in times of emergency.

Border tensions have been diminishing at some points but growing at others, as exemplified by the warming of relations between Malaysia and Singapore on the one hand, and the worsening of the situation in southern Thailand and in the Sulawesi Sea on the other. In East Asia, the question of Taiwan remains a stubborn problem, although some would contend that it is a diminishing, mistrust between China and Japan — perhaps also diminishing — continues despite strong economic ties, while North Korea's isolationism in Northeast Asia keeps its hold on the world's attention. The nuclear test that Pyongyang managed to carry out in October 2006 shook its closest neighbours and the United States. China is expected to be much more proactive in the near future in influencing North Korea's relationship with the rest of the world.

Conflicts from the past, whether from the colonial period, World War II or the Cold War, linger on in very clear and uncomfortable ways. This multi-faceted heritage poses challenges to regionalism in eastern Asia that are just as hard to meet, as national issues of inter-ethnic relations, good governance and economic development are.

Spurred by the awareness that the past must continuously be re-thought if present ills are to be resolved, an uncommon joint initiative was taken by Malaysia's Institute of the Malay World and Civilization (ATMA) of Universiti Kebangsaan Malaysia (UKM) and Taiwan's Fu Guang University, to organize a forum for discussing new ways of healing old wounds, studying old conflicts and dissolving old contradictions. On 16–17 February 2004, "Building on Our Past and Investing in Our Future: An International Seminar on Multi-disciplinary Discourse" was held at UKM in Bangi, Selangor. The subjects were varied, as one would expect. In the end, eleven articles that held relevance to inter-regional relations were chosen to form this present volume. The organizers hope that the others will be printed in other contexts in the near future.

Regional denotations may present a problem to the casual reader, and it should be stated at the outset that while some authors use the terms "East Asia" and "Southeast Asia" to distinguish between two clearly separated regions of Asia, there is a current trend, to subsume Southeast Asia under "East Asia". In other cases, this combined region is merely called "eastern Asia". We judge it better to allow the individual authors to denote as they wish, since it is often obvious within their contexts what the terms actually mean. "Asia" is generally used to denote the landmass east of Europe, while Asia Pacific connotes the lands and coastlines east, west and south of the Pacific Ocean.

This book is divided into four separate sections. The first deals with the impact of Japanese modernization since the Meiji Restoration (1868–1912) on the European colonial enterprise throughout eastern Asia, the destruction of the Qing, and the subsequent struggles of China's Republican period. Hsu Chieh-Lin takes us through the history of Japanese diplomacy during the modern era, showing us in the process that the Japanese Occupation of most of eastern Asia was not a determined course of events. Internal conflicts in Japan during the crucial period before the world wars were symptomatically expressed through different trends of diplomacy. After a string of tragedies were inflicted on the whole region by the adoption of a "Pan-Asian" diplomacy in Japan, a conciliatory and "multi-directional Shidehara diplomacy" managed to regain favour, and continues to inspire Japanese foreign relations to this day.

In Arujunan Narayanan's chapter, the highly-charged issue of Japanese guilt is broached. To Chinese, Koreans and many Southeast Asians, the war against the Japanese still conjure memories of atrocities that seek redress. This ranks alongside Taiwanese independence, and North Korean isolationism as one of the major hurdles to harmonious relations in eastern Asia. Happily, time does heal. We are otherwise surely doomed. Given the speed at which the global economy demands adjustments at all levels of socio-economic and political life, considerations about present paths must depend less and less on memories. As Narayanan reminds us, "there is no permanent enemy or friend in international relations but only permanent interests".

Undeniably, memories of Japanese atrocities will remain among the victims and their loved ones. Some may try to keep the memories alive as a heritage of history or for political advantage. However, time heals, and a new generation that did not experience the atrocities will not give as much importance to them as the generation that experienced them had done. For the young, moving ahead is more important than thinking about matters relating to a war that occurred many decades ago.

Furthermore, the economic influence that Japan exercises over the whole region, China notwithstanding, has helped to soften attitudes about past tragedies.

The second section of this book considers the vital relation between economics and regional integration. Through a close study of the Malaysian case, Tham Siew-Yean reviews issues raised in the aftermath of the Asian Financial Crisis of 1997–98. Different schools have debated how the crisis could have taken place at all. Was the East Asian development model a myth? Tham suggests that "the diversity of experience in the subject of government intervention makes the synthesizing of these experiences into a single East Asian model over-simplistic". Two schools of thought are discernible, the first of which considers "structural imbalances and policy distortions" as the culprits, contending that despite having earlier aided the success of the East Asian economies, these nonetheless contributed in the end to their fall. Tham finds no support for this view. The second school fingers free capital flows and investor panic as the cause of the crisis. Tham concludes that the miracle did occur, that the tigers were no myth, and that growth has but been temporarily hampered.

However, the playing field is found to have changed after the smoke cleared. According to Tham, the Malaysian government, for example, would do well to concentrate on productivity-driven growth, attracting foreign investments, and reducing reliance on protective measures for chosen branches, such as the automobile industry. Above all, enhanced use of "functional interventions such as sound macro-economic management, prudent fiscal policies and investment in infrastructure and human capital" is very much needed.

In Chen Yu-Hsi's analysis of the crisis, the lesson to be learned is that two factors continue to carry considerable impact on the region's economies — the processes of globalization, and the rapid development of information technology. Given this insight, a new paradigm for studying economic processes in eastern Asia is required. What had been happening before the crisis was that a paradigm of "developmentalism", encouraged by a modernist disdain for traditional values, had in effect been challenged by economic growth fashionably ascribed to Confucian or Asian values, and backed by state intervention. This dualism lost most of its relevance after the crisis, according to Chen, and what is needed now is the courage to construct a new paradigm based on the stunning growth and impact of information technologies.

The third section is provocatively entitled "Inter-regionalism and Regionalism" to draw attention to the fact that regions have flexible boundaries. National borders are porous in all sorts of ways — economic, political, cultural or military. Furthermore, multilateralism always exists alongside bilateralism, and bilateralism very often transcends the borders of formal regional bodies. As mentioned earlier, border conflicts still exist throughout the region, and whether or not we brand them leftovers of colonialism or the Cold War, or creations of the nation-state ideology, they are in no hurry to disappear. Thus, regional and inter-regional relations must continue to involve the acquisition of arms and the securing of alliances. Interestingly, how weapons are acquired varies over time, and is a good indicator of changes in the security situation. This is what is studied in Sun Yi-ching's chapter. The cogency of the logic used in Sun's analysis regarding the ratio between arms sale and arms aid from the United States to an ally becomes more apparent the more it is understood.

Studies of regional integration cannot avoid a look at the case of Europe. Surely, the processes started immediately after World War II in Europe to break the karmic circle of wars has succeeded beyond the wildest dreams of its creators. Although one should exercise caution when comparing different countries, let alone continents, with one another, lessons can be learned from the experience of others. In analysing the European Union, Klaus C. Hsu finds that it has succeeded extremely well, having delivered "half a century of stability, peace and prosperity". Political and economic integration has advanced to such a level that Europe now has a single currency — presently excepting those of Britain, Denmark and Sweden — and its politics influences the daily life of people throughout the continent. However, the next major issue that may lead to deep contentions is the existent cultural diversity, now intensified by the many new and poorer members from Eastern Europe, as well as by immigration. "In fact, the economic and political progress of the 1970s made it painfully clear to EU member states that a lot has yet to be done in the field of culture."

The compulsion to compare the EU and ASEAN is further strengthened by the fact that the two have been holding official discussion forums at venues in both Europe and Southeast Asia for quite a number of years. While the EU has expanded to include countries from the former Soviet Union, ASEAN members have found it expedient to negotiate sometimes individually and sometimes as a single unit with its giant neighbours to the north and the west. Given ASEAN's extremely low level of integration, there is a tension between the need for ASEAN integration and bilateral relations fostered by individual member countries with non-member countries. There is in essence no consensus as to how tightly knit the organization is to become. Hsu notes that unlike the EU case, ASEAN forums continue to be hampered by "the continuing importance attributed to the national interests of individual member states, an apparent inability to manage their internal environment, and the need to cope with structural alignments previously associated with bipolarity in international relations".

In his contribution, Khoo Kay Kim reminds us that "Southeast Asia–East Asia relations are not thoroughly studied and thus tend to be understood mainly in economic terms". This is worth keeping in mind. Undeniably, there is a general propensity to allow economic explanations to fill knowledge gaps, especially when complicated matters such as inter-cultural influences occurring outside the official purview are concerned. Given the fact that inter-state and inter-people contacts — cultural, academic, religious or philosophical — have or will quickly develop economic ramifications, or that economic activities will soon lead to cultural exchanges, and furthermore given that the speed of change forces stronger reliance on quantitative rather than qualitative information, inter-regional and intra-regional phenomena will continue to be depicted through statistics, tables and graphs.

Regionalism and East Asia–Southeast Asia relations cannot dismiss the central and historical role played by China and the Chinese. Ming support for the kingdom of Melaka in the fifteenth century was as important to the status and commercial designs of the latter as good relations with Beijing today is to the future of Southeast Asian nation states. No doubt, the reasons for this can be stated in economic terms. However, the long tradition of Chinese migration to, and trade with, the Southeast Asian region has left a Chinese imprint that extends beyond economics. All Southeast Asian nation states have Chinese communities whose impact on the cultural landscape has been considerable. This is regardless of the level of cultural assimilation these communities have experienced. The long history of Chinese commerce and settlement in Southeast Asia, along with the nature of maritime trade, has configured inter-ethnic relations and integrated ethnic groups in unique ways. Khoo contends that the plural society common to the region, popularly understood as a colonial device, was in fact a locally favoured solution:

> The British were not the first to encourage Chinese migration to Malaya and although they brought in the Indians and Jaffnese to work in both the private and public sectors, they were not responsible for the numerous cultural and ethnic associations that multiplied during the late 19th and early 20th century. [...] It would be more accurate to say that Malaya's plural society existed – and continues to exist — because the various ethnic groups desired it.

The last section consists of essays suggesting strategies for change in the emergent regional bodies. While decolonization is often studied as a process within nation states, it is nevertheless true that the end of colonialism profoundly altered the power and trade balance as well as the epistemic structure of the region. This present book and the subjects discussed within it are a function of that tumultuous change. Recently initiated projects at the Institute of the Malay World and Civilization (ATMA) offer exciting examples of the changing infrastructure for the construction of knowledge about eastern Asia. Shamsul A.B., the director of the institute, and one of the minds behind the conference for which these papers were produced, explains in his article the rationale behind the databases his institute has been creating, and also the series of conferences it has been organizing. He also takes issue with Khoo Kay Kim's understanding of a plural society, and suggests that a plurality–plural society continuum is a more valid and powerful device for studying and comparing societies in the region. Shamsul postulates that the social plurality of the pre-colonial period was indeed transformed into coercive and divisive networks of plural societies, a process that today shows itself in the fact that scholars of pre-colonial–Southeast Asia find it necessary to abandon methodologies that they otherwise use when studying the modern period. This occurs because the empirical material requires it:

> Whether or not an orientalist approach is employed, one cannot avoid writing about that period within a plurality framework, and one cannot ignore the region's diversity and traditions. In other words, this social reality to a large extent configures analytical frameworks for the study of that period.

In recent years, ATMA had essentially changed its own academic discipline. From the traditional study of the "Malay *ethnie*", the conceptual nucleus has been switched to the more promising and extroverted "Malay World". Not only does this strategy dismiss nationalistic tendencies, it also gives due attention to the maritime nature of the region and the influence this has had on inter-cultural contacts of all kinds. Projects generated by this intended paradigmatic shift include a formidable series of international conferences about "The Construction of the Malay World by Others", where the comparison of knowledge construction in different scholarly traditions about one and the same region provides insights not only about the region as such but about the very workings of knowledge creation about the region. Another is the collection of databases about the Malay World that ATMA keeps freely available on the Internet <www.malaycivilization.com>.

Just as security along the Silk Route was a major concern for all Chinese emperors, and just as the safety of commercial shipping wrinkled the brows of rulers throughout ancient Southeast Asia, safeguarding the regional infrastructure for commercial and other activities throughout eastern Asia is essential to the welfare of all the countries in the region. This is a Herculean task indeed. Regional growth is highly dependent on the reliability of regional transport and communication networks, and on a powerful regional "security architecture". K.S. Nathan discusses in his chapter the challenges that must be faced by all eastern Asian regimes, both where traditional and non-traditional security issues are concerned. Terrorism is but one of many critical questions they have to deal with. "Piracy, illegal immigration, drugs, religious militancy and environmental pollution" are among some of the non-traditional threats given further currency by globalization, and by the multilateral push for stronger regionalism. Nevertheless, concerns about terrorism are strong, drawing relations with the United States into the picture and adding salience and significance to old tensions within and between nations.

> The answer obviously lies in constructing shared perceptions of a world order in which cultural pluralism encourages multilateral approaches that emphasize not only the military component in combating global terror, but also the political, social, and economic and diplomatic strategies required to harmonize local, national, regional, and global identities.

The U.S.-led fight against terrorism, though recently initiated, has strongly influenced inter-cultural relations and perceptions throughout the region. Mohamad Abu Bakar considers the uncomfortable fact that "due to the lack of nuanced information about Islam, many non-Muslims have become uncomfortable with the Muslims in their midst". Be that as it may, he states, the point must be accepted that "Islam is here to stay". Strategies for the future must recognize this and in the process realize Islam's "commitment to development" and its "art of improvisation". He is optimistic that this is forthcoming. As he puts it,

> Since Muslims and non-Muslims share certain common values, a convergence of cultures is not impossible. With or without the adoption of Western-style democracy and the operation of a market economy, moral principles governing human relations in Asia must remain in place. Respect for authority, the promotion of civil society, and the importance of the family, are some of the perennial concerns of all Asians.

Without a doubt, there is a long list of regional tensions that needs ironing out over the coming decades. Judging from the arguments and perspectives advanced in this book, solutions that rely on multilateral cooperation appear the way to go. It is hoped that the finer points of academic reasoning contained in this volume will not be ignored by politicians and administrators, but will instead influence their decisions for the better.

Notes

[1]   See the anthology *Southeast Asian Studies: Pacific Perspectives*, edited by Anthony Reid, Arizona State University, USA, 2003.

[2]   See *Chinese Studies of the Malay World. A Comparative Approach*, edited by Ding Choo Ming and Ooi Kee Beng, Eastern Universities Press, Marshall Cavendish, Singapore, 2003, and Anthony Reid, *Southeast Asia in the Age of Commerce 1450–1680, Volume Two: Expansion and Crisis*, New Haven and London: Yale University Press, 1988.

PART ONE

Putting Japanese Imperial History to Rest

.

1

THE SUCCESS OF JAPAN'S MULTI-DIRECTIONAL DIPLOMACY IN MODERN TIMES

Hsu Chieh-Lin

PART I

Japan's diplomacy of international conciliation can be traced back to the latter years of the Shogunate. Japanese cooperation with Western Powers began in 1853 when, under the threat of Commodore Perry's "Black Ships", Japan concluded unequal treaties with the United States. The Treaty of Kanawa was signed in 1854, to be followed by the U.S.-Japanese Commercial Treaty in 1858. It also concluded unequal treaties with Holland, Britain, Russia, France, Portugal, Germany, Sweden, Belgium, Italy and Denmark.

Although these treaties were qualified by terms such as "good-will" or "commercial", their actual contents concerned: (1) opening ports for trade; (2) extra-territorial jurisdiction; (3) negotiating a customs-tax rate; and (4) granting of most favoured nation status, etc. These very treaties marked the beginning of the so-called "humiliation diplomacy". The Meiji restoration was carried out under the concept of "*Sonno Joyi*" (Reverence for the emperor and expulsion of the barbarians). Nevertheless, the Meiji government was wont to take over the unequal treaties, signed by the Bakufu in submission to the foreigners.

It is said that the representatives of Britain and France were very active in pursuing economic interests in Japan behind the scenes of the Meiji restoration.

British envoy Harry Smith Parkes supported Satsuma-Choshu in overthrowing the Bakufu, while French envoy Leon Roches stood by the Tokugawa Shogunate.[1] Thus, it may be said, the outcome of the Meiji restoration was Britain's diplomatic victory over France. Accordingly, Japan was in a position to appease Britain after the Meiji restoration. In 1871, Iwakura Tomomi was selected to head a special mission composed of more than one hundred powerful Meiji government officials including Kido Koin, Okubo Toshimichi, and Ito Hirobumi, to mention but a few. Their aim was to have negotiations with the Western powers concerning the revision of the unequal treaties.

However, Iwakura's group was disappointed by the cold reaction of the Western powers to their treaty revision proposals. They had no choice but to alter the purpose of their mission and embark upon a tour of America and Europe to study Western civilization. Iwakura and his companions came to realize that Japan had lots to learn about *bunmei kaika* (civilization enlightenment) and *fukoku kyohei* (rich country, strong army) before she could rank among the Western powers.

In the meantime, the caretaker government of *Sangi* (Councillors) Saigo Takamori and Itagaki Taisuke, etc., had taken charge and passed a resolution calling for Japanese subjugation of Korea for the purpose of extending Japanese influence. Dajo-daijin (Prime Minister) Sanjo Sanetomi, worried by this, called for the return of Iwakura's mission. The mission thus ended its tour of the West and hurried back to Japan. The members of the Iwakura mission were inspired by what they had seen abroad. They firmly asserted that reforms in domestic administration, rather than military expeditions abroad, were Japan's first priority. Therefore, Iwakura's group vehemently opposed military expansion into Korea on the grounds that it would lead to Russo-Japanese hostilities should Japan subsequently fail to secure international conciliation. Furthermore, they doubted Japan's capability to win a war against Russia. In the event, the group succeeded in getting the decision to invade Korea shelved. This turn of events led to the resignation of both Saigo and Itagaki. Saigo returned to his home, Satsuma, and committed *harakiri* after an unsuccessful rebellion in 1877. Itagaki and his supporters, on the other hand, formed the first political party in Japan, the *Aikokuto* [Patriotic Party], in order to continue their attack on "*hambatsu seifu*" [clan government]. Later, the name of the party was changed to *Jiyuto* [Liberal Party] because the party advocated "*jiyu minken*" [liberty and civil rights]. The Liberal Party continued to denounce the "government of oligarchs" and its "humiliation diplomacy".

The officials who assigned top priority to the issue of domestic administration rather than military expansion into Korea did so not because of heartfelt goodwill towards their neighbours. In the midst of the Saga riots that broke out after the defeat of the Korea expansionists, the Meiji government nevertheless launched its first foreign expedition, an assault on Taiwan. The government initiated this expedition in the hope of quelling internal rebellion by diverting public attention to external expansion. As it turned out, the Formosan expedition was Japan's first diplomatic triumph ever. Foreign Minister Terajima Munenori took over the "Taiwan expedition diplomacy" of his predecessor, Soejima Taneomi. Terajima hired General Le Gendre, a former U.S. consular agent in Amoy, to draft a secret plan for the occupation of eastern Taiwan.[2] However, the Chinese government somehow got wind of the plot and objected bitterly.

In response to China's protests, British envoy Harry S. Parkes, and American envoy, John A. Bingham, along with envoys from several other countries, issued a neutrality warning to Japan in an effort to stop the expedition.[3] This warning by the Western powers, however, was to no avail. Saigo Tsugumichi, commander of the Taiwan expeditionary force, was contemptuous of his government's docile submission to the threat of Western intervention and consequently deployed troops on his own initiative, insisting that he revered the Imperial rescript and this transcended his duty to obey orders given by Premier Sanjo. After the fact, the government was left with no choice but to confirm Saigo's action.

The Japanese belief that the occupation of Taiwan would be less expensive than expansion into Korea, and would lead to less international complications, was rudely shattered after the assault on Taiwan. In the face of diplomatic defiance by the Chinese government, Okubo Toshimichi was appointed minister plenipotentiary and sent to Peking to negotiate. At the same time, the Japanese government was actively preparing for war in case negotiations failed. On 9 July 1874, the cabinet passed resolutions for the "dispatch of troops abroad" and "procedures for the proclamation of war"[4] and led national opinion in support of the war. After Okubo arrived in Peking, he firmly refused the Ching government's request for the withdrawal of Japanese troops from Taiwan, and devoted himself to obtaining the understanding of the British, French and other foreign diplomats in China. Thus, in waiting for international opinion to shift in favour of Japan while making only slight concessions to the Ching government regarding the reparation of military expenses through the mediation of British Minister Wade, Okubo won a diplomatic victory.[5]

After assessing Japan's strength at that time, Okubo hoped for peaceful negotiations. He therefore waited until national opinion had shifted in favour of war against China and the military had strengthened its armaments, before undertaking diplomatic negotiations. The success of Okubo's "Taiwan expedition diplomacy" made the world powers marvel at the improvement in Japan's diplomatic skills. In fact, it even led the Ching government tacitly to permit Japanese Occupation of the Ryukyus. The Kianghwa Island Incident of August 1875 was launched under a tacit scheme thought up by the assistant secretary of the navy, Kawamura Jungi, and the captain of the *Unyo-kan*, Inoue Ryokei. In January of 1876, Japan dispatched Ambassador Extraordinary and Plenipotentiary Kurota Kiyotaka and Vice-Minister Inoue Kaoru, and diplomatic negotiations began under the intimidating presence of Japanese warships. The "Japanese-Korean Friendship Treaty" was concluded on 16 February. The so-called "Kianghwa Treaty" was an unequal treaty that demanded the open ports of Fusan, Yuensan (Wonsan) and Jenchuan (Chemulpo), extra-territoriality, and trade privileges. In August, the "Exchange Document Concerning the Elimination of Corrupt Trade Practices in Korea" was drawn up, granting Japan the special privilege of exemption from import and export customs tariffs.[6] These Japanese diplomatic moves were reminiscent of the process surrounding Commodore Perry's "Black Ships", and were thus an imitation of the methods used by America to force Japan to sign unequal treaties, and that compelled Korea to open the country to foreign intercourse. From this time on, acts of aggression against weak Asian neighbours and conciliation with Western powers became the fundamental principle of Japanese foreign policy.

Inoue Kaoru assumed a haughty posture with regard to Korea, but adopted a humble attitude when dealing with Western powers, and thus promoted a courteous "Europeanization diplomacy". Inoue, who became foreign minister in 1880, built the notorious Western-style *Rokumei-kan*. The *Rokumei-kan* cost 180,000 yen to construct and occupied an area of 410 *tsubo* (1 *tsubo* = 3,306 square metres). In order to learn Western etiquette, high society Japanese organized banquets, balls, garden parties, etc. there.[7] The ostensible purpose of all these activities was to make Westerners aware of how civilized Japan was, with the hope that this would be conducive to treaty revisions. Inoue also set up the "Tokyo Club" which held its meetings in English in the *Rokumei-kan,* and built the Imperial Hotel to receive Western guests in the vicinity of the *Rokume-kan*.

Inoue, whom Saigo Takamori contemptuously referred to as a "Mitsui inn keeper", adopted a conciliatory policy with regard to treaty revisions. His obsequious attitude in dealing with foreigners, which went so far as to allow foreigners to serve as judges, was frowned upon even by a government legal advisor, Gustave Emile Boissonade. Moreover, Inoue came under fierce attack from the popular parties and right-wing nationalists, and this eventually cost him his position. His successor as foreign minister, Okuma Shigenobu, amended Inoue's policy of flattering foreigners, specifying that foreign judges be employed only in the *Daishinin* (Grand Council). Nevertheless, he too was censured by the public and forced to resign, and later became the victim of an assassination attempt by a member of the right-wing association *Genyosha*, and lost a leg in the explosion.

In 1869, the second year of the restoration, Okuma was recommended by Choshu leader Kido Koin for the position of vice-foreign magistrate. Later, while serving as assistant secretary in the Ministry of Finance and Home Affairs, Okuma took part in the government's Europeanization policy. At that time, Okuma and Ito cooperated to begin construction of a railroad, taking out a £1,000,000 loan from London at an annual interest rate of nine per cent, with the terms of the loan requiring that customs revenues be used as collateral. However, this railroad project was censured by the public.[8] In 1874, during the "subjugation of Taiwan", Okuma served concurrently as director of the Uncivilized Taiwan General Affairs Bureau and in 1876 as minister of finance. He made every effort to back the Europeanization policy and support Mitsubishi business interests.

In 1892, Mutsu Munemitsu took over as foreign minister in the second Ito cabinet. He also devoted himself to the task of abolishing the unequal treaties, beginning negotiations in July 1893. Mutsu assessed power changes on the Korean peninsula and adopted a conciliatory policy towards Great Britain. It was Mutsu's conciliation with Britain that advanced Japan along the road to war with China. Mutsu was ingenious in taking advantage of the Japanese victory in continental Asia to revise the unequal treaties with the Western powers. Since the Crimean War in 1856, Britain and Russia had been at loggerheads, and Britain was extremely displeased by Russia's entry into the Far Eastern arena, and sought to make use of Japanese resistance to Russia to protect British interests on the Chinese mainland. Consequently, during the Anglo-Japanese Trade Pact negotiations, Mutsu took advantage of British sympathy for the Japanese viewpoint. In order to recover the consular jurisdiction that the Japanese people considered a sensitive issue, Mutsu made concessions to Britain concerning the opening up of the hinterland, and obtained partial recovery of Japan's tax privileges.

These dealings made Japan confident that in the event that Japan waged war with China, and Russia decided to intervene, Japan would receive British aid. Mutsu's *Kenken-roku* (Record of Hardships) and the *Komura Gaiko-shi* (A Chronicle of Komura Diplomacy) edited by the Japanese Ministry of

Foreign Affairs, meticulously record how the joint efforts of Foreign Minister Mutsu, Trade Bureau Director Hara Takashi, Minister to Great Britain Aoki Shuzo, Deputy Minister to China Komura Jutaro, and others, gave impetus to the strategy "Conciliate with Britain, Wage War with China".[9] Let us now take a look at a diary list of events before the outbreak of the Sino-Japanese War: On 16 July 1894, the Anglo-Japanese Trade Pact was signed; on 19 July, the Japanese army began preparing for war; on 20 July, the Japanese Minister to Korea, Otori Keisuke, sent an ultimatum to the Korean government demanding that Korea abandon her suzerain relationship with China; on 23 July, the Korean royal palace was seized: on 25 July, a surprise attack was launched against the Chinese fleet; and on 1 August, war was declared on China. From this journal, it is apparent that the essence of Mutsu's diplomacy was conciliation towards the great powers and the adoption of a tough stance against weak neighbours.

After the war, Mutsu served as envoy plenipotentiary for concluding the 1895 Sino-Japanese peace treaty. In April, the Treaty of Shimonoseki was concluded and Taiwan was ceded to the Japanese along with Liaotung Peninsula and Korea. On 23 April, Russia, France and Germany intervened to reverse the Japanese possession of Liaotung Peninsula. On 24 April, a council was held in the presence of the emperor to decide the Japanese course of action for dealing with this problem. A resolution was passed that the decision made by the great powers on the matter would be followed. However, Foreign Minister Mutsu, who was sick at the time, firmly opposed the decision reached by the council. On 29 April, the British foreign minister notified Japan that Britain was powerless to do anything about the Tripartite Intervention. Thus, Mutsu had no alternative but to yield, and the cabinet complied with the decision to give up the Liaotung Peninsula.[10]

Mutsu retired in May 1896 and died in 1897. However, by the end of 1897, Japan had finally succeeded in getting the great powers to renounce the unequal treaties and end extra-territoriality in 1899. The recovery of the collection of customs revenues was not achieved until 1911, following Japan's victory in the Russo-Japanese War (1905) and her annexation of Korea (1910). Mutsu's diplomatic skills were inherited by his successor, Komura Jutaro. In 1893, Mutsu recommended Komura for a position in Peking. In 1894, when the Sino-Japanese dispute intensified, Komura made great efforts to conceal the Japanese intrigue from the envoys of the great powers in Peking, especially from the British minister. On the other hand, he assumed a resolute posture when approaching China. After Mutsu died, Komura held the post of vice-minister of foreign affairs and in 1901 was promoted to foreign minister in the Katsura cabinet. He adequately extended Mutsu's diplomacy to a policy of "Uniting with Britain to subdue Russia". Komura's ambition was not only to dominate Korea in military, political, and economic affairs, but also to control Manchuria and northern China. Thus, he advocated an alliance with Britain and war with Russia. The Anglo-Japanese Military Alliance concluded in 1902 bypassed Russo-Japanese negotiations for a "*Mankan-kokan*" (through which Russia would control Manchuria in exchange for Japan dominating Korea)[11] In 1904, Japan declared war on Russia.

This war led to Korea becoming a Japanese colony. Japan had behind-the-scene backing from the British and the Americans. Indeed, had Britain, America and some other nations not provided Japan with 800,000,000 yen in loans for military assistance, Japan would probably not have been able to defeat Russia. At that time, America's biggest concern in the Far East was commerce, not territory. Thus, the United States promoted the "Open Door" and "Equal Opportunity" policies in China. President Roosevelt's reason for supporting Japan was to expel Russian influence from Manchuria. In late May 1905, Japan took advantage of her naval victory over the Russian Baltic fleet in the Japan Sea and asked American President Theodore Roosevelt to mediate Russo-Japanese peace talks.

Roosevelt understood that Japan wished to dominate Korea in exchange for U.S. control of the Philippines. Secretary of the Army, William Howard Taft, was sent to Japan, and on 29 July, Taft and Katsura Taro concluded the secret "Taft-Katsura Agreement". The essence of this agreement was that the United States agreed to Japanese dominance in Korea in return for American freedom of action in the Philippines.[12] The first session of the Russo-Japanese peace conference was held on 10 August in Portsmouth. Japanese Ambassador Plenipotentiary Komura harboured ambitions for ceded territory and reparation payments. The negotiations, however, stalemated. In the end, the "Peace Treaty of Portsmouth" was concluded under the good offices of President Theodore Roosevelt. Under the terms of the treaty, Russia was compelled to recognize the "paramount" political, military and economic interests of Japan in Korea. Russia also agreed that all troops were to be removed from Manchuria. The railway lines in South Manchuria constructed by Russia were ceded to Japan without charge. Liaotung Peninsula, containing the ports of Talien and Port Arthur, was turned over to Japan, as was the southern part of Sakhalin. Japan also obtained fishing rights in the waters adjacent to the Russian Far East.[13] As a result, Japan rose to the position of a world power and continued her expansionist policy.

However, the Manchurian railroads created mutual suspicion between Japan and America. The American railroad tycoon Edward Henry Harriman went to Japan with plans for the South Manchuria Railroad to become part of a worldwide transportation network. Harriman suggested collective Japanese-American management of the South Manchuria Railroad to Katsura. Katsura, apprehensive that Japan lacked sufficient funds to operate the railroad after the war, consented to Harriman's proposal immediately. The "Katsura-Harriman Agreement" was concluded on 12 October of the same year.[14] However, Foreign Minister Komura, returning from the Portsmouth Peace Conference, was firmly opposed to it. He saw absolutely no reason why the Americans should alongside the Japanese enjoy rights to the Manchurian railroad that had been procured with Japanese blood.[15] Therefore, the agreement was abrogated.

Komura diplomacy colonized Korea, without yielding an inch to the United States on the scheme for full control of Manchuria. Consequently, the Japanese-American honeymoon period drew to an end, although America, in order to safeguard economic interests in China, continued patiently to seek conciliation with Japan. On 18 December 1909, American Secretary of State Philander Chase Knox put forth a proposal for the neutrality of the Manchurian Railroad. He made inquiries concerning Foreign Minister Komura's plan through the intermediary of the Ambassador to Japan, Thomas J. O'Brien. The content of the proposal called for the elimination of international competition in Manchuria by having Japan, America, Britain, France, Germany and Russia form a consortium in China to buy up Japanese and Russian railroad holdings. The six nations would then collectively operate the railroad for purely commercial purposes, and not for military or political aims.[16] Since Japan not only controlled Korea's economy but dominated her military and political affairs as well, she had by that time already reached the point where she could annex Korea. She thus stubbornly rejected America's proposal for the neutrality of the Manchurian railroad.

Japan passed through the Mutsu diplomacy of the Sino-Japanese War period and the Komura diplomacy of the Russo-Japanese War period, and after Korea was annexed in 1910, the unequal treaties were completely abolished in 1911. However, when Japan severed the bonds of fifty-six years of unequal treaties with the great powers and obtained independence and freedom, she simultaneously turned around and enforced unequal treaties on open ports, extra-territoriality, customs agreements, concessions, and railroad privileges on her Asian neighbours. Moreover, Japan was even more candid than the Western powers about her intentions to annex Korea and colonize China. As far as the Japanese were concerned, Mutsu and Komura were distinguished and meritorious officials who had made great contributions toward renouncing the unequal treaties, occupying Taiwan and annexing Korea. From the viewpoint of other Asians, however, they were the chief offenders who forced Asian nations to sign unequal treaties and implemented the colonization of Taiwan and Korea. Likewise, to the Japanese, Ito Hirobumi was a great statesman who formulated a constitutional government. From the standpoint of the oppressed peoples, however, Ito was a colonial tyrant, the president of the Taiwan Affairs Bureau that began the Japanese rule of Taiwan, and later the "Commander of Korea" who ruthlessly dominated Korea. Therefore, in 1909, at the train station in Harbin, Ito was assassinated by the Korean patriot, An Chung-keun.

Although Japanese-American relations had deteriorated because of disputes over rights to Manchuria, the two countries still fought side by side against Germany in World War I. Taking advantage of the power vacuum in East Asia created by American participation in the European war, Kato Takaaki, foreign minister in the Okuma cabinet, tried to profit from the situation by presenting the "Twenty-One Demands" to Yuan Shih-kai in January 1915. These called for Japan to assume Germany's position in Kiaochow and assume the German leaseholds in Shantung province; for Manchuria and Mongolia to be reserved for Japanese exploitation and colonization; for Japanese control of the main coal deposits in China; for the other powers to be excluded from further territorial concessions; for Japanese guidance of China's military, commercial and financial affairs; for joint administration of the police in strategic locations; and for the purchase of Japanese weapons.[17] These demands completely stripped China of her sovereignty and made China a Japanese protectorate. The Twenty-One Demands made the traitorous warlord government feel uneasy and incited widespread resentment among the Chinese people, fuelling strong resistance to Japanese aggression, and subsequently led to the loud censure of Foreign Minister Kato at home and his removal from office.

Ishii Kikujiro was the next foreign minister appointed by the Okuma cabinet to carry on Kato's work in 1914. He had worked on the Korean annexation treaty in 1911 and continued to follow a positive diplomacy in China after the Twenty-One Demands. However, the vehement climax of the anti-Japanese movement in China aroused such great dissatisfaction among the Japanese people that it finally led to the general resignation of the Okuma cabinet. Afterwards, Ishii found a position as ambassador to the United States in the Terauchi cabinet in 1918. Before that, on 2 November 1917, Ishii and American Secretary of State Robert Lansing had signed an "exchange of notes between Japan and the United States regarding China". In the "Lansing-Ishii

Agreement", the United States recognized Japan's "special interests" in China, and Japan likewise agreed to respect China's territorial integrity and observe the commercial "Open Door" and "Equal Opportunity" policies. In accordance with this agreement, where China was regarded as a fish on a chopping block, Japan and America temporarily reached a compromise. However, in the days that followed, a great discrepancy arose between the two countries' understanding of the phrase "special interests". The United States was under the impression that "special interests" referred only to economic interests. However, the Japanese interpreted this phrase to include political and military interests.[18] During World War I, all the great powers in Europe suffered tragically. Only Japan and America, both fighting in foreign battlefields, became great war profiteers.

PART II

After World War I, international order was based on the Peace Treaty of the Versailles Conference, the Naval Disarmament Treaties, and the Nine-Power Convention of the Washington Conference. In keeping with the domestic trend of a constitution protection movement, the Hara cabinet emerged in Japan, and from its signing of the Versailles Peace Treaty in 1919 to the 1931 Manchurian Incident, with the exception of the Tanaka cabinet's "tough" diplomacy, all successive cabinets upheld the Versailles and Washington orders and implemented conciliatory policies with Britain and the United States. The international conciliation contained in the "Shidehara diplomacy" was representative of Japanese diplomacy during this period.

Shidehara had a long diplomatic career. While serving as vice-minister of foreign affairs, he was responsible for preparing counter-proposals at the Versailles Peace Conference in Paris. While serving as Ambassador to America, he represented Japan at the Washington Conference. The experience Shidehara gained from these conferences convinced him that only the diplomacy of international conciliation could benefit Japan. Beginning in June 1924 with the Kato cabinet, and until the collapse of the second Wakatsuki cabinet in December 1931, Shidehara served five years and three months as foreign minister — the only break being the Tanaka period — implementing the so-called "Shidehara diplomacy". Shidehara upheld the Versailles Treaty because the great powers sided with Japan during the Paris Peace Conference in 1919 and rejected China's request that the Twenty-One Demands be abolished and that Shantung and the former German concessions in Kiaochow be returned. When China again requested the annulment of the unequal treaties, including the Twenty-One Demands, at the Washington Conference (1921–22), the great powers and Japan made common cause and once again refused the request.

The product of the Washington Conference was the two Nine-Power Treaties. Though these stressed respect both for China's sovereignty and territorial integrity and for the Open-Door and Equal Opportunity policies, they did not actually repudiate the existing privileges of the great powers in China. At the Far East General Committee meeting on 2 February 1922, Japanese Envoy Plenipotentiary Shidehara emphasized the legality of the Twenty-One Demands and advocated that this treaty should not be annulled. He declared that, due to "changing circumstances", three revisions would be made:[19]

1. Japan would open to the recently organized international financial consortium the right of option, which had been granted exclusively to Japan, to loans for the construction of railways in South Manchuria and Eastern Inner Mongolia, and to loans to be secured on taxes in that region;
2. Japan would not insist that China engage Japanese advisors or instructors on political, financial, military, or police matters in South Manchuria;
3. Japan would withdraw the reservation she made when signing the Sino-Japanese treaties and postpone Group V of her original proposals (for Japanese control of Chinese policy) for future negotiations.

In other words, in conformity with this revision of the Twenty-One Demands, China's sovereignty and the principle of equal opportunity would be upheld.

The above "Statement of Plenipotentiary Shidehara Concerning Problems with the Twenty-One Demands" highlights the basic posture of Shidehara diplomacy. Although Mutsu and Komura adopted a diplomacy of international conciliation, they gave undue weight to the acquisition and monopoly control of Japanese colonies. Not only economic domination of Korea and Manchuria, but also military and political domination, were established as goals. Mutsu diplomacy had aroused the Triple Intervention, and Komura diplomacy had incurred the displeasure of the United States. The essential difference between Shidehara diplomacy and its predecessors was that Shidehara sought to eliminate all impasses Japan encountered on the international scene through the use of a conciliatory diplomacy with the great powers for the promotion of economic interests.

Shidehara diplomacy was highly esteemed in America because, in this spirit of international conciliation, Shidehara opened up Manchuria and Mongolia and made them accessible to the consortium of the great powers. Shidehara used economic means to advance the interests of the powers and, in the event, to relinquish Japan's military and political domination of Manchuria. The "Treaty Concerning the Resolution of the Pending Issue of Shantung" on 4 February 1922 stipulated that Japan must return the Kiaochow concessions, withdraw occupation troops, and give up the Shantung railroads. However, this forced the Chinese Government on the other hand to recognize that "the former German concessions in Kiaochow must be totally opened up to foreign trade", and that "in the former German concessions in Kiaochow, the existing privileges which were legally and fairly acquired under the Germans or any other foreigners, or during the period of Japanese administration, must be upheld".[20]

The spirit of Shidehara's international conciliation won the respect of Americans, and they supported him completely in rejecting China's request to abolish the unequal treaties. American Delegate John Van Antwerp MacMurray stated:

> I am speaking under instructions from the Secretary of State. The U.S. government cannot recognize the claims of the Chinese plenipotentiary. Even if Japan and China do reach an agreement which is contained in the claims of the Chinese envoy, from the position of its vested rights, the United States is unable to yield on a single point to follow the example of the Sino-Japanese agreement. I hope all of you will understand this point.[21]

Common interests led both the British and American representatives to support the Japanese position at the Shantung Conference.

After Russo-Japanese negotiations collapsed and the Anglo-Japanese alliance was abrogated, Japanese diplomacy had no alternative but to follow a pro-Anglo-American course and to respect the Versailles-Washington orders. As long as Japan observed international treaties and respected the Open-Door and Equal Opportunity policies in China, Japan could maintain a balanced position among the great powers and avoid direct conflict. The China problem became the major source of friction or conciliation between Japan and the Anglo-American powers. Shidehara's "economic diplomacy" sought to maintain a peaceful co-existence with Russia as well, which now had an essentially different political system. Japan promised the new Russian government that it would respect Russia's territorial integrity, would not intervene in domestic politics, and would esteem equal economic opportunity in Siberia. Furthermore, Japan agreed to an early withdrawal of the Japanese troops that had been sent to Siberia in 1918 to intervene in the Russian revolution. Then, on 20 January 1925, Japan and Russia signed an agreement to restore diplomatic ties, and on 14 December, they signed the Russo-Japanese Agreement Regarding Coal and Oil Privileges in North Sakhalin.[22]

The key to Japan's willingness to conform to the Washington order and maintain friendly relations with the British and the Americans was the heavy dependence of the Japanese economy on Britain and America at that time. According to a 1925 *Asahi Yearbook* report, America was Japan's number one trading partner from 1919 to 1923, with an average of 39 per cent of its annual imports coming from America and 33 per cent of its annual exports going to America.[23] Domestically, Shidehara claimed he practised non-partisan diplomacy, and that politically he was without party affiliations. However, his international conciliation diplomacy influenced his relationship with his brother-in-law Kato Takaaki and his *Kenseikai* (Constitutional Association) profoundly. Generally speaking, the *Seiyukai* (Landlords' Party) promoted positive policies and the *Kenseikai* adopted conciliatory policies. The *Seiyukai* drew its support from rural villages and inherited the *Jiyuto* (Liberal Party) tradition of a tough foreign policy, while the *Kenseikai* had an urban base and inherited the constitution of the *Kaishinto* (Progressive Party) for protecting the economic interests of the capitalists.

During World War I, Japan's cotton industry gradually began making investments along the Peking-Hankow railroad line and in Shantung to secure supplies of raw cotton.[24] When Shidehara was appointed foreign minister, Japanese textile capital experienced unprecedented progress in the period after the Great War. In order to advance its interests through economic means, Japan had to comply with the Anglo-American Open-Door policy. Moreover, in order to overtake Anglo-American competitors, Japan had to adopt a much friendlier attitude towards China, and thereby avoid becoming the target of a boycott movement.

In *Gaiko-Dokuhon* (Diplomacy Reader), Ito Masanori made the following comments on the special features of Shidehara diplomacy. First, Shidehara's actions never left the framework sanctioned by world opinion. Second, he used conciliatory methods as a means for advancing Japan's interests. Third, he adhered unswervingly to his doctrines and principles.[25] International conciliation that conformed to Anglo-American policies within the scope of the Versailles-Washington orders was considered apt for maintaining the international balance of peace. Shidehara diplomacy became famous because of the four principles it adopted with regard to China: non-interference in

China's domestic struggles; the use of economic cooperation for mutual prosperity and co-existence, the expression of magnanimity and sympathy at the situation in China, and rational support for reasonable Japanese privileges.

Instead of stating "non-interference in domestic affairs", Shidehara diplomacy especially emphasized "non-intervention in domestic struggles". On the grounds that it might be necessary at times to interfere in domestic affairs in order to protect Japan's interests, Shidehara very prudently used the diplomatic expression "domestic struggles" instead. For example, in October 1924 during the Chinese civil war between the warlords of Fengtien and Chili, as the battlefront drew near to Shanhaikwan, Foreign Minister Shidehara solemnly stated to the two belligerent armies that Japan would absolutely not intervene in China's domestic struggles, but neither would Japan permit the slightest encroachment upon its interests. In November 1925, when Kuo Sung-ling rebelled against Chang Tso-lin, Shidehara also repeatedly warned both parties that they must respect Japan's existing privileges in Manchuria.

Although Shidehara diplomacy was one of conciliation with the Anglo-American powers, it sometimes transcended the course set by British and America. In October 1925, in accordance with the stipulations of the Nine Power Tariff Treaty, a special tariff conference was convened in Peking. At the conference, China requested that her tariff autonomy be restored. Japan expressed approval, in principle, of China's request in order to wrest the initiative from the hesitant nations.[26] This request certainly curtailed Anglo-American benefits, but Britain and America had no choice but to yield to it. Japan noticed that tariff autonomy was a trend of the times, and sooner or later each nation had to recognize this. Therefore, Japan took the initiative and made friendly overtures to China.

Japan adopted a magnanimous and sympathetic attitude toward China with the hope of alleviating anti-Japanese feelings, and expected to turn the brunt of China's negative feelings towards Britain and America. Japan's Twenty-One Demands and the Shantung problem were the cause of the 1919 May Fourth Movement, which aroused the Chinese masses to advocate the overthrow of Japanese imperialism. However, during the May 30 Incident of 1925, while workers in Japanese textile factories in Shanghai went on strike, there were more cries of "down with British imperialism" than there were of "overthrow Japanese imperialism". To a large extent, however, Japan's expression of magnanimity and sympathy towards China was a move to further its own interests.

Since the fundamental principle of Shidehara diplomacy was to advocate Japan's special privileges, it could not in the long run hope to escape being blocked by China's patriotic movement. To the Japanese, the Twenty-One Demands were "reasonable privileges". To the Chinese, however, they represented a most "unreasonable loss of rights". In November 1927, the Chinese nationalist government declared that it wanted to abolish the unequal treaties within the shortest possible time. The Chinese government even set up a timetable for this to happen that included other issues such as the recovery of tariff autonomy, the abolishment of extra-territoriality, the recovery of foreign concessions and leases, the recovery of railroad privileges, the recovery of navigation rights to inland rivers, and coastal trading privileges. Japan's special privileges in Manchuria and Mongolia were also seen, without exception, as national rights that China must recover.[27]

Confronting the passionate movement to recover national rights in China, domestic opinion in Japan was split into two factions. One advocated that Japan accommodate itself to the Versailles-Washington orders, and through conciliation with Anglo-America, expand trade all over mainland China to advance Japanese interests. This was a foreign policy for maintaining the *status quo*. The other rejected the Versailles-Washington orders because they were based on an Anglo-American standard. Japan should exclude these orders and establish a "Pan-Asianism", with Japan as its base. This was a foreign policy to destroy the *status quo*. The former was represented by the conciliation diplomacy of Shidehara, while the latter was symbolized by the drastic diplomacy of Tanaka. Conciliation diplomacy maintained that Japan should act in concert with Anglo-America in order to promote "national interests", advocating expansion through economic means. The alternative diplomacy espoused a "Pan-Asianism" and wished to use military adventurism to achieve its goals. The former was rather ingenious, but was powerless to prevent a boycott movement in China, while the latter was blatant military aggression, and led to an ever more fervent anti-Japanese movement in China.

During the time of Mutsu and Komura diplomacy, when the national goal was to abolish the unequal treaties, the Ministry of Foreign Affairs and the military authorities in Japan worked together. The military did not interfere in politics, rather it served as a diplomatic prop, working in concert with the diplomats for Japan's independence. However, as Japan continued with foreign wars, the influence of the military gradually began to grow. Soon the military was intervening in politics to the point that it was directing diplomacy. Originally, the function of diplomacy was to maintain the international balance of power. However, the military, with its tendency toward expansionism, could not restrain itself from destroying the *status quo* and taking more positive actions. Under pressure from the military initiative, Japanese diplomacy became hopelessly subordinate. After the Manchurian Incident of 1931, it gradually toed the direction the military chose.

On the night of 18 September 1931, staff officers of the Kwantung Army Itagaki Seishiro, Ishihara Kanji, and others demolished a section of the Manchurian railroad in the Liutiaokou suburb of Mukden (Shenyang). The commander of the Kwantung Army, Honsho Shigeru, regarded this as the work of the Chinese Army and issued an order for a general attack. However, on 19 September, the consul-general in Mukden, Hayashi Kujiro, sent an "urgent top secret" telegram to Shidehara, reporting that this incident had been planned by the Japanese military. (First telegram): "From the synthesis of intelligence reports from all directions, we have conjectured that troops all along the Manchurian railroad have been activated on a prearranged course to take offensive action." (Later telegram): "According to the secret reports of Manchurian Railroad director Kimura, the Manchurian Railroad Company has already dispatched engineers to repair the section of railroad which was reported to have been destroyed by the Chinese. However, the troops on the scene have asked that no one be allowed to approach the spot. We can imagine that the incident was a planned action proceeded with by the military".[28]

On 19 September, China protested to Japan about the Manchurian Incident. However, the Kwantung Army, which intended to "occupy Manchuria", had already taken possession of Mukden, Feng-Hwang, and Pen-Hsi-Hu. On 21 September, troops were dispatched to Kirin and the commander of the army in Korea, Hayashi Senjuro, moved troops in Korea toward Manchuria. On 22 September, American Secretary of State Henry Lewis Stimpson, citing the Anti-War Pact and the Nine-Power Treaty, summoned Japanese Ambassador Debuchi and notified him that Japan must assume complete responsibility for the "Manchurian Incident". On 23 September, the Council President of the League of Nations, Monsieur Lerroux, gave both the Chinese and Japanese foreign ministers some advice regarding the Manchurian Incident. On 24 September, the United States sent the Chinese and Japanese envoys a memorandum expressing the hope that force would not be used to resolve the incident. Consequently, the Japanese government began to espouse a policy of non-expansionism. On 24 September, the government issued "The First Official Statement on the Manchurian Incident":

> The Imperial Government frequently strives for a close friendship between China and Japan. Co-existence and co-prosperity has been set as a policy

goal and the government consistently takes great pains to realize this goal. Unfortunately, during the past few years both the words and deeds of the Chinese government and people have often hurt the feelings of our people. Especially in the Manchurian-Mongolian areas, which have very close relations with Japan, several unhappy incidents have occurred recently, so that the friendly and just policies of Japan have not been received in China with a corresponding spirit of gratitude. These impressions have given a blow to the general mentality of our people, resulting in agitation and a dissatisfaction of public feelings. It so happens that on the night of September 18, some part of the Chinese army destroyed the South Manchuria Railroad in the vicinity of Mukden, and attacked Japanese defense troops, which consequently led to a clash.[29]

Although both the consul-general in Mukden and the president of the South Manchuria Railroad Company, Uchida Kosai, had transmitted the truth about the incident to the authorities, the Japanese government still issued a statement claiming that the Chinese army had demolished the Manchurian railroad and attacked Japanese troops. Prime Minister Wakatsuki and Foreign Minister Shidehara switched responsibility for the whole incident over to China, gave a poor excuse to the great powers, and sought understanding from America. During this period, the Japanese government did not take any concrete measures to stop the Japanese Army. On 8 October, the Kwantung Air Force bombed Chinchow. On 10 October, the British, American, French, and Italian ambassadors in Tokyo respectively protested against the bombing. On 24 October, the Council of the League of Nations, led by Chairman Aristide Briand, decided by a vote of 13 to 1, that Japan should withdraw her troops from Manchuria. Thereupon, on 26 October, the Japanese government issued a "Second Statement" as a pre-condition for withdrawing her troops. This statement also laid the blame on China, and justified the presence of Japanese troops in China:

> The recent Manchurian Incident was provoked entirely by the Chinese troops. The Imperial Government has explained this several times. Currently, out of sheer necessity, there are a few imperial troops remaining along the outer regions of the South Manchuria Railroad to protect the lives and property of Japanese nationals.[30]

Outwardly, the Japanese government intoned a policy of non-expansion in response to the protests of the great powers. However, the cabinet voted unanimously for an emergency expenditure of reserve funds for military action. If Prime Minister Wakatsuki and Foreign Minister Shidehara had been absolutely opposed to the exercise of military force, they would have voted against the bill and obstructed these military expenditures. Although they were worried about aggravating international opinion, they stood by and watched the military's adventurism with folded arms. Then, when they saw that the military was succeeding smoothly, they gave their approval to a *fait accompli*. On 18 November, the cabinet decided to dispatch more troops to Manchuria, and the Japanese Army occupied Chichihar. On 19 November, American Secretary of State Stimpson again notified Japanese Ambassador Debuchi in Washington that the Japanese Occupation of Chichihar defied the Nine-Power Treaty and the Anti-War Pact. However, due to the worldwide economic crisis, America was powerless to take effective measures to restrain Japan. Therefore, Japanese aggression in China did not change at all during the period of Shidehara diplomacy. On the contrary, it advanced further. The so-called "weak-kneed diplomacy" and "follower diplomacy" of Shidehara found expression domestically in a tendency to accept military lead.

The Manchurian Incident led to the collapse of Shidehara diplomacy, and Japan had to convert to the so-called "resuscitative Asia diplomacy" (*Koa gaiko*). On 1 March 1932, the military set up the dethroned emperor Pu Yi and established the puppet state of "Manchukuo". Before the "Report of the Commission of Enquiry of the League of Nations into the Sino-Japanese Dispute" — The Lytton Report — was issued, the Japanese government recognized Manchukuo on 15 September and signed the "Japanese-Manchukuo Protocol" which certified and upheld Japan's interests. The protocol specified a mutual defence arrangement between Japan and Manchukuo and an unconditional stationing of Japanese troops, thereby justifying Japan's occupation of Manchuria and Japan's expanding aggression. On 20 September, the Chinese Government declared that Manchukuo was a puppet organization and that Japan's recognition of Manchukuo was an insulting challenge to the League of Nations. In January 1933, the American government notified the powers that the United States did not recognize Manchukuo. In February, a general meeting of the League of Nations approved, by a vote of 42 to 1, the council's decision to advise Japan to withdraw its troops. In March, Japan resolutely withdrew from the League of Nations.[31] Consequently, Japan sank into the mire of the "scorched earth diplomacy" (*Shyodo gaiko*) of Uchida Kosai and the "Axis diplomacy" (*Sujiku gaiko*) of Matsuoka Yosuke. Subsequently, this led to war against America and Britain and to Japan's total defeat.

After World War II, in early October 1945, the imperial cabinet of Prince Higashi-no-kuni retired from power. Shidehara, returning once again to the political arena, was appointed to form a cabinet. Now famous for his pre-war conciliation with Anglo-America, he was judged trustworthy to faithfully and unhesitatingly carry out the orders of Supreme Allied Commander MacArthur. Similarly, the former ambassador to Britain, Yoshida Shigeru, was also returned to the political scene. The general criticism of Yoshida was that he was a "yes-man" for the Americans. During the war, Yoshida was condemned for having collaborated with the British and was imprisoned for his pro-Anglo-American activities. However, after the war, Yoshida was appointed foreign minister in the Prince Higashi-no-kuni cabinet and the Shidehara cabinet, finally rising to the post of prime minister in 1946.[32]

An example that may be contrasted with the ones above is Togo Shigenori, who served as foreign minister both at the outbreak of the war with the British and the Americans, and at its conclusion. Although he had no experience of being an ambassador to Britain or America, he had served as ambassador to Germany and to Russia. In 1941, he served as foreign minister, making every possible effort in Japanese-American negotiations to avoid the outbreak of war. However, Togo laboured in vain and was forced to go to war with America. In 1942, when the government set up a Ministry of Great East Asia, Shigenori took a stand against it and resigned. In April 1945, when Suzuki Kantaro organized a new cabinet, Togo again served as foreign minister and worked hard to conclude the war. In Togo's manuscripts, *An Aspect of the Times*, he frankly recorded that he had done his best to prevent Japan from declaring war on America. When he received the Hull Note from the American secretary of state, which was the equivalent of an ultimatum forcing Japan to give up all of its interests abroad, he felt profound disappointment and even considered resigning.[33] After the defeat, Togo was named a Class A war criminal. He was tried incessantly for his part in the planning of the Pacific War. He was sentenced to twenty years imprisonment and died in prison in 1950. In comparison with Shidehara and Yoshida, Togo was indeed unlucky.

After the war, pro-Anglo-American bureaucrats were praised as pacifists and rationalists, and those without Anglo-American connections received unequal treatment. Changes in the value system under the American occupation force were to result in corresponding value changes among the Japanese people. When Japan's pro-Anglo-American standard-bearer Shidehara accepted his appointment as prime minister, he revealed his conservative personality by retaining all the bureaucrats from the former imperial cabinet in the foreign, justice, army, navy and education ministries. However, MacArthur's headquarters issued the Shidehara cabinet with democratization and non-militarization directives one after another, including instructions on the necessity of revising the constitution. As a result, Shidehara abolished the special police, released political prisoners, and repealed the Peace Maintenance Law.

The greatest contribution of the Shidehara cabinet was its introduction of a new pacifist constitution. However, this new constitution was enacted through the amending of the Meiji constitution, and provided for the "preservation of the emperor system" and the "maintenance of national polity" as the prerequisites for "renouncing war":

> Frankly speaking, there is no doubt that in the beginning Prime Minister Shidehara was very conservative in his way of thinking. He even hesitated about revising the constitution, though he had drastic views about the command of the army and navy. He understood that at first the Allies' occupation policy sought to dismember Japan and destroy the emperor system in order to make Japan a republic. This caused Prime Minister Shidehara to waver a great deal. Then he considered that in order to preserve the emperor system, Japan would have to make great sacrifices. Yet, he was worried about the future of a new Japan. As it turned out, he resolved that in order to preserve the emperor system and maintain national polity, he would renounce war and firmly establish a pacifist Japan.[34]

Shidehara's minister of state, Matsumoto Joji, originally presented the following points for the revision of the constitution: (1) "The emperor is supreme, his imperial authority must not be encroached upon"; (2) "In order to execute the laws and accomplish administrative goals, the emperor must have the prerogative to issue, or transfer to others the right to issue, necessary orders"; (3) "The emperor is the commander-in-chief of the military". Since this outline made only a minimum of necessary revisions to the Meiji constitution, it was rejected by General Headquarters. The Japanese government then had no choice but to comply with the so-called "MacArthur constitution" drafted by MacArthur's staff. The important points in this constitution were: (1) Japan was to renounce war forever, abolish its armed forces and pledge never to revive them; (2) While sovereignty was to be vested in the people, the emperor was to be described as a symbol of the state; (3) The peerage was to be abolished and the property of the imperial household was to revert to the state.[35]

This was the origin of the "symbolic emperor system" and of the "renunciation of war" constitution. Since the Shidehara cabinet lacked the autonomy to anchor the goals of "popular sovereignty" and "renunciation of war", there are still those in Japan today who embrace the old value system and regard the new constitution as a "compulsory constitution" or "foreign-made constitution". They use this as reasons for revising the constitution. In any case, the pacifist Japanese constitution not only repudiates wars of aggression; it also renounces all sorts of wars, and proclaims lofty human ideals. Most Japanese are proud of it and consider it Shidehara's achievement.

More than thirty years after the war, the new value system of the Japanese constitution has penetrated deeply into Japanese society. Democracy and pacifism are the fundamental safeguards of order in Japanese society. Consequently, Japanese diplomacy has also adopted the principles of "pacifist" diplomacy and "international conciliation" diplomacy, striving to cultivate the country's economic power and firmly establish its international status.

PART III

Since the war, Japan has consistently kept to the international conciliation of "Shidehara diplomacy". In the pre-war period, Shidehara diplomacy conformed to the Versailles-Washington orders and adopted a policy of conciliation with Britain and America and peaceful means for dealing with the China problem. Had Japan merely followed Britain and America, and remained the Number Three power in the world and used economic means alone to pursue its interests, then all blame for evil deeds would have remained with "Western imperialism", and only Britain and America would have been the targets of Chinese nationalism. In the meantime, Japan could have stayed a good neighbour and surely enjoyed economic benefits. Yet, proponents of "resuscitative Asia diplomacy" sought eagerly to destroy the international order under Anglo-American leadership in order to establish a "New East Asia Order" and a "Great East Asian Co-Prosperity Sphere" with Japan as its centre. Their goal of making Japan the Number One power in the world led to war with Britain and America. As a result, Japan experienced the pain of being a subjugated nation.

After the war, Japan did some soul-searching, and has consistently been practising Shidehara diplomacy. She conformed to the Washington-Moscow orders, sought U.S. and Soviet conciliation, and upheld international peace for the development of world trade. During the Cold War, Japan was but the third economic power in the world after the United States and the Soviet Union, and did not bear the brunt of accusations of wrongdoing on the international scene. Instead, it has quietly enjoyed economic prosperity and has not been censured at all. The ingenuities of Shidehara diplomacy, conciliatory in all directions and thus acceptable to most, are plainly celebrated.

Japanese Diplomatic Chronology

- 1853   Perry's "Black Ships" arrive in Japan.
- 1854   Perry returns. Treaty of Kanagawa concluded between Japan and the United States.
- 1858   Three ports — Kanagawa, Nagasaki, and Hakodate — opened to foreign trade.
- 1868   Meiji restoration.
- 1871   Negotiations with Western powers on revision of the unequal treaties.
- 1873   Conscription begun.
- 1874   Taiwan expedition.
- 1875   The Kianghwa Island Incident.
- 1876   The Japanese-Korean Friendship Treaty (Kianghwa Treaty).
- 1894–95 Sino-Japanese War; Japan annexes Taiwan and claims right in Korea.
- 1899   Extraterritoriality ended for foreigners.
- 1900   Participation in suppression of Boxer Rebellion.
- 1902   Anglo-Japanese alliance.
- 1904–05 Russo-Japanese War.
- 1910   Korea annexed.
- 1915   Twenty-One Demands made on China.
- 1919   Versailles Treaty hands over German concessions in China to Japan.
- 1921   Washington Conference.
- 1930   London Naval Treaty.
- 1931   Manchurian Incident.
- 1932   Puppet state of Manchukuo established as Japanese Colony.
- 1933   Japan withdraws from League of Nations.
- 1937   Marco Polo Bridge Incident provokes Japan to invade China.
- 1940   Rome-Berlin-Tokyo Axis established.
- 1941   Neutrality agreement with Soviet Union; Anglo-Dutch oil embargo; Japan attacks Pearl Harbour.
- 1941–45 Greater East Asia War.
- 1945   Japan accepts Potsdam Proclamation and surrenders to the Allies.
- 1946–48 International Military Tribunal for the Far East.
- 1950   Korean War; National Police Reserve created.
- 1951   San Francisco peace treaty not signed by China, Soviet Union, India.

- 1952   Peace treaty in effect, Japan regains sovereignty. Administrative agreement with the United States.
- 1954   Mutual Defence Assistance Agreement signed. Safety Forces renamed Self-Defence Forces; Safety Agency becomes Defence Agency.
- 1956   Japan and U.S.S.R. formalize diplomatic relations without agreement on peace settlement. Japan admitted to United Nations.
- 1965   Japan and South Korea normalize diplomatic status.
- 1969   Sato-Nixon Communiqué; grant of Okinawa negotiated.
- 1972   Okinawa returned to Japanese sovereignty, but with American bases.
- 1973   Tanaka visits Peking, establishes diplomatic relation with China.
- 1978   Sino-Japanese Peace Treaty.

Notes

[1] Ishii Takashi, *Meiji Ishin no Kokusai-teki Kankyo* [The International Environment of the Meiji Restoration], Tokyo: Yoshikawa Kobunkan, 1966, ch. 5 and 6; *Meiji Ishin no Butaiura* [Behind the Scenes of the Meiji Restoration], Tokyo: Yuwanami Shoten, 1960, pp. 104 ff.

[2] Leonard Gordon, "Japan's Abortive Colonial Venture in Taiwan, 1874", *The Journal of Modern History*, XXXIIV, no. 2 (June 1965): 171–85.

[3] Gaimusho Chosabu, ed., *Dainippon Gaiko Bunsho* [Diplomatic Documents of Great Japan] vol. VII, Tokyo: Nihon Kokusai Kyokai, 1939, pp. 30–32, 38–41, 65–67.

[4] Okuboke (copyright), *Okubo Toshimichi Bunsho* [Documents of Okubo Toshimichi] vol. VI, Tokyo: Nihon Shiseki Kyokai, 1928, pp. 30–35.

[5] *Dainippon Gaiko Bunsho*, vol. VII, pp. 293–95.

[6] Gaimusho, ed., *Nihon Gaiko Nenpyo narabi Shuyo Bunsho* [Japanese Diplomatic Chronology and the Main Documents, hereafter cited as "NGNSB"] vol. I, Tokyo: Hara Shobo, 1972–73, pp. 65–70.

[7] Inoue Kaoru-ko Denki Hensankai, Segai Inoue-ko *Den* [A Biography of Marquis Inoue] vol. III (Tokyo: Naigai Shoseki Kabushiki Kaisha, 1934), pp. 766–88.

[8] Okuma-ko 85 nen-shi Hensankai, *Okuma-ko 85 nen-shi* [85 Years History of Marquis Okuma] vol. I, Tokyo: Okuma-ko 85 nen-shi Hensankai, 1926, vol. I, pp. 301–08.

[9] Mutsu Munemitsu, *Kenken-roku [Record of Hardships]* (Tokyo: Iwanami Shoten, 1941), pp. 54–64, 83–86. Gaimusho, ed., *Komura Gaiko-shi [A Chronicle of Komura Diplomacy]* vol. 1, Tokyo: Akatani Shoten, 1953, pp. 47–53.

[10] *Kenken-roku*, pp. 226–42.

11 *Komura Gaiko-shi*, vol. I, pp. 250–56.

12 NGNSB, vol. I, p. 240.

13 Ibid., pp. 245–48.

14 Ibid., p. 249.

15 *Komura Gaiko-shi*, vol. II, pp. 208–10.

16 C. Waiter Young, *Japan's Special Position in Manchuria*, Baltimore, Maryland:
    Hopkins Press, 1931, pp. 125–68.

17 M.E. Cameron, T.H.D. Hahoney and G.E. McReynolds, *China, Japan and the
    Powers: A History of the Modern Far East*, New York: Ronald, 1960, pp. 360–64.

18 Westel W. Willoughby, *China at the Conference: A Report*, Baltimore, Maryland:
    Johns Hopkins Press, 1922, pp. 193–204.

19 Ibid., p. 252.

20 NGNSB, vol. III, p. 6.

21 Shidehara Kijuro, *Gaiko Gojunen [Fifty Years of Diplomacy]*, Tokyo: Yomiuri
    Shinbun-sha, 1951, p. 79.

22 NGNSB, vol. II, pp. 67–71.

23 Asahi Shinbunsha, *Asahi Nenkan 1925 [Asahi Yearbook 1925]*, Osaka: Asahi
    Shinbun-sha, 1924, p. 341.

24 Nawa Toichi, *Nihon Bosekigyo to Genmen Modal Kenkyu* [Studies on Japanese
    Cotton — Industry and the Problems of Raw Cotton], Osaka: Daido Shoin,
    1937, p. 299.

25 Ito Masanori, *Gaiko Dokuhon [Diplomacy Reader]*, Tokyo: Chuo Koronsha,
    1934, p. 118.

26 Negishi Todashi, *Shina Tokubetsu Kanzei Kaigi no Kenkyu* [Studies on China's
    Special Tariff Conference], Tokyo: Jikyokan Shoten, 1926, pp. 173–82.

27 Arnold J. Toynbee, *Survey of International Affairs 1928*, London: Oxford
    University Press, 1929, pp. 418–37.

28 NGNSB: vol. II, pp. 180–81.

29 Ibid., p. 182.

30 Ibid., p. 185.

31 Kokusai Renmei Jimukyoku Tokyo Shikyoku, ed., *Kokusai Renmei ni okeru
    Nisshi Mondai Gifiroku* [Japanese Secretariat of the League of Nations. Tokyo
    Branch Office, ed., Documents of the League of Nations Concerning the Sino-
    Japanese Disputes], Tokyo: Kokusai Renmei Kiroku Kankokai, 1933, vol. II,
    part 4; From the Lytton Report to the Withdrawal of Japan from the League of
    Nations.

32 Tadamiya Eitaro, *Showa Kenryokusha-ron* [A Comment on Men of Power in
    Showa Period], Tokyo: Saimaru Shuppansha, 1972, pp. 132–70.

33 Togo Shigenori, *Jidai no Ichimen [An Aspect of the Times]*, Tokyo: Kaizosha,
    1952, p. 239.

34 Shidehara Heiwa Zaidan, ed., *Shidehara Kijuro*, p. 692.

35 Mafk Gayn, *Japan Diary*, New York: William Sloan Associates, 1948, pp. 125–
    31.

2

WAR MEMORIES AND JAPAN'S RELATIONS WITH EAST ASIAN COUNTRIES

Arujunan Narayanan

INTRODUCTION

East Asia has always been a region that has exerted a strong influence on international history. In ancient times, it was the site of the Chinese civilization and the great Chinese empires. In modern times, it was the place where great powers such as Britain, France, Holland, Portugal, Spain, the United States, Japan and Russia competed for political influence and colonial domination. This struggle led to the Pacific War that left many bitter memories behind. During the succeeding Cold War, it became the arena for ideological conflicts between the East and the West, led by the USSR and the United States respectively. Civil wars dragged on in the Korean Peninsula, the Chinese mainland and in Southeast Asia. With the end of the Cold War in 1989 and the resolution of the Cambodian conflict in 1993, the region became stable and started to experience impressive economic growth. Japan rose like a phoenix from the ashes of war to become an economic giant, second only to the United States. Soon, the four little dragons — Hong Kong, Taiwan, South Korea and Singapore — followed Japan's growth, later to be tailed by Southeast Asian countries such as Thailand, Malaysia, Brunei, the Philippines and Indonesia.

In the meantime, the region also became home to newly established multilateral organizations such as the Association of Southeast Nations (ASEAN), the ASEAN Regional Forum (ARF), the Asia-Pacific Economic Cooperation (APEC) and ASEAN+3 (Japan, South Korea and China). There was even a proposal for an East Asian Economic Grouping that would have excluded Western powers, but which failed because of U.S. opposition. Taken as a whole, the region was an economic powerhouse until it was hit by the 1997 financial crisis. Since then, it has been recuperating and most signs show that it is re-emerging as an area of high growth. Although the security scenario has changed since the collapse of the USSR, some Cold War remnants still remain. U.S.-Japan relations are still central to regional security, and U.S. bilateral security frameworks in the region still remain intact. The United States retains its military presence in Okinawa and South Korea, and overall U.S.-China bilateral relations still remain cordial despite hiccups over human rights, and fears of a power struggle between the two.

There are unresolved security issues that can destabilize the region. Among these are the divided Koreas, the North Korean nuclear question, the Taiwan Straits issue and the conflicting territorial claims in the Spratly Archipelago in the South China Sea involving China, Vietnam, Malaysia, the Philippines and Brunei, the Senkaku/Diaoyutai Islands dispute between Japan and China, and the Takeshima Island dispute between Japan and South Korea. There is also the possibility of a new cold war in Northeast Asia between the United States and its allies, and China. Japan can also quickly turn into a military power if for some reason, the United States decides to withdraw from Pacific Asia.[1]

Another important issue that threatens the region, especially Northeast Asia, is the bitter World War II war memories that countries in the region have of the Japanese military. Japan's refusal to apologize for atrocities in the most remorseful terms, official visits by Japanese leaders to the Yasukuni Shrine, Japanese history textbooks that treat the atrocities as simple war events, the issue of compensation for comfort women and Asian labourers, and the issue of equal treatment of Koreans in Japan, have all been injuring relations between Japan and its neighbours from time to time. The objective of this article is to examine to what extent the issue of war memories will affect Japan's relations with countries in East Asia and the overall stability of the region in the immediate future.

HISTORICAL BACKGROUND

Japan had chosen to be an isolated kingdom until it was forced to open its doors by Western powers, especially after the demonstration of U.S. naval power by Commander William Perry in 1853. It was realized that the only way to escape U.S. occupation was for Japan to reform its socio-economic system and adopt Western science and technology. During the Meiji Era, Japan acquired relevant military and civilian technology and soon emerged as an important industrial and military power. Its defeat of Russia at the Battle of Tsushima in 1904 made it the first non-White nation to be victorious over a White power. This greatly boosted its military morale. Its role during World War I as an ally of the victorious powers, its inclusion as a party in the 1919 Treaty of Versailles, and its appointment as trustee for the German territories in China and the Pacific Ocean further fueled its ambition to achieve a Greater Japan. All this caused Japan to identify itself with the West and feel contempt for the other peoples in the East.[2]

The Great Depression that hit in 1929, and the restrictions placed by colonial powers to maintain their colonial territories as private markets, forced Japan to look to new regions for raw materials for its industries, for markets for its manufactured goods, and for food for its teeming population.[3] Since the whole of Southeast Asia was already occupied by Western powers, it turned instead towards China and Korea and started entertaining the ambition of acquiring them as colonies. Korea became Japan's colony in 1910. In 1937, Japan manufactured the Marco Polo Bridge Incident and started a war on China. The war spread quickly, and Japan easily occupied huge chunks of Chinese territory. The League of Nations then requested Japan to withdraw. Not only did the latter refuse, it left the League of Nations on 27 March 1933. In September 1940, it proceeded with the conquest of Indochina in a move calculated to cut off supplies to Chinese troops.

The United States was now becoming aware of the Japanese threat and demanded that Japan withdraw from Indochina and occupied Chinese territories. Japan refused, feeling that the "sacrifices" it had made thus far would become meaningless if it were to succumb to the demand. The United States launched a trade embargo, especially on oil, iron and other raw materials that were essential for Japan's industries. Soon, other colonial powers joined in and Japan's survival as an industrial state was seriously threatened. Japan had either to meet the U.S. demand or face an economic strangulation. Despite knowing that Japan would not be able to withstand U.S. military might in the long run, Japanese military leaders took a calculated risk and opted for war. On 7–8 December 1941, Japan launched simultaneous attacks on Pearl Harbour, Hong Kong, Malaya, and the Philippines, and later on the Dutch East Indies, to crush the military might of the colonial powers in the Far East. Within a period of six months, Japan had conquered vast territories stretching from Burma in the west to the Pacific islands in the east. These were to remain under its control for almost three-and-a-half years, while it desperately fought enemy forces on many different fronts. The Japanese Military Administration encountered serious resistance from anti-Japanese forces in occupied areas such as Malaya, Singapore and Borneo, especially from the overseas Chinese. Over the subsequent two years, the United States gradually defeated Japanese forces in an island-hopping war. Finally, atomic bombs were dropped on Hiroshima and Nagasaki on 6 and 8 August 1945, respectively. Japan surrendered on 15 August 1945, and on 30 August 1945, the U.S. occupied Japan, and remained in control until 28 April 1952.

During the war, Japanese forces committed atrocities on prisoners-of-war and civilians. After it ended, many civilian and military leaders and members of the Japanese military were brought to justice. In line with the classification of war criminals in Class A, B and C as specified in the 1945 Nuremberg Charter, and as agreed upon at the Potsdam Conference on 26 July 1945, Japanese war criminals were tried by major and minor tribunals. Between 3 May 1946 and 12 November 1948, the International Military Tribunal for the Far East (IMTFE) tried and sentenced twenty-eight "Class A" war criminals. These included major political and military leaders. Hundreds of Japanese Classes B and C war criminals were tried and punished at many locations throughout the Far East by the United States, Britain, Australia, the Netherlands, France, China and the Philippines. Hundreds were executed and the ashes of some were placed at the Yasukuni Shrine in Tokyo.[4]

The U.S. occupation force under General Douglas McArthur initially adopted a policy of reforming Japan. The influence of the Japanese military was to be eliminated and the emperor was to be stripped of his divine status and would become a constitutional monarch instead. In drafting the new post-war constitution of 3 November 1946, McArthur wanted Japan to renounce both the sovereign right to declare war and the right to its own defence forces. His advisors thought the second condition unreasonable, however, and Japan was allowed to construct a self-defence force. The commencing of the Cold War immediately after the World War II, the rapid expansion of communism in the Far East, and the popularity of the communists within Japan, made the United States reconsider its post-war policy. Japan was needed on the side of the Western Bloc. Given this reality, U.S. policy in occupied Japan was changed from one of rehabilitation to one of reconstruction. War criminals who were useful to the United States were not prosecuted, and some even ended up working for U.S. military intelligence in Japan.[5] The war crimes prosecution programme was soon terminated and Japanese war criminals serving prison terms were granted an early release.[6] Some rose to top positions in post-war Japan's domestic politics. The Korean War in 1950 further increased the relevance of Japan to the United States. This hurried the San Francisco Peace Treaty to be signed on 7 September 1951, bringing the Pacific War to an official conclusion, and Japan regained its sovereignty. This treaty was immediately followed by the U.S.-Japan Mutual Security Treaty of 8 September 1951 that allied the two countries against the Communist Bloc. This treaty was revised to become the Treaty of Mutual Cooperation and Security between the United States and Japan on 19 January 1960. On 17 April 1996, the Japan-U.S. Joint Declaration on Security: Alliance for the 21st Century was signed to determine Japan-U.S. relations for the post-Cold War period.

ATROCITIES, MEMORIES AND LEGACIES

Just like any other war in human history, the Pacific War left bitter and painful memories among both military and civilian victims. Allied soldiers suffered at Pearl Harbour, in Hong Kong, the Philippines, Malaya, Singapore, the Netherlands East Indies, British Borneo, Papua New Guinea, the islands of the Pacific and Burma. They experienced torture and horrible living conditions on the Siam-Burma Death Railway,[7] the Bataan Death March,[8] the Sandakan Death March,[9] journeys in the hell ships, and at prisoner-of-war camps. The loss of fellow soldiers to cannibalism was also a horrible thing to remember.[10] The public humiliation of allied prisoners-of-war, both officers and enlisted men, at Japanese hands has been something that the victims have found hard to forget.[11]

During World War II, more than three million Japanese died.[12] For the soldiers, the war was fought as a service to their divine emperor. However, memories of the atrocities they committed still haunt some of them, and many suffer in silence.[13] When the tide turned against them, they were subjected to tortures and insults at the hands of the victorious allied forces.[14] Some surrendered Japanese soldiers were shot and others were badly treated in POW camps. Bones of the dead were sometimes turned into souvenirs. For them, the military trials were merely a "victor's justice" that in a judicial cloak exterminated hundreds of "innocent" Japanese soldiers. Their allied counterparts who committed similar war crimes were, after all, not tried at all.[15]

For the Japanese civilian population, the war was equally brutal. They were the first and the only victims of the notorious atomic bombs dropped on Hiroshima and Nagasaki. The death and destruction that rained on Japanese cities from the Doolittle U.S. Air Force raids left equally bitter memories, as did the utter poverty and misery suffered in post-war Japan. Hatred against the military for taking the country down the path of destruction remained strong.[16] The occupation of Japan, the presence of American military forces and their misbehaviour in Japan dented Japan's sovereignty and hurt Japanese pride. In lands conquered by the Japanese, life was fraught with fear, torture and death. The Chinese, both in mainland China and Southeast Asia, faced the full wrath of the Japanese military.[17] The Rape of Nanking[18] and the killing of thousands of Chinese under the Japanese Biological and Chemical Warfare Research Programme in Manchuria, especially at Harbin, by Lieutenant General Shiro Ishii, were some notorious examples of Japanese brutalities.[19] According to Sheldon Harris, between 10,000 and 12,000 prisoners died in China and the occupied territories in the name of bio-warfare research. At least 250,000 men, women and children died in field tests during the war.[20] It is estimated that between 1931 and 1945, the Japanese military killed over ten million people in China alone.[21] Chinese bitterness about the 1937–45 Japanese Occupation is still widespread.[22]

For the Koreans, war memories run equally deep. Their women were kidnapped and forced to work as "comfort women" in Japanese military brothels all over the Pacific. Koreans forced to work as guards in the Japanese Army were subjected to brutalities at the hands of Japanese soldiers. Korean coolies working for the Japanese were treated as the lowest in the pecking order. In post-war Japan, Korean soldiers in the Japanese Army were denied military benefits offered to their Japanese counterparts, while Koreans who had become Japanese citizens were treated as second-class.[23]

In Southeast Asia, not all countries experienced the same level of brutality. Atrocities were aimed more at the Chinese, although locals were also subjected to torture and retain bitter memories of it. In Malaya and Singapore, thousands of civilians, especially Chinese, were raped, tortured and killed, especially at the *Kempeitai* centres.[24] The *Sook Ching* operations left indelibly bitter memories in Chinese minds. The resistance of the Malayan Peoples' Anti-Japanese Army (MPAJA) in the jungles of Malaya also left bitter memories.[25] The demand for as much as US$50 million as punishment for supporting China during the 1937 Sino-Japanese War was another example of the miseries the Chinese community suffered at the hands of the Japanese military.[26] For the Malays, it was a political awakening. They were given more opportunities in the administration of the country. It was also the beginning of a strong Malay dislike for the Chinese in Malaya. As members of the Japanese military or police force, they clashed with the Chinese-based MPAJA during and after the Japanese Occupation. This left behind an inter-ethnic animosity that is still reflected in post-war domestic politics.[27] For the Indians, the establishment of the Indian National Army (INA) during the war, its heroic march alongside Japanese forces to Imphal and Manipur at the India-Burma border for the liberation of India from the British were memories of heroic militant nationalism that they still cherish today.[28]

Japanese rule, to the Indonesians, blended into their own nationalist struggle. Japan granted independence to Indonesia just before the end of the war and some Japanese soldiers even fought alongside the Indonesians against Dutch forces after the war. However, for the average Indonesian, Japanese military rule was a painful time. Indonesian men were taken to work in other theatres of war, especially the Death Railway, under despicable conditions. Indonesian women were forced to work as "comfort women" in military brothels at many locations. Thus, Japanese rule in Indonesia is remembered with a mixture of respect and hatred.[29]

Some of the worst atrocities were committed against Filipinos for siding with the United States. The most notorious ones were the Bataan Death March and the Rape of Manila in which thousands of Filipino men, women and children were brutally slaughtered. In Burma, the Japanese encouraged the nationalists to cooperate with them. The Japanese military massacred many in Burma, the most notorious event being the Kalagon Village Massacre. Burmese men were taken by the thousands to construct the Burma-Siam Death Railway. Unlike prisoners from other parts though, they were familiar with the terrain and many managed to escape.[30] Since Thailand was a Japanese ally during the war, its people escaped Japanese brutality. In Indochina, the Japanese committed some atrocities but at the same time, they fostered a successful national movement against the French. Therefore, war memories in Thailand and Indochina are not as bitter as those in some other Southeast Asian countries.

Although it has been almost sixty years since the end of the war and normal diplomatic relations have been established between Japan and its neighbours, painful memories still haunt perceptions of Japan, especially in China and Korea. Japan established normal ties with China in 1972 and the Sino-Japanese Peace Treaty was signed in 1978. Similarly, on 28 April 1952, Japan-Republic of Korea (ROK) relations were normalized and were followed by the Treaty on Basic Relations between Japan and the ROK on 22 June 1965. There is no treaty between North Korea and Japan, although ties are improving despite the nuclear issue.

CURRENT ISSUES RELATED TO WARTIME ATROCITIES

History Textbooks Issue

Japanese textbook narrations about the Pacific War have always been a burning issue in Japan's relations with other Asian countries, especially China and Korea. The first controversy occurred in June 1982. The second one took place in mid-1986, leading the Japanese Prime Minister Nakasone to order a revision.[31] On 3 April 2001, the Ministry of Education approved the general use of the New History Textbook written by a group of nationalist scholars. This sparked a spurious diplomatic dispute between Japan, Korea and China. Although the government officially stated that it did not express the official view of history,[32] the book was criticized in Japan and abroad for not mentioning Japan's war atrocities during World War II.[33] Some history books did not mention the comfort women[34] or the germ warfare project in China, and did not give the death toll for the Rape of Nanking. China and Korea called for major changes in the text. When Japan offered to change only two of the thirty-five revisions demanded by Korea, Seoul temporarily recalled its ambassador, froze all military exchanges, cancelled joint naval exercises, boycotted educational exchanges and shelved plans to further open its market to Japanese goods.[35] Consumer groups called for a boycott of Japanese goods, while lawmakers demanded that Seoul oppose Japan's bid for a permanent seat on the United Nations Security Council. An official of the Korean Ministry of Foreign Affairs said that lasting friendship between Korea and Japan depended on a correct understanding of history.[36] This issue is likely to remain a sensitive point unless the Japanese government accepts the uncomfortable facts. Japan should realize that its attempt to treat past atrocities as insignificant details is a denial of history that can always be used for political advantages by China, and North and South Korea.[37] However, the importance given to economic development by the governments of these countries will not allow the textbook issue to become a stumbling block in enhancing East Asian international relations.

Visits to the Yasukuni Shrine

The Yasukuni Shrine of the Shinto religion in Tokyo is dedicated to the spirits of the approximately 2.6 million who had died since 1853 in Japan's various wars, both civil and foreign. During World War II, it was used to promote Japanese nationalism. After Japan's defeat in 1945, the post-war government was compelled to terminate all support for the Yasukuni Shrine, which was then converted into a private organization. The shrine also honours World War II leaders convicted as war criminals by the IMTFE. Ashes of Class A war criminals are also kept there and there is a memorial tablet for them. In recent years, Japanese leaders have been inclined to visit the shrine. This has thus become an issue in relations with China and Korea.[38] The Chinese and Koreans see the shrine as a monument to militarism, and some Japanese consider the visits a violation of the principle of separation between religion and state. When former Prime Minister Yasuhiro Nakasone decided on an official visit to the shrine in 1985, it created such a row amongst other Asian countries, including large-scale anti-Japanese demonstrations by Chinese students, that he cancelled the visit.[39] When Prime Minister Junichiro Koizumi made plans to visit the shrine, twenty South Korean gangsters chopped off their fingers in front of the Independence Gate in Seoul.[40] On 15 August 2001, Prime Minister Junichiro Koizumi visited the shrine but did not undergo the traditional purification rituals.[41] Chinese Foreign Minister Tang Jiaxuan stated that the visit would gradually affect Sino-Japanese relations.[42] While official visits to the Yasukuni Shrine will remain an issue, hopefully, cooler heads will pave the way for their acceptance. Japan is a sovereign state and the new generation of Japanese tends to interpret the visits as an exercise of Japan's sovereign right. Besides, the shrine was not built for World War II war criminals, but for those who died in earlier wars. The war criminals have been tried and punished, and China and Korea should take a more humane attitude for the sake of the families of the soldiers.

Compensation

The 1952 San Francisco Peace Treaty absolved Japan temporarily from paying compensation for wartime damages since it was then not in a position to do so. China, Korea and other Asian countries affected by Japanese atrocities were not present at the signing. In Article 14 of the Treaty, Japan agreed to pay reparation to the Allied Powers for damages and suffering caused during the war.[43] A nominal sum amounting to £76 for each British service personnel and £45 for each British civilian was paid to prisoners-of-war. The Asians were not compensated. After the war, Japan made separate bilateral arrangements with Asian countries and compensation was paid to the governments concerned. With increasing awareness about human rights, some victims have brought lawsuits against the Japanese government. Japanese courts have, however, stuck to the view that the matter had already been settled through the 1952 San Francisco Peace Treaty and the separate bilateral treaties between Japan and the countries concerned after the war. The courts fear that the award of any compensation would be tantamount to an admission of guilt and may open the floodgates for more claims involving more substantial sums. For instance, Article 14(b) of the September Peace Treaty barred individual claims being made from signatory states. However, legal scholars assert that states, as signatories of the treaty, cannot extinguish such claims.[44] To take an example, Article 5 of the Joint Communiqué of the Government of Japan and the Government of the Peoples Republic of China signed on 29 September 1972 states:[45]

> The Government of the PRC declares that in the interest of the friendship between the Chinese and the Japanese peoples, it renounces its demand for war reparation from China.

Article 3 of the Hague Convention 1907 provides that individuals have rights to make claims for crimes against humanity, which no treaty made between or among nations can waive or abrogate. Given the fact that the governments of the occupied countries had already received compensation, they should handle the issue of compensation as a non-legal matter, and possibly with the cooperation of Japan. For instance, the British government agreed to pay £10,000 to each POW, incurring a total cost of £70 million in the process.[46] The issue of compensation to South Korea was settled by the Agreement between Japan and the Republic of Korea Concerning the Settlement of Problems in Regard to Property and Claims and Economic Cooperation signed in Tokyo on 22 June 1965. Article II (i) states:

> The High Contracting Parties confirm that the problems concerning property, rights, and interests of the two High Contracting Parties and their peoples (including juridical persons) and the claims between the High Contracting Parties and between their peoples, including those stipulated in Article IV(a) of the Peace Treaty which Japan signed at the city of San Francisco on September 8, 1951, have [been] settled completely and finally.[47]

In relation to Malaysia, a negotiated settlement between the Malaysian, Singaporean and the Japanese governments was reached in 1963, and has been accepted as the final settlement for reparation.[48] Japan has also paid reparation to other countries through bilateral treaties.

Comfort Women

Over 100,000 women, especially Koreans, were kept in Japanese military brothels established in the Pacific theatre during World War II.[49] The issue of comfort women was not considered in the war crimes trials, nor was it resolved in the post-war settlements. The victims have instead raised legal suits in Japanese courts. Japan's argument is that the issue of compensation was resolved in the San Francisco Peace Treaty and Japan has therefore no further legal obligation to compensate. On the other hand, North Korea claims that Japan had agreed to pay reparation for its colonial rule in Korea; but Japan denies having made any such commitment.[50] Given that the figure involved is not large, the Japanese should find a way to put the issue behind them.

Apology

When Emperor Hirohito was still alive, Japan avoided discussing war atrocities in order not to risk embarrassing him. Since then, many Japanese leaders have expressed their apologies for Japan's war sins. Prime Minister Morihoro Hosokowa, who led the non-Liberal Democratic government between July 1993 and April 1994, carried the process of apologizing further than any of his predecessors.[51] In October 1998, Keizo Obuchi, then the Japanese prime minister, offered his country's apology for the suffering of the Koreans under Japan's rule. On 15 August 2001, during the fifty-sixth anniversary of World War II, Prime Minister Junichiro Koizumi expressed his remorse to those who suffered from Japanese aggression.[52] In October 2001, during his visit to Korea and China, just before the Asia-Pacific Economic Cooperation Summit in Shanghai, he apologized for Japan's war atrocities.[53] Despite this, there are complaints that Japan has not been truly remorseful since its leaders have not used the most appropriate Japanese terms for such an apology. Unlike China and Korea, ASEAN countries have accepted Japan's apologies.[54] Dr Mahathir Mohamad, the former Malaysian prime minister, even went to the extent of advising Japan not to apologize further.[55]

Chemical Weapons Left in China

The latest issue is related to the 700,000 items of chemical weapons left behind in China by the Japanese military. This was revealed in August 2003 when construction workers accidentally dug up five containers, one of which contained mustard gas. The Japanese admitted it was one of theirs.

One man died from exposure to the gas, while dozens of others were injured. After much negotiation, Tokyo offered 300 million yen ($2.7 million) to dispose of the chemicals at the site, leaving it to China to "appropriately distribute" the money. However, Japan refused to call it "compensation". Just before the gas find, a Tokyo court had ordered Japan to pay compensation to the plaintiffs in another incident. The government is appealing that decision.[56]

Japan's Economic Diplomacy in East Asia

Immediately after the war, Japan was seen as a pariah state and was isolated from regional affairs.[57] Its economic entry into East Asia commenced with its provision of aid under various reparation agreements signed as part of the 1952 San Francisco Peace Treaty and the Colombo Plan. Reparation aid came primarily in the form of exports of outdated technology and industrial plants that allowed Japanese companies to re-enter Southeast Asian markets and create technological linkages between those countries and Japan. Meanwhile, newly independent countries in Southeast Asia were in urgent need of capital, investment, technological aid and trade.[58] It was here that the national interests of Japan and these other countries coincided. Japan needed food for its population and raw materials, especially oil, for its industries, while its neighbours needed Japanese capital, technology and markets for their products. Japan's economic growth in the 1980s was impressive and its GNP was second only to that of the United States.[59] The Plaza Accord of 1985, forced on Japan by the United States, led to a re-evaluation of the yen, and Japan, in order to cut industrial production costs, was forced to move some of its industries to other countries in the region. This helped develop the economies of Taiwan, South Korea, Hong Kong and Singapore. These four were then followed by states such as Malaysia, Thailand, Indonesia and the Philippines. With Japan at the core and the other countries in the periphery, the whole region took off economically, in the pattern that became known as the "Flying Geese Model", with Japan as the pilot goose. After the Asian economies deflated in 1997, Japan donated more than US$40 billion in aid and currency support.[60] It also extended US$5 billion in financial assistance to Indonesia.[61] Despite its own economic stagnation, Japan is still responsible for seventy per cent of East Asia's production, and countries in the region still see Japan as their economic engine. The importance of Japan can be discerned in the following tables.

TABLE 2.1
Economic Dimensions of Southeast Asian States

Country	Economy and Per-Cap GNP (US$)		Size and Population (Million)
Brunei	Rich	$17,475	Tiny (5,800 sq. km); 0.3
Cambodia	Poor	$215	Small (181,000 sq. km); 10.2
Indonesia	Poor	$940	Large (1,925,000 sq. km); 197.6
Laos	Poor	$325	Small (236,000 sq. km); 4.8
Malaysia	Mid	$3,930	Mid (332,370 sq. km); 20.3
Myanmar	Poor	$890	Mid (678,000 sq. km); 47.2
Philippines	Poor	$1,130	Mid (300,000 sq. km); 68.5
Singapore	Rich	$18,950	Tiny (616 sq. km); 3.1
Thailand	Mid	$2,680	Mid (514,000 sq. km); 61
Vietnam	Poor	$220	Mid (329,6000 sq. km); 75.5

Sources: J. Dennis Derbyshire and Ian Derbyshire, *Political Systems of the World*, London: Chambers, 1989; *Asiaweek*, 26 April 1996, pp. 56–58; da Cunha, Derek, *Southeast Asian Perspectives on Security*, Singapore: ISEAS, p. 136.

OFFICIAL DEVELOPMENT ASSISTANCE (ODA)

Japan's ODA expanded rapidly from the mid-1970s, rising from US$1.42 billion in 1977 to US$13.8 billion in 1995. In 1996, Japan was the main donor to China, Indonesia, the Philippines, Thailand, Vietnam, Burma, Cambodia and Laos. In 1998, the figure was US$9.4 billion. Japan had become the number one donor in East Asia. In 1998, it allocated 29.4 per cent of its ODA to East Asia.[62] The largest proportion of this, around 16 per cent, was provided to Indonesia and China. Furthermore, Japan's position as the main bilateral donor has been reinforced by its strong position within the Asian Development Bank. Japan realized that the only way it could rebuild international relations was to extend its influence in East and Southeast Asia through trade and commerce. However, ODA is tied to the purchase of Japanese goods and services, especially large infrastructure projects, and can thus be considered to have helped Japanese Transnational Corporations to penetrate East Asian markets. The Ministry of International Trade and Industry (MITI) has often conceived of ODA as a means to enhance the vertical integration of regional economies into Japan's own.[63]

TABLE 2.2

Japan's Foreign Direct Investment in East Asian Countries 1951–97 (US$ millions)

	1951–64	1965	1970	1975	1980	1985	1986	1987	1988	1989	1990	1995	1996	1997
China	0	0	0	0	12	100	226	1,226	296	438	349	4,473	2,510	1,987
South Korea	0	0	17	93	35	134	436	647	483	606	284	445	416	442
Taiwan	9	1	25	24	47	114	291	367	372	494	446	457	521	450
Hong Kong	9	2	9	105	156	131	502	1,072	1,662	1,898	1,785	1,125	1,487	695
Singapore	15	2	9	55	140	339	302	494	747	1,902	840	1,152	1,115	1,824
Thailand	33	6	13	14	33	48	124	250	859	1,276	1,154	1,224	1,403	1,867
Malaysia	13	5	14	52	146	79	158	163	387	673	725	573	572	791
Philippines	24	0	29	149	78	61	21	72	134	202	258	718	559	524
Indonesia	35	16	49	585	529	408	250	545	586	631	1,105	1,596	2,414	2,514
North Korea	0	0	0	0	0	0	3	2	13	10	1	0	1	0
Brunei	1	0	0	1	0	1	1	0	0	0	0	0	0	0
Vietnam	–	–	–	–	0	0	0	0	0	0	0	197	319	311
Cambodia	–	–	0	0	0	0	0	0	0	0	0	0	3	0
Laos	–	–	0	0	0	0	0	0	0	0	0	0	0	0
Burma	0	0	0	0	0	0	0	0	0	0	1	0	0	0
Total	139	32	165	1,078	1,176	1,415	2,314	4,840	5,539	8,130	6,948	11,960	13,910	10,601

Source: Hook G.D., Gilson J., Hughes C.W. and Dobson H., Japan's International Relations. Politics, Economics and Security, London: Routledge, 2001, pp. 450–51.

Japan's economic significance can be further seen from its Official Development Assistance Program (1987–91):

Japan's Official Assistance to East Asia

Country	Total (US$ millions)
China	5,394.98
Indonesia	8,212.42
Republic of Korea	1,521.57
Laos	172.12
Malaysia	2,000.71
Myanmar	2,174.75
Philippines	4,598.67
Singapore	179.15
Thailand	4,073.11
Vietnam	247.30
Brunei	21.60
Cambodia	45.25
Total	64,641.63

Source: *Japan's Official Development Assistance 1992, Annual Report*, Ministry of Foreign Affairs. pp. 203–24.

Japan's trade with China for the January–June 2002 period grew by 3 to 4 per cent to US$45.1 billion, compared with the same period in 2001, setting a record for the third straight year. In the same period, imports from China accounted for 17.8 per cent of total imports, nearing the 18.2 per cent share held by the United States, which has always been the biggest trade partner for Japan. Japan's investment in China is also surging.[64] It has also shifted some of its manufacturing to Southeast Asian countries. Some believe that Japan's future function will be that of "Asia's brain".[65] Japan-South Korea trade relations are also of great importance to both countries.

How East Asia will develop will be determined largely by Japan. One scholar suggests that by 2015, Japan's GNP per capita will be four times that of the United States.[66] Although Japan calls itself a cultural state beholden to the principles of liberalism, democracy and peace, its fundamental objective has been economic. Thanks to Japan's substantial increase in aid, investment and trade with the rest of East Asia, and its dominance within the Asian Development Bank, other economies are greatly benefiting. Malaysia, Thailand

TABLE 2.3
Japan's East Asia Trade 1958–98 (US$ millions)

	1950	1955	1960	1965	1970	1975
China						
Exports	20	29	3	245	569	2,259
Import	40	81	21	225	254	1,531
Trade Balance	−20	−52	−18	20	315	728
South Korea						
Exports	18	40	100	180	818	2,248
Imports	16	10	19	41	229	1,308
Trade Balance	2	30	81	139	589	940\
Taiwan						
Exports	38	64	102	218	700	1,822
Imports	38	81	64	157	251	812
Trade Balance	0	−17	38	61	449	1,010
Hong Kong						
Exports	53	88	156	288	700	1,378
Imports	0.5	6	23	35	92	245
Trade Balance	52.5	82	133	253	608	1,133
Singapore						
Exports	14	59	87	124	423	1,524
Imports	0	16	14	33	87	399
Trade Balance	14	43	73	91	336	1,125
Thailand						
Exports	43	63	118	219	449	959
Imports	44	63	72	131	190	724
Trade Balance	−1	0	46	88	259	235
Malaysia						
Exports	4	14	32	75	166	566
Imports	39	93	194	263	419	691
Trade Balance	−35	−79	−162	−188	−253	−125
Philippines						
Exports	18	52	155	240	454	1,026
Imports	23	89	159	254	533	1,121
Trade Balance	−5	−37	−4	−14	−79	−95
Indonesia						
Exports	46	65	110	205	316	1,850
Imports	13	81	70	149	637	3,430
Trade Balance	33	−16	40	56	−321	−1,580

TABLE 2.3 — *continued*

1980	1985	1990	1995	1996	1997	1998
			China			
5,078	12,477	6,130	21,931	1,806	21,689	20,105
4,323	6,483	12,054	35,922	40,370	41,846	37,085
755	5,994	−5,924	−13,991	−18,564	−20,157	−16,980
			South Korea			
5,368	7,097	17,457	31,291	29,338	26,086	15,401
2,996	4,092	11,707	17,269	15,955	14,590	12,117
2,372	3,005	5,750	14,022	13,383	11,496	3,284
			Taiwan			
5,146	5,025	18,430	28,969	25,953	27,552	25,602
2,293	3,386	8,496	14,366	14,971	12,506	10,237
2,853	1,639	9,934	14,603	10,982	15,046	15,365
			Hong Kong			
4,761	6,509	13,072	27,775	25,337	27,241	22,529
569	767	2,173	2,739	2,576	2,252	1,733
4,192	5,742	10,899	25,036	14,251	18,702	20,697
			Singapore			
3,911	3,860	10,708	23,001	20,775	20,261	14,782
1,507	1,594	3,571	6,844	7,325	5,879	4,717
2,404	2,266	7,137	16,157	13,450	14,382	10,065
			Thailand			
1,917	2,030	9,126	19,715	18,285	14,613	9,347
1,119	1,027	4,147	10,134	10,213	9,574	8,170
798	1,003	4,979	9,581	8,072	5,039	1,177
			Malaysia			
2,061	2,168	5,511	16,795	15,326	14,519	9,331
471	4,330	5,402	10, 549	11,746	11,382	8,687
−1,410	−2,162	109	6,245	3,580	3,137	644
			Philippines			
1,683	937	2,504	7,098	8,390	8,691	7,267
1,951	1,243	2,157	3,482	4,513	5,022	4,427
−268	−306	347	3,616	3,877	3669	2,840
			Indonesia			
3,458	2,172	5,040	9,971	9,052	10,188	4,302
13,167	10,119	12,721	14,214	15,186	14,629	10,841
−9,709	−7,947	−7,681	− 4,243	−6,134	−4,441	−6,539

continued on next page

TABLE 2.3 — *continued*

	1950	1955	1960	1965	1970	1975
North Korea						
Exports	0	0	1	17	23	181
Imports	0	0	0.008	15	34	65
Trade Balance	0	0	1	2	−11	116
Brunei						
Exports	0	0	0	0	10	34
Imports	0	0	0	0	1	1,021
Trade Balance	0	0	0	0	9	−987
Vietnam						
Exports	−	−	−	−	−	−
Imports	−	−	−	−	−	−
Trade Balance	−	−	−	−	−	−
North Vietnam						
Exports	−	−	6	4	5	43
Imports	−	−	10	12	6	27
Trade Balance	−	−	−4	−8	−1	16
South Vietnam						
Exports	−	−	62	37	146	39
Imports	−	−	5	7	5	15
Trade Balance	−	−	57	30	141	24
Cambodia						
Exports	−	−	14	13	11	0.1
Imports	−	−	8	8	6	0.6
Trade Balance	−	−	6	5	5	−0.5
Laos						
Exports	−	−	2	1	7	4
Imports	−	−	0	0	0.049	1
Trade Balance	−	−	2	1	6.951	3
Myanmar						
Exports	16	38	65	76	39	61
Imports	18	46	13	26	13	25
Trade Balance	−2	−8	52	50	26	36

TABLE 2.3 — *continued*

1980	1985	1990	1995	1996	1997	1998
North Korea						
374	247	176	255	227	179	175
180	179	300	340	291	302	219
194	68	−124	−85	−64	−123	−44
Brunei						
88	90	86	131	132	149	62
3,245	1,892	1,262	1,349	1,393	1,407	1,028
−3,157	−1,802	−1,176	−1,218	−1,261	−1,258	−966
Vietnam						
113	149	214	921	1,136	1,278	1,333
49	65	595	1,716	2,012	2,189	1,748
64	84	−381	−795	−876	−911	−415
North Vietnam						
−	−	−	−	−	−	−
−	−	−	−	−	−	−
−	−	−	−	−	−	−
South Vietnam						
−	−	−	−	−	−	−
−	−	−	−	−	−	−
−	−	−	−	−	−	−
Cambodia						
25	2	5	77	56	58	45
0.6	0.4	3	7	7	13	16
24.4	1.6	2	70	49	45	29
Laos						
12	12	20	29	39	29	19
6	1	5	30	24	21	20
6	11	15	−1	15	8	−1
Myanmar						
214	184	101	157	254	211	187
76	35	41	94	103	99	89
138	149	60	63	151	112	98

Source: Hook, Gilson, Hughes and Dobson, op. cit., pp. 442–46.

and China are the most recent beneficiaries. Vietnam is expected to be next, followed by Cambodia.

Given the great significance of economic relations between Japan and other countries in the region, it will be interesting to see to what extent war memories will affect mutual relations. The history of international relations shows that in a conflict between morality and national interest, states tend to favour the latter. The Allies, for example, for economic and political reasons adopted an attitude of indifference after World War I when Holland refused to let the Kaiser be tried for war crimes, and Germany made a farce of the Leipzig Trials. Similarly, after World War II, the United States, again for reasons of political expediency, decided not to bring Emperor Hirohito and other Class A war criminals to trial. The Japanese multinational corporations, the *zaibatsus*, which exploited the war for economic gains, were not abolished by the United States, for economic reasons. Similarly, the Allied Powers agreed to show clemency and terminate war crimes trials in order to win Japan and West Germany over to the Western Bloc.

REVIVAL OF JAPANESE MILITARISM AND US MILITARY PRESENCE IN EAST ASIA

The revival of Japanese militarism in East Asia that China and the Koreas fear so much appears to be a distant possibility, given the current security scenario. The Japanese constitution restricts defence expenditure to about 1 per cent of the GNP and the Japanese public is against any military awakening. U.S.-Japan security arrangements assure a nuclear umbrella for Japan, while U.S. bilateral military relations indirectly protect Japan's security interests in Southeast Asia in relation to the friendly countries enumerated in the following table. Given this regional defence arrangement, there is little chance that war memories can become a serious factor in East Asia's international relations.

CONCLUSION

East Asia has changed greatly. The national interests of all countries now rest upon the upkeep of peace and order. This is further facilitated by the existence of new regional institutions such as APEC, ARF and ASEAN+3 (Japan, China and Korea) that can contribute to the region's stability. The challenges of globalization push all these countries together, and Japan is seen as the key player in advancing their interests.[67]

If war memories continue to be an issue, it will only be in countries where they have domestic political significance, particularly China and Korea.

TABLE 2.4
U.S. Defence Ties with East and Southeast Asian States

Country	Year	Types of Agreement
Japan	1954	Mutual Defence Assistance Agreement
	1960	Treaty of Mutual Cooperation and Security
South Korea	1953	Mutual Defence Treaty
Taiwan	1979	Taiwan Relations Act
Philippines	1951	Mutual Defence Treaty
Thailand	1951	U.S. Mutual Security Act
Singapore	1990	Memorandum of Understanding allowing U.S. rotational access to Singapore facilities
Brunei	1994	Memorandum of Understanding on Defence Cooperation
Malaysia	1984	Bilateral Training and Education Cooperation
Indonesia	1992	Facilities for U.S. naval repairs

Source: da Cunha, Derek, *Southeast Asian Perspectives on Security*, Singapore: ISEAS, p. 146.

TABLE 2.5
Ethnic Chinese in Southeast Asia as
Percentage of Total Population

Brunei	16.0
Cambodia	1.0
Indonesia	3.0
Laos	0.4
Malaysia	29.6
Myanmar	1.4
Philippines	1.3
Singapore	77.7
Thailand	8.6
Vietnam	1.5

Source: da Cunha, Derek, ed., *Southeast Asian Perspectives on Security*, Singapore: ISEAS, 2000, p. 140.

However, these countries need close economic relations with Japan and there is inter-dependence with regard to trade and investment. In Southeast Asia, the issue will not become important for two reasons. Firstly, the overseas Chinese are not an important domestic political force except in Singapore,

for whom economic survival is too important for them to start antagonizing
Japan for the latter's historical sins.

The war criminals whose ashes are kept at the Yasukuni Shrine have already
paid with their lives. Undeniably, memories of Japanese atrocities will remain
among the victims and their loved ones. Some may try to keep the memories
alive as a heritage of history or for political advantage. However, time heals,
and a new generation that did not experience the atrocities will not give as
much importance to them as the generation that experienced them had done.
For the young, moving ahead is more important than thinking about matters
relating to a war that occurred many decades ago. In accordance with the
adage "there is no permanent enemy or friend in international relations but
only permanent interests", countries in the region will come to employ war
memories less and less as a political tool. The countries in East Asia need each
other, and they need Japan, for their economic growth. Japan cares more than
any other country in the region about good relations within the region, since
that secures the supply of raw materials.[68] In turn, Japan needs to address its
guilt daringly, or the issue will linger and might resurface to garner hatred
against Japan in the event of a deterioration of relations between Japan and
China or Korea. Even Japan does not seem to be giving as much thought to
its historical sins as it did in the past. For instance, during the meeting
between Prime Minister Obuchi and President Jiang Zemin in Tokyo in
December 1998 and in Beijing in July 1999, Obuchi refused to kowtow to
China's usual negotiating tactic of raising the issue of the colonial past in
order to extract a ritual apology from Japan. Given all these, it can be
concluded that war memories will lose their political appeal as time passes.

Notes

[1]   Mearsheimer, John J., *The Tragedy of Great Power Politics*, New York: W.W.
       Norton & Co., 2001. pp. 373–77.
[2]   Peattie, Mark R., *Oppressor or Modernizer? Himeji International Forum of Law
       and Politics*, no. 2 (1995): 351.
[3]   Ibid., p. 350.
[4]   Piccigallo R., Philip, *The Japanese on Trial: Allied War Crimes Operations in the
       East 1945–1951*, Austin: University of Texas Press, 1979.
[5]   Ward, Ian, *The Killer They Called A God*, Singapore: Media Masters, 1996,
       p. 294.
[6]   Pritchard, R.J., The Gift of Clemency Following British War Crimes Trials in
       the Far East, *Criminal Law Forum* 7, no. 1 (1996).
[7]   Kinvig, Clifford, *River Kwai Railway*, London: Brassey, 1992; Roling, B.V. and
       C.F. Ruter, *The Tokyo Judgment: The International Tribunal for the Far East 29th*

April 1946 – 12th November 1948, Amsterdam: APA University, 1977, pp. 403–04.

8   Tanaka, Yuki, *Hidden Horrors: Japanese War Crimes in World War II*, Oxford: Westview, Press, 1996.

9   Ibid., pp, 45–78; Wall, Don, *Kill the Prisoners*, printed by D. Wall, Mana Vale, New South Wales, Australia.

10   Tanaka, op. cit., pp. 111–34; Crasta, J.B., *Eaten by the Japanese*, Singapore: Raffles, 1999.

11   Lomex, Eric, *The Railway Man*, London: Vintage, 1996.

12   *The Star*, 16 August 2001.

13   Gold, Hal, *Japan's Wartime Human Experimentation Program. Unit 731 Testimony*, Singapore: YenBooks, 1999. Soldiers involved in the programme still feel guilty about what they did and have asked the Japanese Government to acknowledge it.

14   Dower, John, *War without Mercy: Race and Power in the Pacific War*, New York, 1986; Mahbubani, Kishore, *Can Asians Think?*, Singapore: Times Books International, 1998, p. 100.

15   Minear, Richard, *Victor's Justice: The Tokyo War Crime Trial*, Princeton: Princeton University Press, 1971; Cook H.T. and T.F. Cook, *Japan at War. An Oral History*, New York: The New Press, 1992, pp. 420–27.

16   Well A., Donald, *An Encyclopedia of War and Ethics*, London: Greenwood Press, 1996, pp. 203–04.

17   Chang, Iris, *The Rape of Nanking: The Forgotten Holocaust of World War II*, New York: Penguin Books, 1997; Buruma, Ian, *Wages of Guilt. Memories of War in Germany and Japan*, London: Vintage, 1995, pp. 112–35; Ward, Ian, op. cit.

18   Chang, ibid; Wickert, Erwin, ed., *The Good German of Nanking. The Diaries of John Rabe*, London: Little Brown & Co., 1998.

19   Harris, Sheldon H., *Factories of Death: Japanese Biological Warfare 1932–1945*, and the American Cover Up, London: Routledge, 1994.

20   Lee, Ivy, Probing the Issues of Reconciliation More than Fifty Years after the Asia-Pacific War, *EastAsia International Quarterly* 19, no. 4 (Winter 2001): 46.

21   Ibid., p. 39.

22   Hawthorn, Geoffrey, "A New Japan? A New History?" in *Statecraft and Security. The Cold War and Beyond*, edited by Ken Booth, Cambridge: Cambridge University Press, 1998, p. 213.

23   Ibid., p. 215; Howard, Keith, ed., *True Stories of the Korean Women*, London: Cassel, 1995; McCormack G. and H. Nelson, *The Burma-Thailand Death Railway*, Chiengmai: Silkworm Books, 1993; Schmidt, Petra, Disabled Colonial Veterans of the Imperial Japanese Forces and the Right to Receive Social Welfare Benefits from Japan, *Sydney Law Review* 21, 2 June 1999.

24   Deakon, Richard, *Kempetai: A History of Japanese Secret Police*, New York, 1983; Mallal, B.A., "The Double Tenth Trial, War Crimes Court in re Lt. Col. Sumida Haruzo and Twenty Others", Malayan Law Journal Office, Singapore, 1947.

25   Choon B.K. and Kuan Y.H., *Rehearsal for War. The Underground War Against the*

Japanese, Singapore: Horizon Books, 2002; Fook, Ho Tean, *Tainted Glory*, K.L.: University of Malaya Press, 2000; Karthigasu, Sybil, *No Dram of Mercy*, Singapore: Oxford University Press, 1983; Chapman, F.S., *The Jungle is Neutral*, London: The Reprint Society, 1949; Kheng, Cheah Boon, *Red Star Over Malaya, Resistance and Social Conflict During and After the Japanese Occupation of Malaya 1941–1946*, Singapore: Singapore University Press, 1983.

26   Ward, op. cit.; Mallal, B.A., op. cit.; *Files WO 235/931 (Penang Kempetai Trial), WO 235/89 (Double Tenth Trial), WO 235/1004 (Singapore Chinese Massacre Trial)*, Public Records Office, Kew, London; Kratoska, H. Paul, *The Japanese Occupation of Malaya. A Social and Economic History*, Hurst & Co., London, 1998.

27   Ahmad, Abu Talib, The Malay Community and Memory of the Japanese Occupation in Huen L.P. and Wong D., eds., *War and Memory in Malaysia and Singapore*, Singapore: ISEAS, 2000, pp. 45–89.

28   Gerald, Corr, *The War of the Springing Tigers*, London: Osprey, 1975; Ramasamy P., Indian War Memory in Malaysia in Huen P.L.P. and Wong D., ibid, pp. 90–105; *Netaji Subhas Chandra Bose. A Malaysian Perspective*, Kuala Lumpur: Netaji Centre, 1992.

29   Tanaka, op. cit., pp. 79–110; Lam, Peng Er, Perceiving Japan: The View from Southeast Asia, in da Cunha, Derek, ed., *Southeast Asian Perspectives on Security*, Singapore: ISEAS, 2000. p. 141.

30   Piccigallo, op. cit., p. 109; Kinvig, op. cit.

31   Ibid., p. 169.

32   *New Straits Times*, 18 July 2001.

33   *New Straits Times*, 1 August 2001; 9 August 2001.

34   *Economist*, 24 April 2001, p. 26.

35   *Far Eastern Economic Review*, 7 August 2001; *The Economist*, 14 April 2001; *New Straits Times*, 1 August 2001.

36   *Economist*, 14 April 2001, p. 26.

37   Buruma, op. cit., pp. 189–201; *Far Eastern Economic Review*, 7 June 2001.

38   *Far Eastern Economic Review*, 30 October 2003.

39   Hook, op. cit., p. 169.

40   *New Straits Times*, 1 June 2001.

41   *New Straits Times*, 31 May 2001.

42   Ibid.

43   *Treaty of Peace with Japan, with Declaration and Protocol — San Francisco*, 8 September 1951, Vol. 158, HMSO, 1961, pp. 543–44.

44   Lee, op. cit., p. 48.

45   Hook, op. cit., p. 482.

46   *The Times*, 9 July 2000.

47   Hook, D., op. cit., pp. 498–99.

48   Cheah, Boon Keng, "Memory as History and Moral Judgement. Oral and Written Accounts of the Japanese Occupation of Malaya", in Huen L.P. and Wong D., op. cit., p. 36.

[49] Christie, Kenneth, Memories of War Crimes in Asia and Europe: A Review Article, *Contemporary Southeast Asia* 19, no. 4 (March 1998): 422.
[50] *The Straits Times Interactive* <http://straitstimes.asia1.com/asia/ea13_0408.html 08/04/00>.
[51] Sheridan, op. cit., p. 207.
[52] *The Star*, 16 August 2001.
[53] Lee, op. cit., p. 47.
[54] Hawthorn, op. cit., p. 213.
[55] Cheah, Boon Kheng, Memory as History and Moral Judgement. Oral and Written Accounts of the Japanese Occupation of Malaya in Huen, L.P. and Wong D., op. cit., p. 35.
[56] *Far Eastern Economic Review*, 30 October 2003.
[57] Hook G.D., Gilson J., Hughes C.W. and Dobson H., *Japan's International Relations. Politics, Economics and Security*, London: Routledge, 2001, p. 154.
[58] Hawthorn, op. cit., pp. 217, 220.
[59] Ibid., p. 209.
[60] Sheridan, op. cit., pp. 193, 194, 199.
[61] Lam, Peng Er, op. cit., p. 145.
[62] Hook, op. cit., p. 194.
[63] Ibid., p. 195.
[64] *Far Eastern Economic Review*, 5 September 2002, p. 21.
[65] Hawthorn, op. cit., p. 213.
[66] Ibid., p. 209.
[67] Hook, op. cit., p. 154.
[68] Hawthorn, op. cit., p. 214.

References

Books

Barber, Noel. *Sinister Twilight. The Fall of Singapore*. London: Arrow, 1988.

Best, A., J.M. Hanhimaki, J.A. Maiolo and K.E. Schulze. *International History of the Twentieth Century*. London: Routledge, 2004.

Booth, Ken. *Statecraft and Security: The Cold War and Beyond*. Cambridge: Cambridge University Press, 1998.

Buruma, Ian. *Wages of Guilt: Memories of War in Germany and Japan*. London: Vintage, 1994.

Choon B.K. and Y.H. Kuan. *Rehearsal for War: The Underground War against the Japanese*. Singapore: Horizon Books, 2002.

Cook H.T. and T.F. Cook. *Japan at War: An Oral History*. New York: The New Press, 1992.

Cooper, C. Bryan. *Decade of Change. Malaya and the Straits Settlements 1936–1945*. Singapore: Graham Brash, 1998.

Crasta, John Baptist. *Eaten by the Japanese*. Singapore: Raffles, 1999.

da Cunha, Derek, ed. *Southeast Asian Perspectives on Security*. Singapore: Institute of Southeast Asian Studies, 2000.

Dower, John W. *Embracing Defeat: Japan in the Aftermath of World War II*, London: Penguin Books, 1999.

———. *War Without Mercy: Race and Power in the Pacific War*. New York, 1986.

Eichi, Hoshino. *Human Rights and Development Aid. Japan after the ODA Charter in Ness, Peter Van, Debating Human Rights. Critical Essays from the United States and Asia*. London: Routledge, 1999.

Eiji, Takemae. *Inside GHQ: The Allied Occupation of Japan and Its Legacy*. New York: Continuum, 2002.

Fallows, James. *Looking at the Sun: The Rise of the New East Asian Economic and Political System*. New York: Pantheon Books, 1994.

Fook, Ho Thean. *Tainted Glory*. Kuala Lumpur: University of Malaya Press, 2000.

Harris, Sheldon H. *Factories of Death. Japanese Biological Warfare, 1932–45, and the American Cover-up*. London: Routledge, 1994.

Hicks, George. *Japan's War Memories: Amnesia or Concealment?*. Aldershot: Ashgate, 1998.

Hook, G.D., J. Gilson, C.W. Hughes and H. Dobson. *Japan's International Relations. Politics, Economics and Security*. London: Routledge, 2001.

Howard, Keith, ed. *True Stories of the Korean Women*. London: Cassel, 1995.

Huen, L.P.P., and D. Wong, ed. *War and Memory in Malaysia and Singapore*. Singapore: Institute of Southeast Asian Studies, 2001.

Jackson, Sergeant-Major Charles R. *I Am Alive. A United States Marine's Story of Survival in a World War II Japanese POW Camp*. New York: Ballantine Books, 2003.

Li, Peter, ed. *The Search for Justice. Japanese War Crimes*. New Brunswick: Transaction Publishers, 2001.

Mahbubani, Kishore. *Can Asians Think?* Singapore: Times Books International, 1998.

Masuyama S., D. Vandenbrink and C.S. Yue, ed. *Restoring East Asia's Dynamism*. Singapore: Institute of Southeast Asian Studies, 2000.

Mearsheimer, John J. *The Tragedy of Great Power Politics*. New York: W.W. Norton & Co, 2001.

Md. Khalid, Khadijah, and Ping, L.P. *Whither The Look East Policy*. Bangi: Penerbit Universiti Kebangsaan Malaysia, 2003.

Morley, James W., ed. *Driven by Growth. Political Change in the Asia-Pacific Region (revised edition)*. New York: East Gate Book, 1999.

Pearson, Judith L. *Belly of the Beast. A POW's Inspiring True Story of Faith, Courage, and Survival Aboard the Infamous WWII Japanese Hell Ship Oryoku Maru*. New York: New American Library, 2001.

Piccigallo, R., Philip. *The Japanese on Trial: Allied War Crimes Operations in the East 1945–1951*. Austin: University of Texas Press, 1979.

Ping, Lee Poh. *The Japanese Model and Southeast Asia Beyond the Asian Crisis, Working Paper Series, No. 17 (June)*. Bangi: Institute of Malaysian and International Studies, Universiti Kebangsaan Malaysia, 2000.

Preston, P.W. *Understanding Modern Japan: A Political economy of Development, Culture and Global Power*. London: Sage Publications, 2000.

Roden G., K. Hewison and R. Robinson, ed. *The Political Economy of South-East Asia: Conflicts, Crises and Change*. Melbourne: Oxford University Press, 2002.

Sajima, Naoka. Japan's Strategic Culture at Crossroads. In *Strategic Culture in the Asia-Pacific Region*, edited by Booth, K. and R. Trood. London: Macmillan Press, 1999.

Sheridan, Greg. *Asian Values Western Dreams*. Understanding the New Asia. St. Leonards: Allen & Unwin, 1999.

Stares, Paul B., ed. *The New Security Agenda: A Global Survey*. New York: Japan Center for International Exchange, 1998.

Storry, Richard. *A History of Modern Japan*. London: Penguin Books, 1979.

Tanaka, Yuki. *Hidden Horrors. Japanese War Crimes in World War II*. Oxford: Westview, 1996.

—— *Rape and War: The Japanese Experience*, Melbourne: Japanese Studies Centre, 1999.

Wall, Don. *Kill the Prisoners*, published by Don W. Australia: Mona Vale, 1996.

Warren, Alan. *Singapore: Britain's Greatest Defeat*. Singapore: Talisman, 2002.

Waterford, Van. *Prisoners of the Japanese in World War II: Statistical History, Personal Narratives and Memorials Concerning POWs in Camps and on Hellships, Civilian Internees, Asian Slave Laborers and Others Captured in the Pacific Theater*. North Carolina: McFarland & Co, 1994.

Wickert, Erwin, ed. *The Good German of Nanking: The Diaries of John Rabe*. London: Little Brown & Co, 1998.

Wong, Anny. *Japanese Comprehensive National Security Strategy and its Economic Cooperation with the ASEAN Countries, Research*. Monograph No. 6, Hong Kong: Institute of Asia-Pacific Studies, The Chinese University of Hong Kong, 1991.

Yahuda, Michael. *The International Politics of the Asia-Pacific, 1945–1995*. London: Routledge, 1996.

Articles

Cropsy, Seth. "On the Pearl Harbour Anniversary, Japan Still Says 'Don't Blame Me' ", *The Heritage Lectures 353:*

Martin, Bernd. "From the Pacific War to a Policy of Good Neighbourliness: Japan's Way of Dealing with the Past". *Dialogue + Cooperation*, Occasional Papers, Southeast Asia Europe, Friedrich Ebert Stiftung.

Christie, Kenneth. "Memories of War Crimes in Asia and Europe: A Review Article". *Contemporary Southeast Asia* 19, no. 4 (1998).

Lu, Catherine. "Justice and Moral Regeneration: Lessons from the Treaty of Versailles". *International Studies Association* (2002).

Martin, Bernd. "Japan's Dealing with its Past". *Dialogue + Cooperation*, Occasional Papers Southeast Asia Europe 2, Friedrich Ebert Stiftung.

Ott, Marvin C. "East Asia: Security and Complexity". *Current History* (April 2001).

Peattie, Mark R. "Oppressor or Modernizer? Reflections on Japanese Colonialism". *Himeji International Forum of Law and Politics 2* (1995).

Price, John. "Cold War Relic: The 1951 San Francisco Peace Treaty and the Politics of Memory". *Asian Perspective* 25, no. 3 (2001).

Schmidt, Petra. "Disabled Colonial Veterans of the Imperial Japanese Forces and the Right to Receive Social Welfare Benefit from Japan". *Sydney Law Review* 21 (1999).

Thurow, Lester. *The Future of Capitalism. How Today's Economic Forces Shape Tomorrow's World*. London: Nicholas Brealey Publishing, 1997.

Towle P., M. Kosuge and Y. Kibata, ed. *Japanese Prisoners of War*. New York: Hambledon, 2000.

Tutu, Anglican Archbishop Desmond. "War Crimes Tribunals May End Impunity, But They Can't Heal Hatred". *New Perspective Quarterly* 19, no. 2 (2002).

Wilson, Dick. "Did Japan Declare War?", *Journal of Royal Society for Asian Affairs*, vol. 31, no. 1, March 2000.

Yahuda, Michael. *The International Politics of the Asia-Pacific, 1945–1995*. London: Routledge, 2000.

Yoshimura, Akira. *One Man's Justice*. San Diego: Harvest Book, 2001.

Magazines

Japan and Korea are Tied by a Painful Past, *Far Eastern Economic Review*, 24 August 1995.

Japan's Sins of Omission, *The Economist*, 14 April 2001:

History on Fire, *Far Eastern Economic Review*, 7 June 2001.

Memories of Horror, *Far Eastern Economic Review*, 5 September 2002.

Toxic Past, *Far Eastern Economic Review*, 30 October 2003.

Imperial Japan Inc. on Trial, *Asiaweek*, 15 November 1996.

Newspapers

The Daily Telegraph, 1 April 1999.

New Straits Times, 29 April 2001.

New Straits Times, 5 May 2001.

New Straits Times, 25 May 2001.

New Straits Times, 31 May 2001.

New Straits Times, 14 June 2001.

New Straits Times, 18 July 2001.
New Straits Times, 1 August 2001.
New Straits Times, 9 August 2001.
The Star, 16 August 2001.

Internet

The Straits Times Interactive, 8 April 2000 <http:straitstimes.asia1.com/asia/ea
13_0408.html>.

PART TWO

The Economics of
Regional Integration

3

MYTHS AND MIRACLES OF ECONOMIC DEVELOPMENT IN EAST ASIA
Policy Lessons for Malaysia in the Twenty-first Century

Tham Siew-Yean

INTRODUCTION

In its broadest sense, economic development deals with improving the quality of life of people. It is thus not just the goal of developing countries alone. Rather, it has been the central quest of all modern nations. Malthus, for example, calls the study of the causes of poverty and wealth of nations to be the grand object of all inquiries in political economy. The focus on economic growth is motivated by the fact that increases in Gross Domestic Product (GDP) per capita over time can have a significant impact on the reduction of hunger and poverty. As summarized by Easterly (2002: 13), empirical evidence shows clearly that "fast growth went with fast poverty reduction, and overall economic contraction went with increased poverty". The pursuit of economic growth has led to an extensive research interest in East Asian development, even before the publication of *The East Asian Miracle* (World Bank 1993). The 1993 World Bank study turned out to be controversial and stimulated many countering studies, especially on the issue of an East Asian model of development.[1] However, the Asian Financial Crisis (AFC) in 1997 provoked considerable rethinking on this "East Asian model".[2] Post-crisis, the debate continues to engage the minds of both academics and the public even as some of the miracle economies continue to struggle to recapture the golden years of growth.

The objective of this chapter is to review the factors that contributed to rapid growth in East Asia before the AFC in order to provide some policy suggestions for Malaysia. The chapter is organized as follows: After the introduction, the East Asian miracle is explained in Section 2; Section 3 analyses the sources of growth that underpinned the miracle while Section 4 discusses to what extent the miracle was a mirage in light of the AFC; in Section 5, some policy lessons for Malaysia's long-term development are suggested; Section 6 summarizes the main findings of this chapter.

THE EAST ASIAN MIRACLE

As stated in the *Overview of the World Bank* (1993: 1), the miracle in East Asia consisted of a record of high and sustained economic growth between 1965 and 1990, more so because it was associated with poverty reduction and declining inequality.[3] Growth in Miracle Asia between 1961 and 1996[4] clearly outperformed other countries, including those in Southeast Asia such as the Philippines, South Asia, Latin America, the Caribbean as well as Sub-Saharan Africa (Table 3.1). More importantly, this was found to hold in terms of GDP growth, GNP per capita growth as well as in absolute GNP per capita.[5]

This growth was certainly accompanied by significant reductions in poverty as shown in Table 3.2. These reductions were striking, whether understood in terms of US$1 per day or of national poverty line for the time periods shown, when compared to, for example, South Asia. However, the claim that rapid growth in East Asia was one of "shared growth" is more controversial. Quibria (2002: 11), for example, reported that the Gini coefficient had showed little improvement between the 1970s and 1993 for Singapore, while it deteriorated for Hong Kong and Taiwan. It improved for Malaysia for the same period, but deteriorated for Thailand. Although income distribution improved for Indonesia over that period, it deteriorated in the 1990s. It was therefore superior growth performance and poverty reduction in East Asia during the period 1960–90 that motivated the search to identify common policies that may have contributed to these outcomes, an effort tantamount to a search for an East Asian model of development.

TABLE 3.1

Economic Indicators, Selected Asia Economies and Selected Regions, 1961–96

Economy and region	GDP growth (%)					GNP per capita growth (%)					GNP per capita (constant 1995 US$)					
	1961–70	1971–80	1981–90	1991–96	1961–96	1961–70	1971–80	1981–90	1991–96	1961–96	1960	1970	1980	1990	1995	1998
Miracle Asia																
Hong Kong, China	9.87	9.38	6.63	5.21	7.77	7.06	6.73	5.32	3.46	5.64	3,022	5,947	11,290	18,813	22,619	21,726
Korea, Rep.	8.26	7.67	9.08	7.35	8.09	5.18	5.53	8.03	6.23	6.24	1,322	2,171	3,686	7,960	10,844	10,972
Singapore	9.96	9.04	7.36	8.88	8.81	7.16	6.40	5.99	6.97	6.63	3,145	6,208	11,516	20,465	28,794	32,602
Taipei, China	–	9.70	7.96	6.48	8.04	5.20	9.20	7.70	–	7.37	1,489	2,797	5,839	12,652	–	–
Indonesia	4.18	7.87	6.41	7.83	6.57	1.83	4.91	4.46	6.27	4.37	250	298	481	741	992	896
Malaysia	6.49	7.87	6.00	8.67	7.26	3.61	5.30	3.00	5.74	4.41	959	1,366	2,283	3,051	4,032	4,107
Thailand	8.17	6.89	7.89	8.05	7.75	5.41	3.90	5.95	6.49	5.44	451	762	1,115	1,977	2,771	2,579
Average	*7.82*	*8.35*	*7.33*	*7.49*	*7.76*	*5.06*	*6.00*	*5.78*	*5.86*	*5.73*	*1,520*	*2,793*	*5,173*	*9,380*	*11,675*	*12,147*
Philippines	4.93	5.93	1.80	2.80	3.86	1.70	3.46	–0.51	1.17	1.46	701	829	1,164	1,091	1,114	1,182
South Asia																
Bangladesh	4.06	1.79	4.77	4.53	3.79	1.11	–0.57	2.54	2.95	1.51	214	237	219	281	324	361
India	4.10	3.06	5.87	5.66	4.68	–	0.87	3.46	3.81	2.71	–	216	234	328	387	441
Nepal	2.52	2.11	4.79	5.22	3.66	0.48	–0.31	2.09	2.56	1.21	150	157	151	185	211	222
Pakistan	7.24	4.72	6.29	4.87	5.78	4.31	1.38	3.43	2.54	2.91	175	266	304	425	486	489
Sri Lanka	4.58	4.43	4.18	5.12	4.58	2.06	2.84	2.86	3.44	2.80	278	340	449	595	712	792
Average	*4.50*	*3.22*	*5.18*	*5.08*	*4.50*	*1.99*	*0.84*	*2.87*	*3.06*	*2.23*	*204*	*243*	*272*	*363*	*424*	*461*
Regions																
East Asia and Pacific	5.20	6.60	7.80	8.90	7.10	3.17	4.71	6.14	7.35	5.34	181	244	386	700	1,002	1,092
Latin America and Caribbean	5.40	5.90	1.21	3.63	4.04	2.68	3.33	–1.05	1.86	1.71	2,060	2,678	3,712	3,327	3,635	3,883
South Asia	4.36	3.12	5.79	5.45	4.67	–	0.81	3.36	3.51	2.56	–	223	240	334	391	437
Sub-Saharan Africa	5.22	3.64	1.75	1.84	3.11	2.57	0.59	–1.07	–0.62	0.37	456	587	620	555	526	535
World	*5.47*	*3.79*	*2.94*	*2.28*	*3.62*	*3.37*	*1.79*	*1.19*	*0.77*	*1.78*	*2,638*	*3,674*	*4,383*	*4,931*	*5,048*	*5,276*

Note: – Not available
GDP– Gross domestic product
Source: M.G. Quibria (2002).

TABLE 3.2
Incidence of Poverty, Selected Asian Economies, Selected Years (Headcount Index)

Economy	US$1 per day				National Poverty Line				
	1975	1985	1995	1998	1965	1970	1975	1985	1996
Miracle Asia									
Hong Kong, China	–	–	–	–	–	21.0[a]	14.0[b]	–	–
Korea, Rep.	–	–	2.0	–	41.1	23.0	14.6[b]	5.0[c]	9.6
Singapore	–	–	–	–	–	31.0[d]	–	10.0[e]	–
Taipei, China									
China	–	–	–	–	47.0	30.0	23.0	3.0	–
Indonesia	64.3	32.2	11.4	15.2	–	58.0	40.0[b]	28.0[c]	11.3
Malaysia	17.4	10.8	< 1.0	–	–	49.0	43.9	24.0	8.2[f]
Thailand	8.1	10.0	< 1.0	< 2.0	57.0[g]	39.0[h]	32.0[b]	26.0[i]	11.4
Philippines	35.7	32.4	25.5	–			52.0[i]	52.0	36.8[f]
South Asia									
Bangladesh	–	–	29.1	–	–	–	73.0[i]	52.0[l]	35.6
India	–	–	47.0[k]	44.2[f]	–	52.0[d]	51.0[l]	45.0[c]	35.0[k]
Nepal	–	–	37.7	–	–	–	–	–	42.0
Pakistan	–	–	31.0	–	–	–	43.0	25.0	22.0[m]
Sri Lanka	–	–	6.6	–	37.0	–	19.0[l]	40.6[l]	21.0[f]

Note: – Not available

a. 1971 d. 1972 g. 1962 j. 1973 m. 1993
b. 1976 e. 1982 h. 1968 k. 1994
c. 1984 f. 1997 i. 1986 l. 1978

Source: M.G. Quibria (2002)

Causes of the Miracle: Is There an East Asian Development Model?

The drive to understand the sources of growth in East Asia is underscored by the sub-title of the 1993 World Bank publication, that is, to draw policy lessons, especially in relation to the statistical link between growth and public policy. While this is a noble quest, even when the focus is on economic growth factors alone, the complex nature of economic development inevitably opens it to strong criticism.[6] To quote Sarel (1996: 1), "when practitioners of the Dismal Science have recourse to a Higher Power (*by calling a certain phenomenon "miraculous"*), the reader knows that he is in trouble. Confusion is compounded when he discovers that ideological debate has multiplied even further the analyses of this phenomenon."

Sarel (1996: 12) then proceeds to summarize the three main schools of thought pertaining to the impact of government policy and selective intervention on economic growth. The first school embraces the free market ideology that in turn requires the government to focus on creating the appropriate environment for a free market to flourish, while the second school does not believe in the efficiency of markets. Instead, it asserts the need for selective intervention to moderate the excesses of the market and to jumpstart the industrialization process in developing countries. The third school of thought, in turn, rejects the first two schools of thought in claiming that it is not possible to identify how such policies can spur economic growth.

The differences between these schools are further compounded by differences in opinions within each school over time. For example, the debate within the World Bank itself has seen some changes (see Quibria 2002: 2). While the World Bank (1993: 367) highlighted six factors — stable macro-economy, early education, importance of the agricultural sector even with industrialization, necessity of a sound financial system, openness to foreign ideas and technology, and allowing relative prices to reflect economic scarcities — a subsequent study (Liepziger and Thomas, 1997 as cited in Quibria 2002: 2) highlighted only three factors, that is, outward orientation, macroeconomic stability, and investment in people. A more recent study (Yusuf 2001, as cited in Quibria 2002: 2) emphasized four factors — sound macro-economic policy, an efficient bureaucracy committed to long-term development, an "activist" export-orientated government policy to industrialize, and a flexible and pragmatic government policy incorporating error correction mechanisms.

Empirical evidence has been invoked to support the arguments from the different schools of thought. Hence, the empirical evidence on the sources of growth for Miracle Asia will be reviewed in the following section in order to shed some light on the debate. It will be confined to areas where policy implications drawn from the World Bank study are disputed by subsequent studies. Not all of their policy findings were refuted. For example, the World Bank's findings on getting the "fundamentals" right as in the case of sound macro-economic management, export-orientation, and more education are, in the words of Lall (1994: 646), "neither original nor debatable: no one proposes bad macro policies; the trade strategy debate is no longer alive, ... and the need for primary schooling is hardly in dispute". Neither were the findings on prudent fiscal policies, high investments in human capital, the creation of infrastructure that complements private investment and of an investment-friendly environment controversial. In general, the functional interventions mentioned in the 1993 World Bank study were not disputed. What was disputed was the role of selective interventions, especially at the micro-level, and the contribution of functional interventions in comparison with selective interventions. Debates also abound pertaining to its findings on total factor productivity (TFP),[7] as well as the sources of growth in these economies.

SOURCES OF GROWTH

The change in TFP and its contribution to the growth of East Asian economies were used to ascertain the contribution made by factor accumulation and technical progress to output growth.

TFP Studies: Evidence and Counter-Evidence

The World Bank's findings immediately sparked off a series of other cross-country studies as well as single country studies, as shown in Table 3.3. The variation in the magnitudes obtained can be quite large. For example, the values obtained for Malaysia can range from 0.9 per cent in Sarel's study to 2.3 per cent in the study by Iwata et al. (Table 3.3). Similarly, estimates obtained for Taiwan range from 1.5 per cent to 3.87 per cent. The different results demonstrate the difficulties encountered in the measurement of TFP that can be sensitive to the time period of the study, assumptions about the elasticity of substitution in production and the nature of technical progress, the method of estimation, as well as data problems such as the lack of physical capital stock data in most developing countries and the choice of data on human capital.[8] It should be noted that there is a marked difference between

TABLE 3.3
Growth Rates of TFP (Various Estimates)

Country	Adjusted Young (1994, 1995) 1966–90	Collins and Bosworth (1996) 1960–94	M. Sarel (1997) 1978–96	Kim and Lau (1994)	Iwata et al. (2002) 1960–95	Hsieh (2002)	World Bank 1993 (1960–89)
Indonesia		0.8	1.2		1.9		1.3
Malaysia		0.9	2.0		2.3		1.1
Philippines		−0.4	−0.8		0.5		n.a
Singapore	1.0	1.5	2.2	1.6	3.1	2.16	1.2
Thailand			2.0		3.0		2.5
Taipei, China	1.9	2.0		1.5	3.4	3.87	3.7
Korea	1.3	1.5		1.1	3.3	2.07	3.1
Hong Kong, China	2.4			2.8	3.5	2.92	3.6
PRC		4.6			3.0		n.a.

Notes: Kim and Lau (1994) figures are: 1964–90 for Singapore, 1953–90 for Taipei, China, 1960–90 for Hong Kong, China.
Young (1994, 1995) figure for Hong Kong, China is for 1966–91.
Collins and Bosworth (1996) figure for PRC is for 1984–94.
Hsieh (2002) figures are: 1968–90 using average lending rate for Singapore; 1966–90 using one-year deposit rate for Taipei, China; 1966–90 using deposit rate for Korea; 1973–91 using E-P ratio for Hong Kong, China.
World Bank 1993, p. 64.

Source: Yoshitomi (2003)

TFP estimates obtained for the Asian Tigers and for Southeast Asian economies in general. The former set of countries usually obtained higher TFP estimates.

Apart from higher TFP growth estimates, the World Bank's decomposition on the sources of growth led it to conclude that growth in Japan, Korea, Hong Kong, Thailand and Taiwan was productivity-driven while that in Indonesia, Malaysia and Singapore were investment-driven. This was refuted by Kim and Lau (1994) and Young (1995) who showed that almost all growth in the East Asian economies could be attributed to capital accumulation rather than TFP growth. An entire cottage industry of research on this topic has emerged in response to such divergent results (Quibria 2002: 19) but the overall evidence tends to indicate that capital accumulation (and not TFP growth) was the main contributory factor for the spectacular growth of the East Asian economies, thereby attributing their growth to perspiration rather than inspiration. The World Bank has also revised its views as shown in Yusuf's remark that the miracle as mirrored in empirical research reveals capital (both physical and human) to be the primary growth contributor.

While it has been claimed that the aggregated measure of TFP used in these studies may not show sector gains, especially in manufacturing, country level studies on the manufacturing sector have not necessarily supported this argument for some of the East Asian economies, as summarized in Table 3.4. Rapid growth in that sector was contributed mainly by input growth, rather than growth in TFP.[9] However, this conclusion does not shed much light where policy-making is concerned since it is not clear whether it was domestic or foreign capital that spurred the rapid growth in the manufacturing sector

TABLE 3.4
Growth Rate of TFP for Selected East Asian Economies
(Based on Single Country Studies)

Country	TFP Growth
Indonesia	1.0 (1985–90)
Malaysia	0.3 (1986–91)
Singapore	0.08 (1970–79)
Thailand	0.7 (1987–96)
Korea	−1.6 (1967–89)

Note: TFP growth estimates are for the manufacturing sector.
Sources: Indonesia (Abimanyu 1995), Malaysia (Tham 1995), Singapore (Tsao 1982), Thailand, (Warr 2003), Korea (Kwon 1994)

of these economies. Neither is it clear whether the technology of multinational corporations (MNCs) was assimilated and whether it enhanced domestic technological capabilities.

Capital Accumulation: The Role of Foreign Direct Investment

Although the World Bank (1993: 303) noted in passing that Japan and Korea did set obstacles to FDI, the role FDI played in capital accumulation and deepening technological capabilities were not discussed. Japan is essentially a capital exporter rather than a capital importer. Table 3.5 shows that although developing Asia's share of global FDI trebled from 6.1 per cent for 1975–80 to 18.1 per cent for 1990–95 — largely influenced by East Asia — the importance of FDI in each of these economies differed. Singapore leads in terms of FDI inflows as percentage of GDP as well as gross domestic fixed capital formation (GDFC), followed by Malaysia, Indonesia and Thailand. All four economies actively courted FDI in their industrialization drive, with generous incentives and other favourable FDI policies. In 1993, these four were among the top ten developing host economies, indicating their relative success in attracting FDI. The relatively large inflows of foreign capital to these economies were in the main directed at their respective manufacturing sector, with the exception of Indonesia, which had substantial foreign investment in its petroleum industry.

On the other hand, FDI played a much smaller role in Korea and Taiwan. Korea imposed heavy regulations on foreign firm activities and instead favored a nationalistic route for industrialization (Shin and Chu 2003: 5). It has the lowest ratio of FDI to GDFC of all the East Asian Economies before the AFC (Table 3.5), utilizing instead foreign debt to finance its industrialization. Although Taiwan allowed a bigger role for the MNCs in comparison to Korea, it also imposed several regulations on FDIs such as limits on foreign shareholding and local content regulations, unlike liberal Singapore. Thus while it encouraged local enterprises, it also formed international alliances of equity partnership, thereby balancing the mixture of local and foreign enterprises operating in the economy. This factor has an important bearing on domestic export capacities and the indigenous technological capabilities of the East Asian economies.

While foreign affiliates contributed substantially to the exports of Singapore, Malaysia, Indonesia, and to a certain extent Thailand as well, their contribution was less in the case of Hong Kong, Korea and Taiwan (Table 3.6). Thus even though export promotion was utilized in the trade regimes of

TABLE 3.5

FDI Inflows: East Asia in the Global Context (1980–2000)

	1980–84	1985–89	1990	1991	1992	1993	1994	1995	1996	1997	1998	1999	2000
Value of inflow ($mn)													
World	246,573	642,471	203,812	157,773	168,122	219,421	253,506	328,862	386,140	478,082	694,457	1,088,263	1,491,934
Developed countries	187,230	531,189	169,777	114,001	114,002	133,850	146,379	208,372	219,908	267,947	484,239	837,761	1,227,476
Developing countries	59,339	110,998	33,735	41,324	50,376	78,813	101,196	106,224	152,685	191,022	187,611	225,140	237894
Asia	22,854	53,389	19,803	20,781	27,024	44,835	63,844	68,126	93,331	105,828	96,109	102,779	133,707
East Asia	22,040	51,640	19,339	20,325	26,400	47,813	58,844	63,391	75,832	83,817	73,785		
Brunei	–9	1.8	3	1	4	14	6	13ᵃ	654	702	573	596	600
Cambodia	–	–	0	0	33	54	69	151	586	–15	230	214	179
China	2,324	12,435	3,487	4,366	11,156	27,515	33,787	35,849	40,180	44,237	43,751	40,319	40,772
China: Hong Kong	3,298.3	7,850.3	1,728	538	2,051	3,657ᵃ	4,131ᵃ	3,279ᵃ	10,460	11,368	14,770	24,596	61,938
Indonesia	1,052	2,211	1,093	1,482	1,777	2,004	2,109	4,346	6,194	4,677	–356	–2,745	–4,550
Korea, Rep of	356	3,442	788	1,180	727	588	809	1,776	2,325	2,844	5,412	9,333	9,283
Lao, PDR	–	6	6	7	8	300	59	88	128	86	45	52	34
Malaysia	5,655	3,994	2,333	3,998	5,183	5,006	4,342	4,178	7,296	6,324	2,714	3,895	3,788
Philippines	196	1,945	530	544	228	1,238	1,591	1,478	1,520	1,249	1,752	578	1,241
Singapore	6,934	12,134	5,575	4,887	2,204	4,686	8,550	7,206	8,608	10,746	6,389	11,803	5,407
Taiwan	771	3,945	1,330	1,271	879	917	1,375	1,559	1,864	2,248	222	2,926	4,928
Thailand	1,423	3,659	2,444	2,014	2,113	1,804	1,366	2,068	2,271	3,626	5,143	3,561	2,813
Vietnam	31	12	16	32	24	300	650	1,400	1,803	2,587	1,700	1,484	1,289
As a percentage of GDP													
Asia	0.6	0.9	1.3	1.3	1.5	2.4	2.6	2.5	2.5	2.4	2.5		
East Asia	0.7	1.2	1.6	1.5	1.8	2.9	3.1	3.0	3.4	2.3	3.4		
Brunei	–	–	0.1	0.0	0.1	0.3	0.1	0.1	0.0	0.1	0.0		
Cambodia	–	–	0.0	0.0	1.7	2.4	2.9	5.4	–	3.7	–		
China	0.2	0.8	1.0	1.2	2.7	6.4	6.2	5.1	5.6	5.8	5.6		
China: Hong Kong	2.2	3.1	2.3	0.6	2.0	1.4	1.5	1.5	1.6	1.2	0.8		

Indonesia	0.2	0.5	1.0	1.2	1.3	1.3	1.2	2.1	2.7	2.1	***	
Korea, Rep of	0.1	0.5	0.3	0.4	0.2	0.2	0.2	0.4	0.6	0.7	0.8	11.6
Lao, PDR		0.1	0.7	0.7	0.7	2.3	3.9	5.0	5.2	3.7	3.3	
Malaysia	4.0	2.4	5.5	8.5	9.0	8.0	6.1	6.8	6.7	6.4	6.7	
Philippines	0.1	1.1	1.2	1.2	0.4	2.3	2.5	2.0	2.1	2.0	0.7	
Singapore	9.0	11.1	15.3	11.6	4.5	8.2	12.0	8.4	7.9	9.6	7.6	
Taiwan	0.3	0.8	0.8	0.7	0.4	0.4	0.6	0.6	0.6	0.5	0.7	
Thailand	0.8	1.4	2.9	2.0	1.9	1.4	1.0	1.2	1.3	1.1	1.6	
Vietnam			0.2	0.3	0.2	2.3	4.2	6.9	6.7	3.4	3.7	

As a percentage of GDFC

Asia	2.0	3.2	4.2	4.1	4.9	7.4	7.9	8.0	8.2	9.2	9.5	9.6	
East Asia	2.4	4.0	5.0	4.7	5.5	8.3	8.8	8.8	9.1	7.2	8.1		
Cambodia	–	–	0.0	0.0	17.1	17.0	15.0	16.5	71.9	-2.5	53.5	44.8	37.6
China	0.6	2.2	2.8	3.3	7.4	14.7	15.7	12.7	14.3	14.6	12.9	11.3	10.5
China:													
Hong Kong	7.1	12.1	8.4	2.3	7.2	5.2	4.8	4.2	21.7	19.8	30.0	60.2	144.9
Indonesia	0.9	1.8	3.1	4.1	4.7	3.8	3.5	6.7	9.2	7.7	-1.5	-9.0	-12.2
Korea, Rep of	0.3	1.5	0.8	1.0	0.6	0.5	0.6	1.1	1.2	1.7	5.7	8.3	7.1
Lao, PDR	–	1.0	5.6	5.3				1.1	23.6	18.2	14.4	15.6	9.7
Malaysia	11.5	9.3	16.3	23.7	25.6	22.7	24.7	27.9	17.0	14.7	14.0	22.2	16.5
Philippines	0.4	6.2	5.0	5.9	2.0	9.5	10.3	8.9	7.8	6.2	12.7	4.0	9.2
Singapore	18.9	19.3	38.7	30.4	12.3	23.1	36.1	25.4	24.6	29.4	20.8	42.4	19.8
Taiwan	1.2	3.6	3.6	3.0	1.7	1.6	2.4	2.5	3.0	3.4	0.4	4.4	6.8
Thailand	2.6	4.5	6.9	4.8	4.7	3.6	2.3	2.9	3.0	7.1	20.5	13.9	10.4
Vietnam	–	0.1	1.9	2.2	1.4	11.4	16.4	25.4	29.5	37.3	23.9	20.1	15.0

Notes: GDFC – Gross domestic fixed capital formation.
  – – Data not available or negligible.
  a – Estimates.
  *** – Zero or negligible

Source: Prema-chandra, Authukorala and Hal Hill (2002) and World Investment Report (2002).

TABLE 3.6
Share of Foreign Affiliates in Total manufactured Exports[1] from Developing Host Countries in East Asia (%)

	Source	Criterion of foreign ownership (FDI share in equity capital)	Year of estimate	Approximate share (%)
China	Naughton (1996) and Pomfret (1997)[2]	All firms with FDI	1985	2.2
			1988	7.5
			1990	16.9
			1993	33.6
			1996	47.6
Hong Kong	Nayyar (1978)	All firms with FDI	1972	10
	UNTCMD (1992)	All firms with FDI	1984	16.5
South Korea	Nayyar (1978)	10% or more	1971	15
	Koo (1985)	10% or more	1974	23.6
	Ramstetter (1993)	10% or more	1977	25.3
	Ramstetter (1993)	10% or more	1986	26.1
Taiwan	Nayyar (1978)	10% or more	1971	20
	Ranis and Schive (1985)	10% or more	1974	23.7
	Schive and Tu (1991)	10% or more	1976	31.3
	UNTCMD (1992)	n.a.	1981	25.6
	Ramstetter (1993)	10% or more	1989	18
Malaysia	UNTCMD (1992)	n.a.	1980	41
	UNTCMD (1992)	n.a.	1986	51.2
	Athukorala (1998, Chapter 8)	49 % or more	1988	72
		49 % or more	1992	75.6
Singapore	Chia (1985)	All firms with FDI	1963	57.4
	Nayyar (1978)	All firms with FDI	1970	70
	Huff (1994, Table 11.11)	51% or more	1975	84.1
		51% or more	1980	84.7
		51% or more	1990	85.8
			1991	91.5
Philippines	ITC (1987)	12.5% or more	1980	60.8
			1983	57.5
Thailand	Ramstetter (1997)	All firms with FDI	1974	12
			1986	15
			1988	33
Indonesia	Ramstetter (1999)	All firms with FDI	1992	65
			1994	71

Notes: 1. In all cases manufactured exports have been measured using the ISIC-based definition of manufacturing (that is, ISIC 3) or an approximation of it. Estimates cover direct exports only.

2. Derived from data on exports by foreign invested enterprises given in Naughton (1996), Table 3 and value manufactured exports reported in Pomfret (1997), Table 2. Estimate for 1996 refers to the first six months.

n.a. Information not available.

Source: Prema-chandra, Authukorala and Hal Hill (2002).

the HPAEs (World Bank 1993: 124), the contribution of local firms to their country's export success differed considerably.

Technology Exports and Domestic Technological Capabilities

Table 3.7 shows that Singapore, Malaysia, Taiwan and Korea are the most technologically advanced exporters, with differentiated and science-based exports constituting more than 40 per cent of their total manufactured exports. In the narrower category of high-tech products, the share in total manufactured exports is the highest for Malaysia, followed by Singapore, Taiwan and Korea (Lall 2000: 35). However, the local technological content of such exports can differ between countries. As noted in Lall, high-tech exports from Korea and Taiwan, based on technological learning at the micro level, have significant local linkages (in terms of both equipment and components) and greater local technological input at least up to basic design stages. Of the two, Korea's industrial sector has developed considerable industrial depth, and covers a wide range of activities. More importantly,

TABLE 3.7
Distribution of Manufactured Exports by Technological Categories (%)

	China		Korea		Taiwan		Singapore		Hong Kong	
	1985	1992	1980	1994	1980	1994	1980	1994	1980	1994
Resource-based	4.3	6.3	7.3	3.8	9.4	6.8	6.5	3.3	2.0	3.7
Labour-intensive	66.6	58.4	49.5	27.8	53.9	32.7	16.9	8.5	65.8	54.3
Scale-intensive	17.6	11.2	25.8	27.2	9.4	13.9	20.9	10.5	1.2	4.2
Differentiated	5.3	17.2	14.7	35.6	23.7	30.9	50.3	46.3	16.7	21.4
Science-based	0	1.1	2.7	5.6	3.6	15.8	5.4	31.4	14.3	16.4

	Indonesia		Malaysia		Thailand		India		Pakistan	
	1980	1992	1980	1992	1980	1992	1980	1992	1980	1992
Resource-based	14.7	29.5	11.0	5.4	53.9	20.1	26.5	28.7	15.5	4.5
Labour-intensive	28.9	48.7	18.4	17.4	28.4	38.3	55.4	49.6	84.5	93.8
Scale-intensive	20.2	7.6	4.9	5.3	4.3	5.6	11.2	17.1	0	0
Differentiated	19.0	7.6	60.1	29.6	13.4	15.7	4.1	1.2	0	0
Science-based	0	0.9	3.8	42.3	0	20.3	2.8	3.4	0	1.7

Notes: Figures for Singapore and Hong Kong are for total manufactured exports (including re-exports). No data for China are available for 1980, so the starting year is 1985.
Source: Lall (2000).

these activities developed largely on their own without much reliance on FDI, and are based on indigenous learning and skills, and research and development (R&D). Taiwan, while tapping technology transfer through local content requirements on the MNCs, also provided strong government support to provide incipient local electronics manufactures with requisite technology and information.

Singapore, in emphasizing MNC-driven industrialization, has developed an edge in providing an efficient and high-skill base for MNC activity rather than in using its own technological base. Malaysia also utilized the FDI route but has considerably less local linkages and a lower local technological input in high-tech exports compared to Korea and Taiwan. Similarly, following the FDI-driven route, Thailand and especially Indonesia also have a relatively weak technological base, since they serve mainly as assembly bases for MNC production. Hence micro-evidence seems to show that there is a distinct difference in indigenous technology development between Korea and Taiwan on the one hand, and Indonesia, Malaysia, Singapore, and Thailand on the other.

The Role of Industrial Policies

Since all the economies intervened intensively to promote industrial development, and with differing impact as shown above, it is not surprising that the World Bank's (1993: 312) conclusion on the effectiveness of industrial policies became hotly debated.[10] As in the case of TFP studies, there are evidence and counter-evidence.[11] Similarly, also as in the case of TFP studies, severe measurement problems have appeared. It is exceedingly difficult to quantify the impact of industrial policy, given that there is a whole gamut of selective interventions involved, ranging from tariffs, subsidized credit, selective tax holidays, and tax credits to preferential access to technology licences.

Apart from measurement problems, the empirical evidence on the effectiveness of industrial policy also encounters several interpretive problems: First, while micro-evidence may showcase some success stories, they cannot show the aggregated impact on the overall economy, that is, whether or not gains in targeted sectors translate into net gains for the overall economy when feedback effects are taken into account. Second, even accounts of successful interventions, for example in the form of increased exports or technological development, rarely take the costs of these interventions into consideration. For example, the use of subsidized, guaranteed credit to develop heavy industries in Korea was a high-risk strategy that subsequently ran into moral hazard problems. Third, interventions in Korea and Taiwan need to be differentiated from interventions in Indonesia, Malaysia and Thailand since industrial targeting in Southeast Asia may be influenced more by political than economic factors (Yoshitomi 2003: 38).

More importantly, hugely varied results that emerged from the utilization of the same set of policy instruments in selective intervention suggest that the measures by themselves do not determine success or failure. Rather, their effectiveness is contingent on factors such as human capital, the characteristics of market organizations, and the structure of political institutions (Kwon 1994: 642).

Econometric Studies

In studying cross-country regressions on the sources of total factor productivity growth in East Asian economies, the World Bank (1993: 322) concluded that "openness is consistently associated with superior TFP performance, controlling for other variables." As in the case of its TFP estimates, this finding by the World Bank set off a plethora of other studies that explored the relationship between openness and economic growth.

First, as in the case of TFP studies, severe problems were also encountered in the construction of summary measures of openness. There is a whole range of indicators created for this purpose. These include the Sachs and Warner index, the Leamer index, indices of trade distortion, the average import tariff rates, and the average coverage of non-tariff barriers.[12]

Second, various technical problems also exist, such as: (a) an identification problem in separating the effects of trade restrictions from those of macroeconomic imbalances and bad institutions, since an open trading regime is often a proxy for a host of liberal policies and effective institutions; (b) specification problems, since the impact of trade liberalization depends on numerous variables that may be neither quantified nor quantifiable, and (c) parameter heterogeneity rather than the assumption of common parameters that are required in cross-country regressions (Quibria 2002: 32).

Bearing in mind the above-mentioned problems and the usage of different time periods and data sets in various empirical works, it is not surprising that conflicting conclusions have emerged from the voluminous empirical literature on this issue. Thus while there are studies that have confirmed the positive effect of openness on economic growth, there are also others that have not found such a positive and significant impact.[13] However, there is a consensus that no credible evidence has been found for the converse situation, that is, that trade protection is good for economic growth. In other words, trade restrictions have not been found to be systematically associated with higher growth rates (Rodriguez and Rodrik 1999: 39).

Given the complex inter-relationships between trade policies and other government policies as well as macro-economic variables, it would appear to be futile to search for a relationship between trade barriers and growth alone, in a cross-country context (Baldwin 2003: 30). The focus on empirical research should then be on nuanced, in-depth country experiences that can enable us to understand better the linkage between trade and growth. In particular, in-depth studies should be able to explain better the contingent conditions under which a liberal or restrictive trade policy can affect growth.

WAS THE MIRACLE A MIRAGE?

The Asian Financial Crisis (AFC)

The AFC generated as much research interest as the 1993 World Bank study, with the causes of the crisis being hotly debated. While one viewpoint blames the crisis on poor economic fundamentals and inconsistent policies in the crisis-hit countries,[14] the opposing view points to unabated capital inflows in the form of short-term and foreign currency denominated debts and a panic by domestic and international investors to be the root causes of the crisis (Bosworth and Collins 1999: 2). Although it is likely that both sets of factors played contributory roles in the crisis, the rapid V-shaped recovery in crisis-hit countries suggest that the extreme view of fundamental structural imbalances in these economies is less likely to be valid.

Thus, as shown in Table 3.8, although all crisis-hit countries experienced a sharp reversal in their GDP growth rates in 1998 from positive to negative, they had within the span of one year restored their growth rates to positive by 1999. Furthermore, all of them have sustained positive growth rates since then, with the exception of Singapore in 2001. As noted by Bosworth and Collins, if the causes of the crisis were systemic, recovery would have been gradual and incomplete. Instead, the crisis bore a strong resemblance to a severe downturn in the business cycle. Therefore, there is general agreement within the literature that the AFC was not attributable to any deterioration in the macro-economic fundamentals of a country as in the case of "first-generation models" of crises.

Instead, the AFC emerged because both capital and financial liberalization in East Asian economies preceded the establishment of sound institutions (Yoshitomi 2003: 66). Consequently, a large amount of foreign capital was allowed to flow into these economies before the governments had developed

TABLE 3.8
Growth Rate of GDP (% per year)

	1997	1998	1999	2000	2001	2002	2003*	2004**	Average 1997–2003
East Asia	7.1	2.9	7.3	8.1	4.4	6.5	5.6	6.2	6.0
China, People Rep. of	8.8	7.8	7.1	8.0	7.3	8.0	7.3	7.6	7.8
Hong Kong, China	5.1	–5.0	3.4	10.2	0.6	2.3	2.0	4.0	2.7
Korea, Rep.of	5.0	–6.7	10.9	9.3	3.1	6.3	4.0	5.3	4.6
Mongolia	4.0	3.5	3.2	1.1	1.1	3.9	5.0	5.2	3.1
Taipei, China	6.7	4.6	5.4	5.9	–2.2	3.5	3.7	3.9	3.9
Southeast Asia	4.4	–6.6	4.1	6.2	1.7	4.1	4.0	4.8	2.6
Cambodia	4.3	2.1	6.9	7.7	6.3	4.5	5.0	5.5	5.3
Indonesia	4.7	–13.1	0.8	4.8	3.3	3.7	3.4	4.0	1.1
Lao People's Dem. Rep.	6.5	3.0	6.8	5.9	5.7	5.8	6.0	6.5	5.7
Malaysia	7.3	–7.4	6.1	8.3	0.4	4.2	4.3	5.1	3.3
Myanmar	5.7	5.8	10.9	13.7	11.1	–	–	–	9.4
Philippines	5.2	–0.6	3.4	4.4	3.2	4.6	4.0	4.5	3.5
Singapore	8.5	–0.1	6.4	9.4	–2.4	2.2	2.3	4.2	3.8
Thailand	–1.4	–10.5	4.4	4.6	1.9	5.2	5.0	5.5	1.3
Viet Nam	8.2	4.4	4.7	6.1	5.8	6.4	6.9	7.1	6.1

Note: – Not available
  * Estimate
  ** Forecast
Source: Asian Development Outlook 2003.

adequate prudential regulatory oversight capacities, and before banks had mastered risk management skills. In this regard, it is important to distinguish between the different types of private capital flows into East Asian economies. Short-term bank loans and portfolio capital can be causes of instability, while FDI is a far more stable source of finance. More importantly, FDI inflows have also been surprisingly impervious to transitory financial crises.[15]

However, the large inflows of short-term, dollar-denominated foreign capital channeled into long-term domestic investments in real estate and manufacturing created problems by giving rise to both a currency and maturity mismatch. The subsequent exit of capital in 1997 and the depreciation of East Asian currencies caused balance sheets to collapse. Financial intermediation became restricted, thereby depressing the real estate sector, turning a financial crisis into an economic one.

Historical evidence shows that economies recover relatively quickly from financial crises even before all the financial problems are resolved, as in the case of 1997 AFC. Hence, the financial crisis should be interpreted as an interruption in the growth in East Asia, rather than the end of an era. In view of this, the growth that propelled East Asia to fame is still there, albeit at a slower pace due in part to changes in the external environment such as the slower growth in the United States and the EU, economic stagnation in Japan, 11 September, the Bali bombing as well as other unforeseen external events.

Post-Crisis Challenges

Since the crisis, both internal and external circumstances within the East Asian economies have changed. Internally, the weaknesses in the banking structure as revealed by the crisis has led to bank restructuring to resolve non-performing loans, tightening of prudential regulations as well as corporate debt restructuring. Since firms that borrowed from the banks were not effectively monitored during the years of high growth before the crisis, a need to improve post-crisis corporate governance has been strongly felt. While these countries may have succeeded in their shift toward low-tech industrialization, they are now facing severe challenges in sustaining and upgrading industrialization and/or moving toward a service economy. Some of their industrial sectors are facing a "hollowing out". The need to develop local technological capability is more pressing since the external environment has become increasingly competitive.

In this regard, the economic rise of China poses strong competitive pressures on other East Asian economies since the exports of China continue to penetrate their internal markets as well as third-country markets. China's continued attraction for FDI also stands in strong contrast to the declining attraction of ASEAN-5 as host economies. India's competitive advantage in the information technology (IT) sector also poses new challenges to the aspirations for technological progress in the region, as well as in China. The emergence of the World Trade Organization (WTO) as the international body for global trade governance in 1995 and the subsequent failure of trade negotiations at Cancun in 2003 have led to numerous countries moving toward bilateral trade agreements. This shift from multilateral trade liberalization does not augur well for small economies that have a limited ability to negotiate on a bilateral basis with economic super powers.

Thus in the ten years since the 1993 World Bank study, the internal and external environment of East Asian economies have changed significantly. Clearly then, the future cannot be a replay of the past.

POLICY LESSONS FOR MALAYSIA

While factor accumulation contributed to rapid growth in the past, doing more of the same is unlikely to move the East Asian economies forward. First, capital accumulation has fallen since the crisis, as shown by the fall in Gross Domestic Investment as a percentage of GDP, thereby increasing the need to improve efficiency in the utilization of capital (Table 3.9). Second, the weight of comparative experience shows that except for lower income countries, rapid growth will have to depend more on the push provided by TFP (Yusuf 2002: 10). Malaysia, like the rest of the miracle economies, will have to move

TABLE 3.9
Gross Domestic Investment (% of GDP)

	1997	1998	1999	2000	2001	2002	2003*	2004*
East Asia								
China, People's Rep. of	38.2	37.7	37.4	37.1	38.6	38.5	38.2	38.5
Hong Kong, China	34.5	29.2	25.3	28.1	26.5	24.2	25.0	27.0
Korea, Rep. of	34.2	21.2	26.9	28.3	27.0	26.1	26.0	27.0
Mongolia	–	–	27.0	26.1	28.3	26.7	–	–
Taipei, China	24.2	24.9	23.4	22.6	17.4	16.8	18.1	18.6
Southeast Asia								
Cambodia	14.3	11.3	15.9	13.5	17.9	16.2	16.6	17.0
Indonesia	31.8	16.8	11.4	15.8	17.5	14.3	15.2	16.1
Lao People's Dem. Rep.	26.2	24.9	22.7	20.5	21.0	21.2	22.2	22.6
Malaysia	43.0	26.7	22.4	27.1	23.8	24.4	25.3	27.1
Myanmar	12.5	12.4	13.4	12.4	–	–	–	–
Philippines	23.8	19.3	17.8	17.4	16.6	15.6	17.5	18.5
Singapore	38.6	32.2	32.4	32.3	24.2	20.6	25.0	28.2
Thailand	33.7	20.4	20.5	22.7	23.9	23.8	24.0	24.5
Viet Nam	28.3	22.5	22.2	23.9	25.9	32.0	32.0	31.0

Note: – Not available
　　* Estimated
Source: Asian Development Outlook 2003.

from a factor-driven growth to a productivity-driven growth strategy. In turn, this productivity-driven strategy will have to derive its impetus from the availability of high-level skills and innovations.

Policymakers in Malaysia are very much aware of the need for the above-mentioned shift. Productivity-led growth has been the growth strategy since the Seventh Malaysia Plan (1996–2000). This strategy has also recognized both the role of innovation and IT by highlighting the need to shift from a production-based economy to a knowledge-based economy. Indeed as analysed in Tham and Ragayah (2003: 33), the policies of Malaysia are very up-to-date. However, implementation and monitoring are lacking in this constant drive and search for new policies. Implementation is also constrained by the shortage of appropriate higher order skills. As industrialization in the country strives to move up the value-added chain, the earlier emphasis on primary schooling needs to be complemented with an equal emphasis on higher education, quality of education and higher-order skills. Unfortunately, human capital constraints continue to hinder the shift towards a knowledge-based economy.

Since the post-crisis years have registered lower levels of inflow of FDI in comparison to the pre-crisis years, there have been growing calls for increasing domestic investment. While this call is valid, it does not mean that Malaysia is ready to handle a diminished role for FDI in the economy. On the contrary, the technology of the MNCs are more necessary than ever, given the current drive toward higher value-added manufacturing and services. Moreover, it is important to bear in mind that FDI was a relatively stable source of foreign capital during the crisis, as compared to portfolio flows and bank lending. Prema-chandra (2003: 13) also found that affiliates of MNCs in Malaysia were instrumental in ameliorating the severity of the economic collapse and their exports, especially in the electronics sub-sector that facilitated the recovery in 1999 through the upturn in the global electronics cycle. However, although FDI can contribute positively to the economic growth of a country, the magnitude of this effect has been found to be dependent on the stock of human capital available in the host economy (Borensztein, De Gregorio and Lee 1995: 11). Therefore, in order to maximize the absorption of technology from FDI, Malaysia has to improve its human capital.

Finally, the finding that protection does not have any positive impact on growth is pertinent for Malaysia in the light of the current, continued protection that has been accorded to the automotive sector despite the commitment to liberalize under the ASEAN Free Trade Agreement (AFTA). Although tariffs for completely-knocked-down (CKD) units have been reduced from 42–80 per cent to 25 per cent, this decline has been offset by increases in excise duties. On the other hand, Proton, the first national car, is charged 13 per cent in import duty and is provided a 50 per cent discount on excise duties. Perodua, the second national car, besides receiving the same treatment as Proton, is also fully exempted from excise duties for its Kancil model. Therefore, the national cars continue to be protected, thereby violating the spirit of AFTA that taxes should be imposed impartially on all cars. Since the protection of Proton has lasted for nearly two decades, it is unclear where gains are made, since the export performance of Proton continues to be dismal while it has garnered the lion's share in the domestic market under substantial protection. Even the argument of infant industry protection cannot hold water if the infant shows no sign of growing up.

CONCLUSION

The long years of high growth, coupled with poverty reduction, led to the labelling of the East Asian economies as miracle economies. However, the World Bank created considerable debate around its search for common factors that contributed to the high growth for these economies, and consequently around the myth of an East Asian development model. First, its TFP estimates were challenged by other estimates. Second, the World Bank's findings pertaining to the contribution of productivity to East Asian success raised substantial disagreement on the importance of capital accumulation in relation to productivity growth. Third, while functional interventions in terms of macro-economic management, maintenance of a prudent fiscal policy, and investment in human capital and infrastructure were applauded as contributory factors, it was the conclusion on the relative ineffectiveness of selective intervention at the micro-level that sparked off an even more heated debate.

The review in this chapter shows that there is broad cumulative consensus now that productivity growth played a more modest role relative to capital accumulation. Micro-evidence also supports this conclusion. It is important to note that both TFP and micro-evidence show a distinction between the TFP estimates and technology gains of Asian Tigers and the Southeast Asian countries, as well as among the Southeast Asian nations. In particular, micro-evidence shows that the role of foreign capital also differed. Similarly, although East Asian governments intervened at the micro-level in differing degrees using basically the same set of policy instruments, divergent results were obtained. Hence there are both stories of success and failures in the industrial policies used. It appears that it is not the measures *per se* that determine the outcome, but rather that the effectiveness of these policies are contingent on other factors. There is, however, broad agreement that protection does not yield any positive impact on growth. Moreover, the diversity of experience in the subject of government intervention makes the synthesizing of these experiences into a single East Asian model over-simplistic.

The AFC in 1997 led to many reviews of the East Asian model of development. Debates on the causes of the crisis can be separated into two major camps. In the first, structural imbalances and policy distortions were seen as the primary causal factors. Proponents argued that some of the micro-economic interventions that contributed to the earlier success of the East Asian miracle subsequently contributed to the crisis. The second viewpoint traced the crisis to other factors, such as unbridled capital flows and panic by domestic and international investors. It is the argument of this chapter that the V-shaped recovery of the East Asian economies does not support the view that interventions at the micro-level were the primary causal factors of the crisis. Hence, the crisis does not imply that the growth was a mirage. Rather, the crisis should be viewed as an interruption in East Asian growth and not as the end of an era.

Post-crisis development shows that the internal and external environment has changed substantially. Therefore, while the years of growth and crisis offered lessons for development, future growth cannot be premised on old strategies. In particular, lessons learned from the growth paths of other countries show that the East Asian economies must seek productivity-driven growth. Although Malaysia has mapped out a productivity-driven growth strategy since the Seventh Malaysia Plan, the proposed shift toward a knowledge-based economy is hindered by implementation and human capital problems. Similarly, the call for a greater role for domestic investment in the Malaysian economy does not negate the need for FDI, since MNC technology is still required to assist the move up the value-added chain. Finally, Malaysia should heed the lesson that protection does not contribute to growth, and dismantle the protection of the automotive sector in accordance with AFTA commitments.

It is important to remember that some of the policy autonomy that existed in the pre-crisis period is no longer available. The emergence of the WTO has reduced the scope of micro-interventions such as export subsidies and trade-related investment measures. The more enduring lessons of the East Asian miracle pertain to functional interventions such as sound macro-economic management, prudent fiscal policies and investment in infrastructure and human capital. These lessons do not stir up any controversies and do not go out of fashion, nor will they be outlawed by global governance agencies.

Perhaps the more fundamental lesson from the study of the East Asian miracle and crisis is to pay more attention to functional interventions.

Notes

1   See for example, Special Section in *World Development* 22, no. 4 (1994).

2   See *ASEAN Economic Bulletin* 2002, and Masaru Yoshitomi (2003).

3   The eight high-performing Asian economies (HPAEs) in the 1993 World Bank report comprised Japan, the "Four Tigers" (Hong Kong, the Republic of Korea, Singapore and Taiwan) and the three newly industrializing economies of Indonesia, Malaysia and Thailand.

4   This consists of the HPAEs minus Japan, which was excluded from the post-crisis studies of the Asian Miracle because it was not one of the crisis-hit countries and also because of the prolonged stagnation in the country during most of the 1990s.

5   Note that the GNP per capita for Latin America and the Caribbean was actually higher than that obtained for Miracle Asia in 1960 and almost the same in 1970. However, between 1980 and 1995, the difference between the two region's GNP per capita diverged considerably.

6   Along with economic studies of the East Asian development, there are also numerous other studies that looked at non-economic issues such as East Asian philosophical and historical backgrounds (see for example, Lee and McNulty 2003). However, this chapter will focus on the economic factors alone.

7   TFP measures the efficiency of the use of both labor and capital resources to produce output. Better utilization of factor inputs in the production process will foster TFP increases.

8   It should be noted that data problems are less problematic with regards to developed countries.

9   It is likely that the low TFP estimates obtained was due to the fact that much of the technology is embodied in factor inputs, leaving little to the measurement of disembodied technology (Kwon 1994: 638).

10 Industrial policies as defined by the World Bank (1993: 304) refer to government efforts taken to alter the industrial structure in order to promote productivity-based growth.

11 See for example, Kwon (1994: 637) for his TFP results of the heavy promoted industries in Korea, compared with the TFP obtained for light industries. This directly contradicts World Bank findings. See Quibria (2002: 49) for other empirical evidence that supports World Bank findings and still other data that support Kwon's findings.

12 The Sachs and Warner index classifies an economy as open if (a) import duties average less than 40 per cent, (b) quotas cover less than 40 per cent of imports, (c) the black market premium on the exchange rate is less than 20 per cent,

(d) a state monopoly of major exports is absent, and (d) the economy is not socialist. The Leamer index uses the deviation of the actual from the predicted volume of trade as a measure of openness and the deviation of the actual from the predicted pattern as a measure of intervention.

[13] See for example, Dollar (1992) and Edwards (1998) as an example of the former, and Rodriguez and Rodrik (1999) as samples of the literature in this area.

[14] Namely, Indonesia, Malaysia, Philippines, Thailand, and Korea.

[15] Prema-chandra Athukorala (2003: 7) shows that the behaviour of FDI inflows to the crisis-hit countries were significantly different from portfolio flows and bank credit. While FDI inflows to the five countries contracted by 15 per cent for the period 1996–97, it recovered swiftly to the pre-crisis level by 1998. On the other hand, portfolio and bank credit contracted by 101.2 per cent in 1997–98.

References

Abimanyu, A. "The Indonesian Economy and Total Factor Productivity". *The Singapore Economic Review* 40, no. 1 (1995): 25–40.

Baldwin, R. Openness and Growth: What's the Empirical Relationship? NBER Working Paper Series, Working Paper 9578, 2003.

Borensztein, E., J. de Gregorio and Lee, J.W. "How Does Foreign Direct Investment Affect Economic Growth?" NBER Working Paper Series, Working Paper No. 5057, 1995. <http://netec.mcc.ac.uk/WoPF_c/data/Papers/nernberwo5057.htm/ 31/1/2004>.

Bosworth, B. and S.M. Collins. "From Boom to Crisis and Back Again: What Have We Learned?" Draft paper presented at the ADBI Workshop on Development Paradigms, 10 December 1999. <http://www.adbi.org/PDF/wp0002_7.pdf 14/ 1/2004>.

Dollar, D. "Outward-Oriented Developing Economies Really Do Grow More Rapidly: Evidence from 95 LDCs, 1976–85". *Economic Development and Cultural Change* (1992): 523–44.

Easterly, W. *The Elusive Quest for Growth*. Cambridge (Massachusetts): The MIT Press, 2002.

Edwards, S. "Openness, Productivity and Growth: what Do We Really Know?" *The Economic Journal* 108 (March 1998): 383–98.

Kwon. J. "The East Asia Challenge to Neoclassical Orthodoxy". *World Development* 22, no. 4 (1994): 635–44.

Lall, S. The East Asian Miracle: Does the Bell Toll for Industrial Strategy? *World Development* 22, no. 4 (1994): 645–54.

Lall, S. "Technological Change and Industrialization". Chapter 2, in *Technology, Learning and Innovation: Experiences of Newly Industrializing Economies*, edited by Kim, L. and Nelson, R.R. Cambridge: Cambridge University Press, 2000.

Lee, H-C, and McNulty, M.P. "East Asia's Dynamic Development Model and the Republic of Korea's Experiences". World Bank Policy Research Working Paper, 2987, March 2003. <http://econ.worldbank.org/files/4755_wps2987.pdf 14/1/2004>.

Masaru Yoshitomi and ADBI Staff. *Post-Crisis Development Paradigms in Asia*. Tokyo: ADBI, 2003. <http://www.adbi.org/publications/post_crisis/oocontents.pdf. 14/1/2004>.

Quibria, M.G. "Growth and Poverty: Lessons from the East Asian Miracle Revisited". ADB Institute Research Paper 33. Tokyo: ADB Institute, 2002. <http://www.adbi.org/PDF/wp/rp33.pdf. 14/1/2004>.

Prema-chandra, Athukorala. FDI in Crisis and Recovery: Lessons from the 1997–98 Crisis. Forthcoming in *Australian Economic History Review* (*Special Issue, Financial Institutions and Economic Crisis in Asia*, edited by Hal Hill and Thomas Lindblad), 2003. <http://rspas.anu.edu.au/economics/publish/papers/wp2003/wp_econ_2003_04pdf>.

Rodriguez, F. and d. Rodrik. "Trade Policy and Economic Growth: A Skeptic's Guide to The Cross-National Evidence". NBER Working Paper Series, Working Paper 7081, 1999.

Sarel, M. "Growth in East Asia: What We Can and We Cannot Infer". *Economic Issues, No. 1*, Washington D.C.: International Monetary Fund, 1996. <http://www.imf.org/external/pubs/ft/issues1/index.htm. 14/1/2004>.

Shin, J.S. and Chu, Y.P. "Three Paths for High-technology Catching-Up in East Asia". Paper presented at the East Asia High-tech Drive, Taipei, August 2003.

Tham, S.Y. "Productivity, Growth and Development in Malaysia". *The Singapore Economic Review* 40, no. 1 (1995): 41–64.

Tham, S.Y. and Ragayah H. Mat Zin. "The Shift to High-Tech Industrialization: Case of Malaysia". Paper presented at the East Asia High-tech Drive, Taipei, August 2003.

Tsao, Y. "Growth without Productivity". *Journal of Development Economics* 18 (1985): 25–38.

Yusuf, S. "Remodelling East Asian Development". *ASEAN Economic Bulletin* 19, no. 1 (2002): 6–26.

The World Bank. *The East Asian Miracle: Economic Growth and Public Policy*. New York: Oxford University Press, 1993.

The World Bank. Special Section on "The East Asian Miracle: Economic Growth and Public Policy". *World Development* 22, no. 4 (1994): 615–63.

Warr, P. "The East Asia Development Experience Before and After the Crisis: Lessons for Africa", 2003. <http://www.worldbank.org/wbi/RECT/madagascar/english/warr_plenary.pdf>.

4

TOWARDS A NEW PARADIGM IN EAST ASIAN ECONOMIC STUDIES*

Chen Yu-Hsi

AN OVERVIEW OF PARADIGMS

East Asian economic studies have been based on three alternative paradigms: one mainstream and two rival paradigms. The mainstream paradigm involves basic economic thoughts derived from free-market theory, modernization theory and development economics. It argues, among other things, that economic development in East Asia and other regions can be achieved only through the implementation of a market economy along with free trade and free enterprise systems. Inputs from the West, such as capital, technology, institutions and cultural values, are essential, while traditional cultures and institutions of the Orient are considered to be obstacles to progress. High economic growth in East Asia is credited to the free market system, with the state playing a small role. Proponents of this paradigm include such well-known economists as Milton Friedman, Gustav Ranis, John C.H. Fei and Edward K.Y. Chen.

As early as in the 1970s, the mainstream paradigm was challenged by a neo-Marxist school of thought known as "dependency theory". It asserts in general terms that "periphery capitalism" (that is, the capitalist system in the Third World) will inevitably result in dominance by "core" economies that will deprive the "peripheral" economies of any chance of "autonomous development". Samir Amin and other dependency theorists applied this theory to Asia in the mid-1970s, arguing that none of the Asian economies had come close to "the stage of independent and autonomous development", but on the contrary, "unequal development" and the dependency-dominance relationships in these economies had become a more serious problem than ever before. Some neo-Marxist theorists even went so far as to lump Asian economies together with other Third World regions under the vague category of "under-development", which was said to be the consequence of "over-development" in the core economies of the West. As the economic success of the Four Tigers became increasingly evident, however, this rival paradigm sank into oblivion.

The second rival paradigm came on the scene toward the end of the 1970s when the "economic miracle" of East Asia attracted the attention of the world's academic communities. Many prominent social scientists, including sociologist Peter Berger and political scientist Ezra Vogel, argued that the East Asian model of economic development was different from the free-market model, and undertook to develop an alternative "Asian type of modernization", with emphasis placed on the contribution state interventions and traditional Confucian values make to economic success. Proponents of this "East Asian model" cite evidence to show that free market mechanisms were restricted in many ways in the economies of the Four Tigers, while the state played a decisive and active role in promoting economic development. Confucianism is said to contribute to the economic miracle of Japan and the Four Tigers by inculcating the importance of education, hard work, thrift and discipline. One important conclusion is that economic modernization does not necessarily follow the Western pattern prescribed by modernization theorists. This rival paradigm remained vocal until the Asian financial turmoil in 1997.

This chapter envisions another paradigm shift in the offing. This time the shift is towards an "Information Economy", in which information technologies (IT) are the primary driving force of productivity. The shift is related in part to the financial turmoil and economic crisis of 1997–98, in that it caused an outcry against "crony capitalism" and the inefficient state bureaucracy alleged by Western critics to be the root of the crisis. However, while the financial turmoil and economic crisis in East Asia did undermine the second rival paradigm, they were not the main reasons for a paradigm shift. Rather, the root cause lies in the fact that the East Asian model of economic modernization has become increasingly vulnerable to the rising tide of globalization, along with its auxiliary development of a world financial market characterized by free movement of capital. Globalization thus makes for the emergence of a new paradigm for East Asian economic studies in two ways. First, it contributed to the financial turmoil in 1997 that was followed by a severe economic crisis that laid bare not only the destabilizing forces of international speculative capital, but also the weaknesses and vulnerability of the economic system in East Asia. Second, globalization has helped to spread information technologies (IT) to East Asia and to build an increasingly close linkage of East Asian economies to the IT-based New Economy of the advanced industrial nations, especially the United States, with a potential to influence and transform the region's economic development so radically as to warrant a paradigm shift.

MAJOR CONCERNS OF THE NEW PARADIGM

The new paradigm addresses two major concerns. The first is the changing conditions affecting macro-economic performances in the region in the "information age". Ever since its inception in the late 1970s, the heavily sociology-based paradigm of East Asian economic modernization has generally neglected the impact external capitalist forces have on the region's socioeconomic stability. These include the business cycle and the forces of world commodities and financial markets. Consequently, when an excessive influx of speculative capital and an over-heated economy combined to ferment a major crisis in 1997, scholars of East Asia in general were academically unprepared to tackle the issue.

As globalization, coupled with the rapid development of information technologies, ushers in a new era of closer economic inter-dependence, East Asian research needs to broaden its perspectives and the scope of economic studies, especially in the areas of the business cycle and international trade, investments and financial relations. In this sense, the paradigm shift is a move away from inward-looking and static socio-economic analyses towards a focus on the dynamics of change in East Asian economies understood as an integral part of the global capitalist system. Rather than emphasizing the region's economic development as a model of Asian-styled modernization, the new paradigm needs to address issues arising from its external linkages. Specifically, it needs to inquire into how economic fluctuations and business cycles occur in relation to the free movement of financial capital as well as the forces of "creative destruction" of the Information Economy.

A second concern of the new paradigm is the longer-term impact that information technologies may have on the political economy and the industrial-technological development of the region as a whole. Political economists such as Fernando H. Cardoso (1993) and Manuel Castells (2000) have in recent years put forth a new "Fourth World" proposition in response to the global development of what they call "informational economy". According to these scholars, the rapid development of IT-related industries and the industrial and commercial applications of information technologies bring the more developed among the Third World economies into closer alliance with dominant industrial nations — an alliance based on the new international division of labour along the lines of hi-tech production — while poor Third World countries sink into a "Fourth World" characterized by "de-industrialization" and the "social exclusion" of the general population.[1]

While this new theory can be included as one of the dimensions of the new paradigm, its validity and applicability *vis-à-vis* East Asian economies need to be carefully assessed. One observation is that the "Fourth World" concept does not fit well into the socio-economic settings of East Asia, not only because of the relatively high level of the region's industrial-technological development, but also because its labour-intensive products still enjoy a comfortable niche in world markets even where poorer countries of the region are concerned. Moreover, the formation of an expanding Southeast Asian economic community provides a regional coherence that prevents these poor countries from sinking into a "Fourth World".

Lastly, the new paradigm is concerned with the long-term impact that the New Economy may have on the region's industrial-technological development. Due to the special characteristics of information technologies such as a relatively short product life cycle, fast changing innovations and the greater accessibility of new technologies, the extensive involvement in IT industries in East Asia may disrupt the region's technological hierarchy depicted by the so-called "flying geese model", and shape a new order in which information technologies are widely diffused among East Asian countries. In the long run, a point will be reached where these technologies contribute to economic growth in the region not only through exports of IT products, as they are doing now, but also through their diffusion and application to non-tech sectors of the economy as a whole. At this point, East Asian economies will have been integrated into the Information Economy and will no longer merely be producing for international markets.

'INFORMATION ECONOMY' AS A NEW PARADIGM

The need to establish the "Information Economy" as a new paradigm for East Asian economic studies stems from the fact that the region has been highly integrated into the global production network of semiconductors and other IT-related products. Nearly half of semiconductors on international markets come from East Asian countries, especially Japan, Taiwan, South Korea and Singapore. These and other IT-related products, including consumer-oriented electronic products, account for the lion's share of the exports of many East Asian countries — 60 to 70 per cent for Singapore, 60 per cent for Malaysia, and 50 per cent both for Taiwan and the Philippines. Although South Korea's exports of IT products are not extremely large, the country does own the world's two largest producers of memory chips. The pivotal role that IT industries play in East Asian economic development is not a historical accident. Since the late 1970s, the governments of more developed East Asian countries have chosen microelectronics, semiconductors and computers as the "strategic sector" for upgrading industrial technology. The state and the private sector together have invested heavily in technological infrastructure, R&D, technical training and education, science parks, etc., which are needed for the development of IT industries. U.S. demand for semiconductors, memory chips, computer parts and components and other IT-related products has sharply increased since the mid-1990s, and East Asian countries have also increased investments in these industries and through them forged a successively close linkage to the IT-driven "New Economy" (that is, Information Economy) of the United States.

The concept of the "Information Economy" does not only refer to a new economic system in which the revolution of information technologies has brought about a sustained increase in productivity and other structural changes; it also refers to a new paradigm for economic studies. Already, there has been much debate in American academic and business circles about how forces unleashed by the New Economy may influence micro-economic and macro-economic performance in ways different from the past, and thereby change the laws and principles of conventional economics. For several years before the "technological bubble" in the United States busted in 2000, New Economy optimists argued that industrial productivity generated by the innovations and applications of information technologies could increase without limit, thus challenging the law of diminishing returns. This euphoria was based on the limited empirical data that productivity in the United States increased only an averaged 1.4 per cent annually during 1973–95, while by contrast it doubled to 3 per cent during 1996–2000. Moreover, it was asserted that new technical innovations in the management of production and distribution, such as just-in-time supply chain management (SCM), the integration of order placements with production lines, quick inventory adjustment technique, etc., could ensure a balance between supply and demand to such an extent that the law of the business cycle could be negated. In the words of *The Economist*, "Thanks to the wondrous new technology, the business cycle was supposedly consigned to history books, and productivity would grow forever at a miraculous rate."[2]

Curiously, the supposed negation of the business cycle was accompanied by a revival of the long-dismissed Say's Law in classical economics that "supply can create its own demand." Because IT equipment and products are characterized by rapid innovation and a shortened product life cycle, business firms and consumers, it was argued, have no choice but to keep placing orders for new equipment and products so as to survive tough competition and to keep up with the times. As Federal Reserve Chairman Alan Greenspan put it, computers and software are "productivity-boosting assets that depreciate rapidly and get replaced quickly", so that there would be "no major pull back in IT spending".[3] In other words, the expansion of production capacity under the New Economy will be sustained by a synchronized increase in demand. While this modern-day version of Say's Law served to reinforce the "theory" about the "demise of the business cycle", it was quickly refuted by weakened demand, excessive inventories and decreased capital spending in the technology sector, as well as the consequent economic downturn that began in the second half of 2000. Obviously, supply does not create its own demand under the New Economy, and the age-old problem of over-production remains as much a reality as before.

Another theoretical point about the New Economy concerns inflation. It is pointed out that sustained productivity gains and improved efficiency in marketing will yield such significant cost savings that corporations will be able to cut product prices. Consequently, inflation is supposedly no longer a threat to the U.S. economy. Low inflation in turn will give the Federal Reserve greater flexibility in exercising its monetary policy to stimulate the economy. This hypothesis about low inflation has not been challenged so far. However, the low inflation rates in the United States during the past few years are accounted for by a number of factors, notably economic downturns since the later part of 2000 and cheap imports from Asia, especially China. Strong economic revival in 2004 brought about the threat of inflation to such an extent that the Federal Reserve is likely to raise interest rates in the second half of the year. Whether or not low inflation is a sustainable characteristic of the Information Economy is now open to question.

The validity of "New Economy" as an explanatory concept is also disputed. Northwestern University professor Robert Gordon and some other economists, for example, cite official data from the Department of Labour to argue that the increase in productivity during the second half of the 1990s came primarily from the IT sector, and that the "ripple effects" (namely, productivity gains in the non-tech sectors as a result of the application of computers and other information technologies) are minimal. They point out that the impact of information technologies on the U.S. economy cannot be compared to the technological revolution during the second half of the nineteenth century, when the inventions and applications of electricity, the internal-combustion engine and other technologies radically changed the American economy and society.[4] On the other hand, other economists and analysts argue the opposite case that productivity gains come in large part from the widespread applications of information technologies to e-commerce, e-banking and other service and manufacturing industries. In this sense, the New Economy can be touted as a new economic system in which structural transformation is evident as a result of IT revolution.[5] Furthermore, we need to broaden our perspectives on the New Economy issue to include the earlier theory of the "post-industrial society" put forth by Daniel Bell and the voluminous empirical studies on "information economy" conducted by Marc Porat. Drawing on these earlier academic studies, it dawns upon us that as early as the late 1960s or early 1970s, a new type of economy had already emerged in American society in which information and theoretical knowledge played a key role in social and economic progress, independent of whether or not we called it "information economy" or "new economy" or something else. As Bell put it, "The 'economics of information' is not the same thing as the 'economics of goods', and the social relations created by the new networks of information.... are not the older social patterns' or work relations — of industrial society." Writing in the early 1970s, Bell was already speaking of the main dimensions of the post-industrial society as "the dominance of [the] professional and technical class in the labour force" and "the centrality of theoretical knowledge and the expansion of the service sector as against a manufacturing economy".[6]

DIMENSIONS OF THE NEW PARADIGM

These theoretical issues and perspectives contain useful implications for East Asian economic studies, and can be borrowed to form a major dimension of the new paradigm under the assumption that factors affecting the New Economy in advanced industrial countries can also affect the macro-economic performances of East Asian economies. Take the business cycle for example. It is well-known now that the quick recovery of East Asian economies from the financial and economic crisis in 1997–98 was due to the strong demand of the U.S. economy for IT products from East Asia, and that the economic slump during 2001–03 in East Asia was a direct result of the busting of the "technological bubble" in the United States. It is thus important to understand how the patterns of the business cycle may change under the New Economy. To claim the demise of the business cycle is obviously going too far, but we must also realize that the business cycle since the end of World War II no longer behaves the same way the historical patterns preceding the Great Depression of the 1930s did. Instead of a four-stage cycle, what we have seen in modern times are often irregular up-and-down fluctuations, with "boom" generally lasting longer than "bust" and without depressions or drawn-out recessions. The Japanese experience of a decade-long "growth-recession" following more than a decade of prosperity is another example that defies the conventional pattern of the business cycle. The principle of the business cycle cannot be negated, but its behavior patterns can change under different socioeconomic settings.

One lesson learned during the financial turmoil and economic crisis of 1997–98 is that economists and analysts generally lose sight of the business cycle as an explanatory concept in the study of East Asian economic development. For almost two decades, amid the euphoria of the "Asian miracle," sociological and political economists stressed statism (the central role of the state in economic development) and Confucian values as key factors that contributed to the miracle, while neo-classical economists stuck to the free market system and non-intervention by the state as the simple causes of the East Asian success. Neither of these paradigms ever discussed the possibility that an "economic miracle" could be undermined by dynamics inherent in the capitalist economic system. No one seemed to have predicted — on the basis of the business cycle theory — the coming of a financial turmoil even amid the irrational exuberance and excesses of the stock and real estate markets on the eve of the crisis. Furthermore, after the crisis broke out, Western economists and analysts were quick to dismiss the "Asian miracle" as a "hoax", a "myth" or a "tower built on sand". Many of them blamed "crony capitalism" and state interventionism, and the prestigious business journal, *The Economist*, even went so far as to attack Confucianism as the caprice of the economic disaster. Some of them, inspired by Paul Krugman's 1994 article entitled "The Myth of Asia's Miracle", attributed the crisis to a development model that relied on "inputs" (labour and capital) rather than technological progress and efficiency as a source of economic growth.[7] The common fallacy of these arguments lies in the assumption that the economic miracle is not subject to cyclical change — an assumption resulting from ignorance about the business cycle.

A second dimension of the new paradigm deals with international economics. Over the past decades, international trade, foreign loans and foreign investments have been important external factors contributing to the economic development of East Asia. However, unlike earlier decades when foreign loans and investments were directed towards productive manufacturing and service industries and infrastructure projects, the international financial market since the 1980s has been replete with a huge pool of financial capital seeking unproductive, speculative "investments" in currency exchange, stock markets, real estate markets, etc. To find outlets for this surplus capital that is mostly owned by American financial institutions, the United States has been championing free capital movement as an integral part of globalization, and puts pressures on East Asian countries to open up their financial markets. The massive inflow of international financial capital created price bubbles in the stock and real estate markets of Southeast Asian countries prior to the financial turmoil, and its massive withdrawal in the second half of 1997 amid currency devaluation caused a sudden collapse of these markets, giving rise to the financial turmoil and economic crisis.

The free capital movement, facilitated by the application of information technologies, has thus become a formidable force that makes for the booms and busts of East Asian economies. A recent study by IMF finds that as cross-border flows of international capital are accelerated by information technologies and the relaxation of capital market controls, the correlation among equity prices in different countries has become closer and global factors have become more important relative to local factors in determining share prices. On the basis of this finding, a *Business Week* article concludes that the globalization of capital markets helps explain why worldwide stock markets and the American stock market simultaneously surged in 1999 and collapsed in 2000 and 2001.[8]

For various reasons, East Asian economic studies need to be concerned with the cost and benefit of opening up to globalization and the New Economy. First, in a matter of less than four years, East Asia has suffered two major economic setbacks stemming from these external linkages — the financial and economic crisis of 1997–98 and the economic downturn of 2001–03. Second, the financial and economic crisis has resulted in the IMF interfering with the economic policies of some East Asian countries, and in Western MNCs taking control over local companies and financial institutions. The economic autonomy of East Asian countries seems to erode increasingly as their involvement in the process of globalization and the New Economy intensifies. Above all, the financial turmoil of 1997 alarmed East Asian leaders to the danger of the "domino effects" of a volatile global financial system. When these concerns are coupled with the rising tide of economic regionalism in the Americas and Europe, some East Asian countries at least are seeing a need to balance globalization with strengthened regional economic cooperation, including free trade agreements and mutual support for currency stabilization. Moreover, their unfinished structural reforms are caught in the dilemma of meeting the demand for financial deregulation while opening up to international capital movement on the one hand and strengthening control and supervision against a repetition of financial turmoil on the other. To address these policy issues would require a great deal of study on international economic relations in the "information age".

The third dimension of the new paradigm is the "silicon cycle". Researchers of the worldwide semiconductor industry have recently discovered a regular ten-year cycle that contains two sub-cycles in the demand and supply of semiconductors, memory chips and other related IT products in international markets. Since the mid-1970s, cyclical changes have been observed and analysed as follows: (1) The first cycle began in 1975, when the global demand and trade volume of semiconductors suffered a shrinkage of –6 per cent, and ended in 1984 with a robust growth of 46 per cent, with an averaged annual growth of 20.4 per cent for the ten-year period; (2) The second cycle began in 1985 with a –16 per cent growth and ended in 1995 when the cycle peaked with a growth rate of 42 per cent, with an averaged annual growth of 20.8 per cent; (3) The third cycle began in 1996 when global demand began falling from its peak until late 1998, to be followed by less than two years — from 1999 to mid-2000 — of intermediate recovery; the current downturn that started in late 2000 was forecasted to last until 2002, and thereafter to climb upward until another peak was reached in 2005, with a growth rate forecasted at 40 per cent.[9]

The "silicon cycle" theory is useful in predicting future trends of the global semiconductor industry that may affect the performance of East Asian economies. It also helps explain what has happened to East Asia since 1997. Although the financial turmoil was not caused by the downturn (1996–98) in the third silicon cycle, we know that the semiconductor and related IT industries of East Asia suffered a sharp decline in sales revenues and earnings during this downturn period, especially in 1998. It was doubtless a factor that aggravated the current accounts problem of Southeast Asian countries and South Korea, making their currency markets more vulnerable to speculative attacks, which touched off the financial turmoil in the first place. Moreover, the dramatic recovery of East Asian economies in 1999 and 2000 is explained not only by the strong demand of the U.S. market, but also by the fact that this period coincided with the intermediate recovery of the global silicon cycle. In other words, if the cyclical over-supply of the global semiconductor industry had lasted into 1999–2000, the U.S. market would have experienced a glut of cheap semiconductors and related IT products, thereby making the East Asian recovery more difficult, if not impossible. It is from this larger global perspective that we need to address East Asian economic issues in relation to the New Economy.

The fourth dimension of the new paradigm concerns the structural change in the stratified "world system" — a change characterized by the emergence of the "Fourth World". As globalization spreads and IT industries are developed in different parts of the world, they pose two challenges to the less developed countries known as the Third World. First, the rapid technological progress and constantly changing innovations have caused a large number of traditional industrial firms to close down, restructure or undertake mergers. Some labour-intensive industries have been wiped out because their products were no longer competitive or needed when alternative new products with more technological contents and better functions came into the market. The consequences are "de-industrialization" and widespread unemployment and poverty in many Third World countries. Second, national governments in the Third World tend to neglect public policy aimed at a more equitable distribution of wealth, income and public service rendered to low-income groups in connection with medical care, child education, welfare, etc., because they need to allocate their resources to improve infrastructure and productive efficiency to compete globally.

Consequently, the traditional Third World is said to have separated into two polarized sets of societies. On the one hand, the more developed countries of the Third World have been integrated into the system of international division of labour in line with the "information economy". On the other hand, poor countries and impoverished segments of more developed countries are deprived of industrial development and are alienated from the process of globalization. The latter category is said to be sinking into a "Fourth World", where the traditional inputs of cheap labour and land have become "unexploitable", that is, they are not even worthy of being exploited by industries because these countries and locations lack the infrastructural facilities and the educated or skilled manpower needed for industrial development. The general population suffers from "social exclusion", and is denied the basic human rights of economic participation both as worker and consumer, and a decent and healthy social life free from drugs, crime, child labour and the sexual exploitation of children. According to Castells' detailed analysis, sexual exploitation and abuse of children are rampant in the "Fourth World" as a direct consequence of economic impoverishment combined with the widespread application of information technologies to the "sex industry" and "sex market".[10]

This "Fourth World" theory is useful for East Asian economic studies, but needs to be applied with reservation. First, there is empirical evidence that information technologies as a driving force for economic growth are widening the gap between the poor and the rich, and East Asian countries are no exception. Second, the more developed East Asian countries — Taiwan, Korea, Singapore and Hong Kong — are indeed closely linked to the New

Economy of the United States. Even Malaysia, the Philippines and China are jumping on the IT bandwagon. East Asia as a whole reportedly supplies nearly half of the world's demand for semiconductors and memory chips. The three largest foundries (contract-chip manufacturers) in the world are located in Taiwan and Singapore, while the world's largest and second largest DRAM producers are Korea's Samsung and Hynix Semiconductor (formerly Hyundai) respectively. According to reports, China will become the world's number one producer of personal computers and computer hardware in a matter of years. This close alignment and integration with the global "information economy" have pushed these East Asian countries away from the orbit of the traditional Third World, where the economy is either stagnant or mainly supplies the international market with raw materials and relatively low value-added labour-intensive products on unequal terms of trade determined primarily by the advanced countries.

The next issue to discuss is whether the poorer countries of East Asia, including the Philippines, Indonesia, the three countries of Indochina and the hinterland of China, are sinking into a "Fourth World" excluded from the process of globalization. As stated above, the "Fourth World" is defined not only in terms of countries, but also includes economically stagnant and socially excluded areas of otherwise wealthy countries such as the United States.[11] By this definition, we can identify segments of poorer countries in East Asia, such as parts of the hinterland of China, Indonesia and the Philippines, as parts of the "Fourth World", on which meaningful sociological-economic investigations can be conducted with regard to economic impoverishment and social exclusion. However, taking the poorer countries of East Asia as a whole, we do not see any of these countries sinking into the "Fourth World". First, as these countries open up to foreign trade and foreign investment, they export labour-intensive products demanded by world markets, where these countries still occupy a comfortable niche thanks to their competitiveness in labour costs and other inputs. Second, the poorer countries in Southeast Asia are members of the Asian Free Trade Area (AFTA) under ASEAN, and are participating in regional economic cooperation in trade and investment. Even if they play no part in the international division of labour for the production of IT industries, they are involved in the intra-regional division of labour for the production of lower value-added parts and components of manufactured goods, including cars and electronic products. Third, some poorer countries, especially China, have a diversified industrial structure, including a large sector for electronics, computer and other IT-related industries. In other words, poverty does not necessarily lead to alienation from the global process of IT production as far as East Asia is concerned.

Consequently, the concept of "Fourth World" is not relevant to East Asian economic studies, except for the case study of how the development of an information economy may socially and economically affect the population within a country.

The fifth dimension of the new paradigm deals with what I term the "parallel development" of information technologies that may disrupt the existing regional technological hierarchy depicted by the "flying geese model". To introduce this new line of thought, we must begin with a brief review of the existing technological order. Since the early 1960s, the development of industrial technologies in East Asia is known to have followed a hierarchical pattern, in which less developed countries acquired mature or routine technologies from more developed countries, especially Japan, with a time lag, normally ten years. For example, labour-intensive manufacturing technologies of textiles, consumer electronics and plastics industries were transferred from Japan to Taiwan, Korea, Hong Kong and Singapore in the 1960s, and the Four Tigers transferred these technologies to China and Southeast Asian countries in the 1970s while they concentrated on higher-level technologies such as petrochemicals, automobiles and heavy industries. Meanwhile, Japan had already moved one step further towards knowledge-intensive industries. Three factors account for the hierarchical order and time lag: first, labour-intensive and capital-intensive manufacturing technologies require heavy investments in infrastructure facilities such as transportation, energy and telecommunications, and also in education and manpower training. The less developed countries are not in a position to develop these industries until they can meet these requirements. Second, the full development of these industries takes time because they require complex investments in land, buildings, machinery, facilities of transportation, energy and telecommunications, and because a whole system of auxiliary or supporting enterprises is needed to supply raw materials, intermediate products, parts and components; and downstream firms are also needed to absorb the new industrial products for further processing or manufacturing. Third, these technologies, being the results of expensive R&D, take on a monopolistic character, and the proprietors transfer them on highly demanding terms and in a cautiously guarded manner. Hence a "flying geese model" has emerged with Japan as the "leading goose" and the Four Tigers and the Four Little Tigers (Malaysia, Thailand, the Philippines and Indonesia) following with a respective time lag.

Information technologies can constitute a different story. Rather than adopt a hierarchical character, they are relatively capable of "parallel development" in countries with different degrees of industrialization, and they diffuse more easily than traditional manufacturing technologies. As early as 1973, Daniel Bell was already talking about information and scientific knowledge as a "'collective good' in that once it has been created, it is by its character available to all". The secrecy of an information technology is harder to guard and its patent or copyright is susceptible to infringement.[12] Moreover, the "hardware" requirements (land, buildings, machinery, etc.) of an IT enterprise are not as complicated as when a manufacturing firm is concerned, and the investment fund is primarily used to retain expertise. Since information technologies are constantly changing and their product life cycles are relatively short, late-comers do not need to start from the bottom, but can simply latch onto any particular technology that offers comparative advantage. Being knowledge-intensive in nature, IT industries do not entail a complex system of supporting enterprises the way manufacturing industries do, so that a less developed East Asian country can succeed in developing one or two IT industries with a shorter time lag than it can in developing traditional manufacturing industries.

The theory of "parallel development" is borne out by the fact that less developed East Asian countries such as China, Malaysia and the Philippines have established a solid base for IT industries, with IT-related products accounting for a substantial portion of their respective exports. Moreover, South Korea has succeeded in its semiconductor and DRAM industries within a relatively short period of time. Looking beyond East Asia, we find that a poor country like India has won worldwide recognition for its advanced software industry, which is now providing European and American corporations with sophisticated and high-quality software service and products, ranging from e-banking and e-commerce platforms to the designing of supply-chain management systems and all-round IT solutions. According to *Business Week*, India may soon threaten the competitiveness of the U.S. software industry.[13]

Ultimately the "parallel development" of IT industries can thus result in the disruption of the regional technological hierarchy of "flying geese". With Japan's economy mired in a long-standing recession and its IT supremacy being challenged by other Asian countries, the model is losing its "leading goose", and Asian countries can now compete in IT industries without much time lag and without having to follow a hierarchical order of development.[14] In the long run, we may expect a new technological order to emerge in the region, in which giant countries with abundant human resources such as China and India are likely to occupy a considerably higher niche, and information technologies are diffused among different countries of the region. One important implication of this development is that the effects of IT industries on macro-economic performance will not only come — as they do now — from the exporting of semiconductors and other IT-related products to world markets, but also from the diffusion and application of information technologies to non-tech sectors, including the manufacturing and service sectors. In that event, we can talk about these economies being integrated into the Information Economy, and not as mere producers meeting the demands of advanced industrial countries.

CONCLUDING REMARKS

A paradigm shift is a radical change in the dominant thought or ideology underlying a particular field of studies. The pressures for such a change build up when social, political or technological revolutions usher in a new order for which the old paradigm loses its explanatory power. In the history of economic thought and theory, paradigm shifts are highly correlated with social changes. For instance, the liberalist paradigm of *laissez faire* in Adam Smith's *Wealth of Nations,* which represented a radical shift from the mercantilist thought of wealth accumulation, was not his own invention, but resulted, rather, from the political liberalism that had been in vogue since the seventeenth century, and also from the bourgeoning productive forces made possible by the early stage of the Industrial Revolution during Smith's times. On the other hand, the paradigm of class conflict in Marx's economic thought had its origin in the growing socio-economic injustice under industrial capitalism in the nineteenth century.

As far as East Asian economic studies are concerned, "developmentalism" inevitably became the dominant paradigm from the 1950s to the middle of 1970s when the theme of economic development was actively championed by the United States and multinational corporations eager to export manufacturing capital and technology, and when the capitalist system urgently needed to demonstrate its economic supremacy over communism. "Developmentalism" then incorporated a dimension of modernization theory that rejected traditional culture as an obstacle to socio-economic progress. A paradigm shift, however, began to emerge towards the end of the 1970s as the economic performance in East Asia stood out as a "miracle" among developing countries. The shift was towards perceiving traditional Confucian values and the interventionism of the state as two essential explanatory concepts in the East Asian model of economic modernization. As a logical consequence, the new paradigm criticized modernization theory and the neo-classical idea of non-interventionism for their failure to explain the success story of that region. It needs to be pointed out that this new paradigm did not overthrow the legitimate position of neoclassical economic theory, but only served as a "rival paradigm" that had gained influence until recent years under the aegis of prominent scholars such as Ezra Vogel of Harvard University. Neo-classical economists, notably Milton Friedman, John C.H. Fei and Edward K.Y. Chen, continued to espouse non-interventionism and the free market as the primary driving forces of economic growth in the region. Thus the "Asian miracle" gave rise to two mutually conflicting paradigms.

As the financial and economic crisis during 1997–98 laid bare the weaknesses of "crony capitalism" and statism in East Asia, it also called the "rival paradigm" into question. Today there is little talk about the "Asian type of modernization" driven by Confucian cultural values and state planning. The dramatic boom and bust in the East Asian economies after 1999 have opened our eyes to the reality that the region's economies are under the strong influence of two external factors: globalization and the rapid development of information technology. Although no scholars of East Asia have spoken of globalization or Information Economy as a new paradigm thus far, it may be time now to envision a paradigm shift in that direction, given the formidable impact of the IT-driven New Economy and the fact that information technologies are becoming a focal point for economic studies in the West. In an era when global economic integration is pressing ahead with great momentum, East Asian economic studies cannot hope to grasp the full dynamics of the regional economy, especially the forces that often capriciously drive its boom and bust, unless they come to grips with this central issue.

Notes

*   An earlier version of this chapter was published in Japan as "A New Paradigm Shift in East Asian Economic Studies" in *Ritsumeikan Journal Asia Pacific Studies* 10 (December 2002): 1–13. The present chapter is a substantially revised and updated version, published here with permission from *Ritsumeikan Journal of Asia Pacific Studies*.

1   Strictly speaking, no theory on the "Fourth World" has been formulated, but political economist Manuel Castells devotes 101 pages to a detailed description and analysis of the "Fourth World" in the third volume entitled *The End of Millennium* of his voluminous book *The Information Age: Economy, Society and Culture*, second edition, Malden, Massachusetts: Blackwell, 2000. See chapter two of that volume, "The Rise of the Fourth World: Informational Capitalism, Poverty and Social Exclusion," pp. 68–108. For the concept of the "Fourth World", see also Fernando Henrique Cardoso, "North-South Relations in the Present Context: A New Dependency?" in *The New Global Economy in the Information Age*, edited by Martin Carnoy, et al. Pennsylvania State University Press, 1993, pp. 149–59.

2   The data on productivity and the quotation here are respectively from two articles of *The Economist*, "Productivity, Profit and Promises: Will America's New Economy Survive the Downturn?" 10–16 February 2001, pp. 22–24, and "To Cut or Not to Cut?" 10–16 February 2001, pp. 61–62.

3   Remarks by Alan Greenspan are quoted in *Business Week*, "A Crisis in Capital Spending?" 5 March 2001, pp. 34–37.

4   The views of Robert Gordon and others against the new economy are quoted from Louis Uchitelle, "In a Productivity Surge, No Proof of a New Economy", in the *New York Times* (electronic edition), 8 October 2000. See also an *AP* news release on Robert Gordon's research report on the New Economy, 4 June 2001.

5   There are a number of articles arguing a case for the new economy, including Christopher Farrell, "The Case for Optimism", in *Business Week*, 9 October 2001, pp. 182–84.

6   See Daniel Bell, *The Coming of Post-Industrial Society*, New York: Basic Books, 1973/76. Many passages in the book mention theoretical knowledge and information as key factors in the post-industrial society, including p. xv, p. xix, and p. 125. For "information economy", see the first volume of Marc Porat's book, *Information Economy: Definition and Measurement*, U.S. Department of Commerce, Washington D.C., 1977. According to Porat, 46 per cent of the GNP of the U.S. was bound up with "information activity" and nearly half of the labour force held an "informational job" and earned 53 per cent of total labour income in 1967. See Chapter One of the book.

7   Paul Krugman's article "The Myth of Asia's Miracle" was published in *Foreign Affairs* 73, no. 6 (November–December 1994): 62–78.

8   For an account of how other stock markets are linked to the U.S. stock market through the globalization of financial capital, see Laura Tyson, "Why the New Economy Is Here to Stay?" in *Business Week*, 30 April 2001, p. 26.

9   For a detailed account of the "silicon cycle" theory, see Su Shih-chieh, et al., *The Semiconductor Industry Marching towards the 21st Century*, [*Ying-hsiang er-shih-yi shih-chi te pan-tau-ti chan-ye*] Taipei: Electronics Times Publishing Co., 2000, pp. 52–53.

10   For a lengthy analysis of "social exclusion" and the exploitation of children by the "sex industry" in the "information age", see Castells, op. cit., Chapter Two, "The Rise of the Fourth World: Informational Capitalism, Poverty and Social Exclusion", pp. 68–168. See especially the sections on "The New American Dilemma: Inequality, Urban Poverty and Social Exclusion in the Information Age" pp. 128–52, and "Globalization, Over-exploitation and Social Exclusion: the View from the Children", pp. 153–65.

11   Castells devotes twenty-five pages to discussing urban poverty and social exclusion in the United States as part of "Fourth World" problems. See ibid.

12   Quoted from Daniel Bell, op. cit., "Foreword: 1976", p. xiv.

13   For an account of India's software industry, see *Business Week* article "India 3.0 — Its Software Outfits Take on the World", 26 February 2001, pp. 44–46. See

also a special report on India's software industry in *Commonwealth Monthly* [*Tien-hsia*] Taipei, 1 April 2001, pp. 48–59. This point is raised in an article by Chu Yun-peng, "The Information Economy Breaks Down the Fatalism of the 'Flying Geese Theory' " [*Chih-shih ching-chi ta-po yen-hsing li-lun te su-ming*], in *Business Weekly* [*Shang-yeh chou-kan*], Taipei, 15 January 2001, p. 84.

References

A Crisis in Capital Spending? *Business Week*, 5 March 2001.

Bell, Daniel. *The Coming of Post-Industrial Society*. New York: Basic Books, 1973/76.

Cardoso, Fernando Henrique. "North-South Relations in the Present Context: A New Dependency?" In *The New Global Economy in the Information Age*, edited by Martin Carnoy, et al. Pennsylvania State University Press, 1993.

Castells, Manuel. *The Information Age: Economy, Society and Culture*. Malden Massachusetts: Blackwell, 2000.

Chu Yun-peng. "The Information Economy Breaks Down the Fatalism of the Flying Geese Theory". *Business Weekly*, 15 January 2001.

Farrell, Christopher. "The Case for Optimism". *Business Week*, 9 October 2001.

"India 3.0 — Its Software Outfits Take on the World". *Business Week*, 26 February 2001.

Krugman, Paul. The Myth of Asia's Miracle. *Foreign Affairs* 73, no. 6 (November–December 1994).

Porat, Marc. *Information Economy: Definition and Measurement*. Washington D.C.: U.S. Department of Commerce, 1977.

"Productivity, Profit and Promises: Will America's New Economy Survive the Downturn?" *The Economist*, 10–16 February 2001.

Su Shih-chieh, et al. *The Semiconductor Industry Marching towards the 21st Century*. Taipei: Electronics Times Publishing Co., 2000.

"To Cut or Not to Cut?" *The Economist*, 10–16 February 2001.

Tyson, Laura. "Why the New Economy Is Here to Stay?" *Business Week*, 30 April 2001.

Uchitelle, Louis. "In a Productivity Surge, No Proof of a New Economy". *New York Times* (electronic edition), 8 October 2000.

PART THREE

Inter-Regionalism
and Regionalism

5

ALLIANCE AND ARMS
A Study of the Change in U.S. Arms Transfer to East Asian Allies, 1950–2001[*]

Sun Yi-ching

INTRODUCTION

In the fall of 1949, the American Congress passed the Mutual Defence Assistance Act that led to a programme commonly known as "security assistance". In accordance with this act (and later revisions), the United States came to export almost US$500 billion in arms and related military services from 1950 to 2001. The transfer of military equipment to allies and friendly states has remained a consistent feature of U.S. foreign policy, although there was a significant change in how arms were supplied. The United States provided arms free of charge in the beginning, but gradually began to demand payment. In other words, there was a shift from military aid to military sales (the aid/sale transformation).[1] The transition was remarkable: in 1950, for example, only 4 per cent of the total agreements on weapons exports were sales; but in 1984, military sales accounted for more than 90 per cent of all U.S. arms exports.[2] Even after the Cold War, this percentage was never lower than 63 per cent. The purpose of this study is to develop a consistent explanation of this increase in the percentage of arms sales, after which the data is tested on the case of U.S. arms exports to East Asia.

World Military Expenditures and Arms Transfer (WMEAT), one of the most cited and commonly used statistical sources, defines "arms transfers" as follows:

> Arms transfers (arms imports and exports) represent the international transfer (under terms of grant, credit, barter or cash) of military equipment, usually referred to as "conventional", including weapons of war, parts thereof, ammunition, support equipment, and other commodities designed for military use.[3]

This involves two important features. First, arms transfer is an "international" activity between at least two states or international actors. In other words, arms transfer involves cooperation between states, and requires a supplier to export arms and a recipient to import them. If either the supplier or the recipient is not capable or not willing to cooperate, no arms transfer can occur.

This chapter contends that U.S. arms transfers cannot be adequately studied by examining the supplier side alone. The supplier and the recipient are equally important in understanding the pattern of U.S. arms transfer. With the above definition in mind, the key question about the aid/sale transformation is why the United States was willing to bear the cost of arms transfers in the 1950s and 1960s, and why the ally was willing to pay for weapons in the 1970s and 1980s?

Current studies of aid/sale transformation can be represented by two lines of reasoning found in the literature on arms transfer. The "political economy argument" claims that the increase in arms sales occurred because the United States changed the objective of arms transfer from the promotion of national security to the boosting of the domestic economy in the 1970s (Klare 1984; Chan 1980; Ron, Humm and Fontanel 1985; Daffron 1991). This change occurred because of the increase in oil prices, the trade deficit, the budget deficit, the high unemployment rate, and the decrease in defence spending, etc. On the other hand, the "security argument" contends that the rationale for arms transfer was and will continue to be an instrument to promote U.S. security interests, and to ensure the regional balance of power (Louscher and Salomon 1988). In other words, the motivation for U.S. arms transfer did not change throughout the Cold War and the post-Cold War period, and economic factors do not help explain U.S. arms transfer behaviour (Sanjian 1988).

However, neither the security argument nor the political economy argument offers a plausible or consistent explanation for the aid/sale transformation. The security argument contends that the major reason for increasing arms sales was the decline of military aid, but does not explain why military aid declined. The explanation offered by the political economy argument is also weak. According to it, the economic benefit of arms sales helps to alleviate domestic difficulties. Thus, during economically hard times, the United States will be motivated to sell more military equipment to foreign countries. However, arms sales are always a better arms transfer method than military aid, even when there is no economic crisis; obviously, it is always better to be paid for weapons than to give them away for free. Why then did the United States not prefer arms sales earlier? Why did U.S. arms sales not decrease dramatically in the 1980s and the 1990 when the economic situation had improved?[4]

This chapter develops three arguments to explain this change. First, the necessary condition of arms sales is that the ally is able to pay for its weapons. Thus, until the ally has improved its economy to such a level that it is able to pay for arms, military sales are not a feasible option. However, even if the ally is able to pay, this does not necessarily mean that the ally will be willing to purchase arms. This chapter develops two additional arguments to explain further the aid/sale transformation. First, the credibility of U.S. commitment may affect the financial arrangements of arms transfer, since the ally has more to lose than the United States in case of military defeat.[5] Thus, when U.S. commitment loses credibility,[6] the ally may wish to import more arms to increase its ability to defeat its enemies on its own. As a result, it will be more likely to concede to the United States in arms transfer negotiations and agree to pay for arms. Second, the strategy adopted by the United States may also explain the aid/sale transformation. When the United States adopts a strategy that makes it more likely that the ally will suffer serious damage in a conflict between the United States and the enemy,[7] the ally may want to import more arms to defeat the enemy on its own. This may weaken the ally's position in asking for military aid. At a very general level, these two arguments contend that the party (the United States or the ally), who is less tolerant to the consequence of no arms transfer, is likely to concede to its partner in arms transfer negotiations.

This chapter is divided into five sections. The one following the introduction illustrates arms transfers within a context of potential conflict involving three actors, and discusses the benefit of arms transfers for both the United States and an arms recipient. The third section develops explanations of the aid/sale transformation, while the fourth provides some empirical evidence from Asian states in support of arguments advanced in the first three sections. The conclusion discusses U.S. arms transfer behaviour in the period after the Cold War.

THE CONFLICT PROCESS AND THE BENEFITS
OF ARMS TRANSFERS

The context in which arms transfers occur is a process of potential conflict. This section first illustrates this process, and then discusses how the ally's ability to resist the enemy benefits the ally itself and the United States.

A. The Conflict Process

The conflict process in this study involves three actors — the enemy, the United States and the ally. In real terms, the enemy during the Cold War was largely the Soviet Union, and after the Cold War, it was mainly Iraq. The United States and the ally view themselves as defenders who use military resources to prevent the enemy from achieving its objective. Figure 5.1 depicts the conflict process between two rival blocs and shows how the United States and the ally interact in a conflict. The enemy has the first move, in which it chooses between mounting a conventional attack (A1) and doing nothing (Q1). If the enemy chooses to do nothing, there will be no conflict and the *status quo* (S) remains. If the enemy attacks (A1), the ally will immediately decide either to resist ($R1_a$) or not to resist the attack ($NR1_a$). If the ally chooses to resist the attack and its military force is capable of doing so ($R1_a$), it can prevent the enemy from advancing into its territory. At this moment, the enemy must decide to continue attacking (A2) or to quit (Q2), and the United States does not have to involve itself in the conflict ($NR1_{US}$). In contrast, if the ally decides not to or is not able to resist the attack ($NR1_a$), the United States has two alternatives — to join the conflict ($R1^*_{US}$) or to do nothing ($NR1^*_{US}$). If it chooses to do nothing, the enemy will win the conflict (a losing outcome (L) for the United States and the ally), since the United States and the ally both do not resist the attack. If the United States chooses to respond to the attack ($R1^*_{US}$), the conflict continues, and the enemy must choose to attack or quit ($A2^*$ or $Q2^*$). This suggests that the only time the United States must decide whether to fight or not is when the ally fails to resist the attack. Why is this the only time that the United States must make a decision about joining the conflict? It seems obvious that if the United States perceives that the ally can handle the attack alone, there is no reason for the United States to enter the conflict.[8]

   After encountering the resistance offered by either the ally or the United States ($R1_a$ or $R1^*_{US}$), the enemy must decide to continue the conflict (A2 or $A2^*$) or quit (Q2 or $Q2^*$). If the enemy chooses to quit, the conflict will end with a winning outcome (W) for both the United States and the ally. If the

FIGURE 5.1
Conflict Process Involving Three Actors

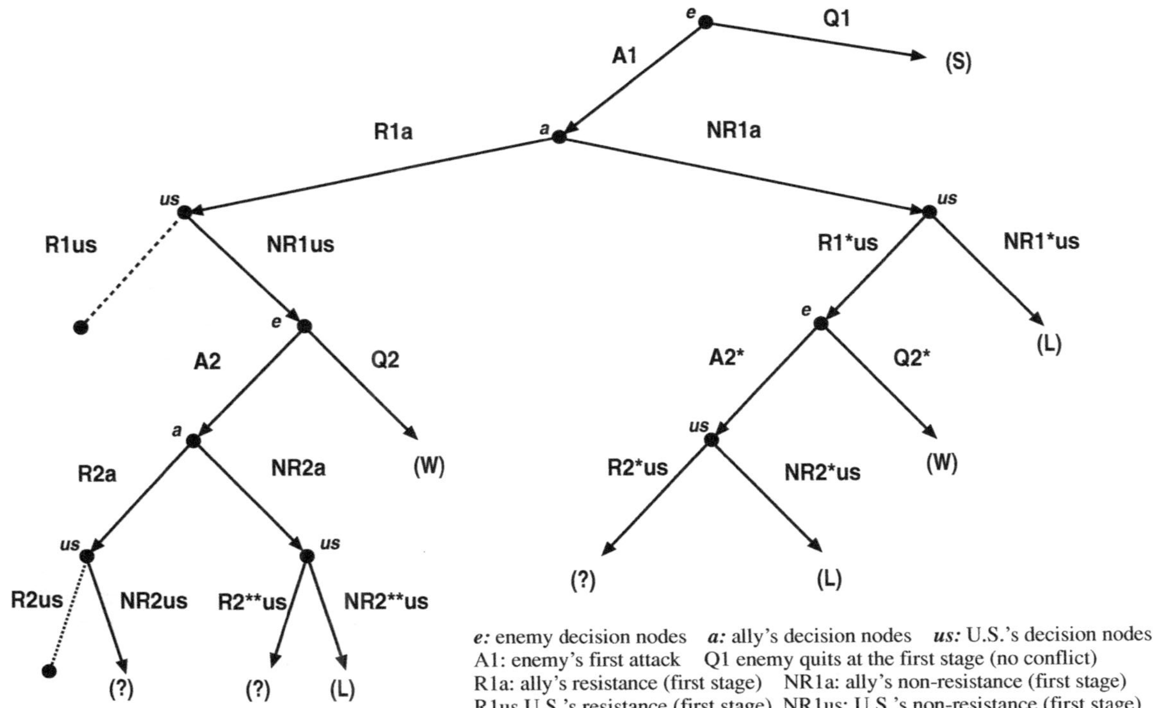

e: enemy decision nodes   *a:* ally's decision nodes   *us:* U.S.'s decision nodes
A1: enemy's first attack   Q1 enemy quits at the first stage (no conflict)
R1a: ally's resistance (first stage)   NR1a: ally's non-resistance (first stage)
R1us U.S.'s resistance (first stage) NR1us: U.S.'s non-resistance (first stage)
(S) Status quo   (L) The U.S. and the ally lose the conflict
(W) The U.S. and the ally win the conflict   (?) Undetermined

enemy chooses to continue (A2 or A2'), the conflict will not end. At this point, the United States or the ally must decide to fight or back down. If the ally is unable to resist the attack in the first stage (NR1$_a$), it will certainly not be able to resist in the second stage of the conflict. In this situation, if the enemy chooses to continue the conflict (A2'), the United States has to decide to continue to resist (R2'$_{US}$) or to quit (NR2'$_{US}$). If the United States chooses the latter (NR2'$_{US}$), the United States and the ally lose the conflict (L). Otherwise, the conflict goes on and the enemy must choose to continue the war or back down.

If the ally is able to resist the initial attack (R1$_a$) and the enemy chooses to continue the conflict (A2), the ally may or may not be able to resist the attack again. If the ally cannot resist the attack any longer (NR2$_a$), the United States must decide to fight (R2''$_{US}$) or not fight (NR2''$_{US}$). If the United States quits, the conflict will end with a loss for both the United States and the ally. If the United States chooses to resist the enemy, the conflict will continue. Then, the enemy must choose its next move (A3'' or Q3''). If the ally is still capable of defending itself (R2$_a$), the United States can continue observing the fighting and not involve itself in the conflict; the enemy must decide to continue the conflict or quit.

The process of potential conflict can develop in one of three ways: 1) the enemy chooses not to initiate an attack, 2) one side loses its willingness to fight, or 3) one side is completely destroyed by the other side. The third way can lead to a special scenario where both sides lose in a nuclear disaster (D). Except for the early Cold War years, both the United States and the Soviets possessed a certain degree of second-strike capacity. This means that even if one side suffered a defeat, it would still have the ability to launch a final attack that would impose extremely high costs upon the adversary. In other words, if one side had nothing left to lose, it would try to annihilate its adversary. Thus, for each side, this process can end with one of four payoffs: 1) *status quo* (S), 2) winning (W), 3) losing (L), or 4) disaster (D). For both sides, winning is considered better than losing, and losing better than disaster (W > L > D). The *status quo* is also assumed to be better than losing and disaster. Even if the United States and the ally do not challenge the *status quo*, they suspect that the enemy prefers winning to the *status quo* (W > S > L > D). Thus, the United States or the ally will threaten to use force to prevent the enemy from achieving a winning outcome. If they can make their adversary feel that it has no chance of winning, it will choose to keep the *status quo*. In contrast, when the enemy believes that it has a high probability of winning, it may choose to attack.

B. Benefits and Motivation of Arms Transfers

The most obvious contribution that an ally can offer the United States is to allow the United States to stay out of the fighting. As long as the ally is able to resist the attack, the United States does not have to choose to fight or accept a losing outcome. In what ways does the United States benefit if the ally is able to resist the enemy on its own? To answer this question, we shall examine the basic form of cooperation between the United States and the ally in the conflict, which can be represented by the initial stage (R1) of the conflict. In stage one of Figure 5.1, the choices of the United States and the ally form four different resistance patterns: 1) only the ally resists the attack $(R1_a-NR_{US})$; 2) only the United States responds to the attack $(NR1_a-R1^*_{US})$; 3) neither the ally nor the United States resists the attack $(NR1_a-NR1^*_{US})$; and 4) both the ally and the United States resist the attack $(R1_a-R1_{US})$. However, the last possibility — $R1_a-R1_{US}$ — is included for analytical completeness only because if the United States observes that the ally is effectively resisting the attack, as assumed earlier, it will not involve itself in the fighting.

If the enemy attacks, the ally can expect to suffer at least one of the following types of costs. As assumed earlier, the ally is geographically closer to the enemy than the United States. If the enemy attacks, there will be an immediate cost to the ally because the battlefield will be in the ally's territory. If the ally cannot resist the attack, it will suffer even more. When the ally does not stop the enemy and the United States chooses to fight $(NR1_a-R1^*_{US})$, the ally will bear the cost of a "firebreak"[9] until the enemy comes into contact with the resistance offered by the United States. Third, even if the United States chooses to fight $(NR1_a-R1^*_{US})$, the ally will suffer the cost of a conflict between the United States and the enemy since it will be fought on its soil. If the United States chooses not to respond to the attack or is defeated by the enemy, the ally will suffer conquest by the enemy. To avoid suffering such damages, the ally will obviously resist the attack. However, the question is whether the ally is able to do so. If the ally is unable to offer any effective resistance, the enemy will continue to advance without needing an additional decision. This is similar to the case in which the ally chooses not to resist $(NR1_a)$. If the ally's resistance is strong enough to contain or defeat the attack $(R1_a)$ (for example, if it can encircle a great portion of the enemy's troops), the ally can temporarily limit its damage. At this moment, the enemy must decide to send in reinforcements to continue the attack (A2) or quit fighting. If the enemy decides to quit, the ally wins the conflict with a cost that is much less than that of non-resistance. However, if the enemy continues the attack, the ally's payoff is uncertain because the conflict has not ended. Resisting the attack ($R1_a$) offers a better payoff to the ally than not doing so ($NR1_a$). To avoid the high cost of not resisting is an important motivation for the ally to import arms.

What are the payoffs to the United States in these different resistance patterns? If the ally effectively resists the attack ($R1_a$) alone, the United States benefit is that it need not use its own forces to respond to the attack ($NR1_{US}$). If the enemy quits at this point, the United States wins the conflict without any cost to itself. In contrast, when the ally cannot resist the attack ($NR1_a$), the enemy will continue advancing into the ally's territory. In this case, the United States must choose to confront the enemy ($NR1_a$-$R1^*_{US}$) or accept a losing outcome ($NR1_a$-$NR1^*_{US}$). If the United States decides not to fight, the ally will be conquered by the enemy, and the United States will lose the ally. However, if the United States is not willing to accept a losing outcome, it has to use its own forces to confront the enemy ($R1^*_{US}$). Since the enemy may decide to fight back ($A2^*$), the United States may suffer certain costs in this case.

Table 5.1 summarizes the payoff of each resistance pattern in the first stage of the conflict (except for the fourth one which is included for analytical completeness only). Both the United States and the ally will receive a losing outcome in the third resistance pattern ($NR1_a$-$NR1^*_{US}$), because neither of them resists the attack. In this situation, the ally will be conquered by the enemy, and the United States will lose its ally. The first ($NR1_a$-$R1^*_{US}$) and the second ($R1_a$-$NR1_{US}$) resistance patterns appear to produce a payoff similar to that in Figure 5.1. However, the first pattern is better than the second for both the ally and the United States, because the United States does not have to use its own forces to fight the enemy and the ally temporarily suffers less

TABLE 5.1
Resistance Patterns in the First Stage of the Conflict

Resistance Patterns	Enemy's choices	Payoff for defenders
1. $R1_a$-NR_{US}	A2	?[*]
	Q2	W
2. NR_a-$R1^*_{US}$	$A2^*$	?[*]
	$Q2^*$	W
3. NR_a-NR^*_{US}		L

[*] The payoff of the conflict is uncertain, since it depends upon the choices made by the United States, the ally and the enemy in later stages of the conflict.

damage. Conversely, in the second resistance pattern, the United States must use its own forces and become engaged in an overt conflict. Furthermore, the ally will suffer more because of "firebreak" and some other costs.[10]

If the ally can resist the attack in the first stage and the enemy decides to continue the conflict (A2), the resistance pattern and payoffs for the succeeding stages (R2, R3...Rn) are similar to those of the initial stage (R1). As long as the ally can continue to resist subsequent attacks (A2, A3...An) the United States can remain uninvolved, and the ally can prevent massive damage. However, if the ally fails to resist the attack in any subsequent stage of the war, it will suffer a high cost. Once this occurs, the United States must decide whether to fight or not. If the United States chooses not to fight, the conflict will end with a losing outcome for both the United States and the ally. If the United States decides to confront the enemy, the conflict will continue until either the United States or the enemy loses its capacity or willingness to fight.

In conclusion, the basic motivation for arms transfer is to equip the ally to win a probable conflict; this benefits both the United States and the ally. This corresponds to the assertion offered by the security argument that arms transfers function as an extension of American defence of U.S. interests.

EXPLANATIONS OF THE AID/SALE TRANSFORMATION

As discussed earlier, for both the United States and the ally, the best outcome of a conflict is that the ally defeats the enemy. Thus, when the United States and the ally suspect that the enemy may launch an attack, the ally's defensive abilities will be evaluated. If the United States and the ally think that the ally is unable to defeat the enemy, arms transfer negotiations are likely to take place. In other words, the occurrence of arms transfer negotiations suggests that the United States and the ally agree that 1) there is a possibility that the enemy may attack;[11] and 2) the ally is not likely to defeat the enemy with its current military capability. If the United States or the ally disagrees with either one of these two conditions, an arms transfer is unlikely. If the likelihood of a conflict increases and if the ally's chances of defeating the enemy decrease, the likelihood of arms transfer will also increase. In contrast, if the likelihood of a conflict decreases or if the ally's chances of defeating the enemy increase, the likelihood of an arms transfer will also decrease.

Arms transfer negotiations have two possible outcomes: successful or unsuccessful. A successful arms transfer is one in which the United States and the ally reach an agreement to transfer arms that will enhance the ally's ability to defeat the enemy in a conflict. An unsuccessful arms transfer is one in which the United States and the ally do not agree to transfer arms. In this case, the ally cannot improve its military capability or its chances of defeating the enemy. The transfer of arms can range from being entirely military aid to being entirely arms sales. This study assumes that the United States always prefers arms sales to military aid, while the ally always prefers military aid to arms sales. A successful transfer of arms requires cooperation between these two parties. Thus, the United States or the ally (or both of them) must make concessions about who will bear more of the costs of the weapons. If neither side concedes, there will be no arms transfer. Thus, the answer to the question why arms are transferred *via* military aid or *via* military sales is provided by the answer to the question why one party makes more concessions than the other in arms transfer negotiations. In general, if the ally is able to pay, the party that has more to lose if no transfer of arms is agreed upon will be more likely to concede to its partner in a negotiation.

This explanation of the aid/sale transformation consists of two parts. The first part examines the necessary condition for an arms sales agreement — the ally must be able to pay. The second part contends that the credibility of U.S. commitment and the chosen U.S. strategy for fighting a war affect the expected cost of no arms being transferred for both the United States and the ally, which in turn influences the aid/sale transformation.

A. Economic Advancement and Aid/Sale Transformation

As ascertained above, the best option for both the United States and the ally in a conflict is for the ally to defeat the enemy alone. To make this option feasible, the ally must be supplied with sufficient arms. That is why the United States and the ally are willing to cooperate with each other to reach an arms transfer agreement.[12] Both the United States and the ally will benefit from arms transfer regardless of whether it occurs via military aid or arms sales. However, military aid is always a better deal for the ally, while arms sales are always a better deal for the United States. Why did the United States give military aid in the 1950s and 1960s and why did the ally agree to purchase arms in the 1970s, and 1980s? The most direct answer to this question is that it is impossible for the United States to sell arms to an ally who is not able to pay for them. If the United States insists on selling arms to an ally that cannot afford them, there will be no agreement between the United States and the ally. This will substantially increase the possibility that the United States will need to use its military forces to protect the ally. Thus, when the ally is too poor to purchase arms, the only way that the United States can help the ally possess more arms is to offer military aid. It is up to the United States, in such a situation, to decide between 1) offering military aid, 2) using its military resources to protect the ally, or 3) accepting the losing outcome. In this situation, offering military aid is the best option available to the United States. This suggests that the economic capability of a recipient not only constrains its ability to purchase weapons but also restricts a supplier's choice of using aid or sales. When an arms recipient has insufficient economic resources, arms sales will not be a feasible option for the United States. Thus, the ally's economic condition is an important factor in explaining why arms sales were not the major arms transfer method in the 1950s and 1960s (when most U.S. allies could not afford to buy arms).

However, economic advancement will only mean that an ally can afford to buy arms; the ally's wealth alone will not motivate the ally to buy arms or prefer arms sales to military aid. From an ally's perspective, military aid is always a better option than arms sales, even if the ally can afford to pay for weapons. Therefore, the ally's possession of a good economic situation is a necessary but not sufficient condition for arms sales. What, then, are the other factors that explain the aid/sale transformation after the ally's economic condition has improved?

B. The Expected Costs of No Arms Being Transferred

If the enemy attacks, the ally is either able or unable to defeat the enemy. If the ally defeats the enemy, it limits its cost of conflict while the United States wins the conflict without incurring any cost. If the ally fails to defend itself, it will incur a tremendous cost. At this time, the United States will decide to accept a losing outcome or to fight against the enemy using its own forces. Obviously, if the ally is able to defeat the enemy, both the United States and the ally will be better off. A necessary condition for the ally to defeat the enemy is that the ally possesses enough arms. Since arms transfer negotiations suggest that the ally is not able to win in a possible conflict, a failure to reach an agreement carries certain risks for both the United States and the ally. But what exactly is the cost of no arms being transferred for the United States and the ally, and how does it relate to U.S. commitment?

If the ally fails to defend itself in a conflict, one of four possible situations may occur: 1) the United States does not keep to its commitment, 2) the enemy defeats the United States, 3) the United States defeats the enemy, or 4) disaster. Each of these outcomes creates different payoffs for the United States and the ally. If the United States decides not to carry out its commitment (the first situation), it won't suffer any cost of fighting. However, the cost for the United States in this situation is the possible loss of the ally to the enemy. If the United States chooses to fight and loses the conflict (the second situation), it not only loses the ally to the enemy, but also incurs costs for the conflict. Costs for the conflict depend upon how the United States fights the enemy and when it decides to give up.[13] If the United States carries out its commitment and wins the conflict (the third one), it saves the ally from being occupied. However, there is a certain cost associated with this winning outcome, which depends upon how the United States fights the enemy and when the enemy decides to give up. Finally, if the United States or the enemy first launches a massive nuclear strike, the cost of the conflict will be extreme on both sides. When one side considers itself having nothing left to lose, it will attempt complete destruction of its adversary.

For the ally, these situations also bring different payoffs. First, if the United States does not carry out its commitment, the ally will be eliminated. Second, if the enemy defeats the United States, the payoff for the ally is the same as the first situation, or even worse.[14] Third, if the United States defeats the enemy, the ally wins the conflict. However, the price of winning includes not only the cost of the firebreak, but also the destruction caused by the fighting between the United States and the enemy. Fourth, if the conflict ends with disaster, it is not clear what will happen to the ally, since it is difficult to conclude how a massive nuclear war between the United States and the enemy will impact on the ally. However it is assumed the ally will suffer less than the United States if the conflict ends in a disaster.

This study argues that two properties of U.S. commitment may have an impact on the cost of no arms transfer being agreed to. The first is the credibility of U.S. commitment, which is defined as the likelihood that the United States will win the conflict. The second is how the United States plans to fight a war. If the ally fails to defend itself and the United States carries out its commitment, the conflict continues. Both the United States and the ally expect certain costs to be associated with the continuation of fighting. The cost of fighting for the United States and the ally will vary depending on how the United States escalates the conflict. For example, if the United States plans to continue the conflict in the ally's territory (for example, a conventional war), the ally will expect a high cost for not having defeated the enemy on its own. This situation suggests that the ally may want to import in advance more arms to improve its chances of winning the conflict by itself. Thus, the ally is likely to concede to the United States to attain an agreement on arms sales. In contrast, if the major battleground shifts away from the ally's territory to that of the United States' (for example, a nuclear war), the United States expects to suffer serious damage for carrying out its commitment. If the ally knows that the United States expects to suffer greatly for fighting against the enemy, the ally is in a better position to ask the United States for military aid. In the next section, these two properties of U.S. commitment will be used to develop arguments concerning the aid/sale transformation.

C. The Credibility of U.S. Commitment and the Aid/Sale Transformation

There are three conditions under which the ally may partially lose its confidence in U.S. commitment, which in turn will create an environment favoring arms sales. When the enemy is able to inflict significant damage on the United States, the United States may be less willing to go into battle, and U.S. deterrence may fail. This suggests that when the enemy has no capability to impose cost on the United States, the latter will consider fighting to be better than not fighting. Thus, every time the enemy increases its military power and reduces the degree of U.S. military superiority,[15] the cost of fighting for the United States increases. As the cost for defending the ally rises, the ally will become more suspicious about U.S. determination to win a conflict. Since the ally has more to lose, it will be more likely to agree to pay for U.S. arms when the enemy significantly improves its military capability.

If the United States considers the ally to be important to its own security, it will have a strong incentive to keep its commitment credible.[16] Therefore, if the enemy enhances its military capability to challenge U.S. military supremacy, the United States is likely to respond in order to maintain its credibility. For example, it may develop new technology or persuade the ally that the United States still has the determination to win the conflict in spite of the damage that the enemy can inflict upon the United States. For example, the United States can send troops into the ally's territory to guarantee its involvement and to demonstrate that there is a high cost to the United States if it does not fight. Such behaviour may regain ally confidence in U.S. commitment. As a consequence, the level of arms sales may go down again. Thus, as the enemy enhances its military capability, the level of arms sale may fluctuate.

The second condition that might cause the ally to lose confidence in the U.S. commitment is when the United States has little at stake. In this condition, the United States is less likely to escalate a conflict than it otherwise would be. Thus, if the ally believes that its survival is no longer of vital importance to the United States, it may suspect that the United States will not be willing to defend it.[17] The ally must then import more arms to increase its chances of defeating the enemy on its own. Thus, it is likely to concede to the United States in arms transfer negotiations.

The third condition that may undermine ally confidence in U.S. commitment is when the United States does not have a reputation for winning conflicts with the enemy. This is worth mentioning even if the context goes beyond our present one.[18] Let us assume for a while that there are two allies — Ally 1 and Ally 2. If Ally 1 observes that the United States defeats the enemy and saves Ally 2, then Ally 1 may retain a high level of confidence (or may even increase its trust) in U.S. commitment. However, if the United States loses the conflict and allows the Ally 2 to be conquered, Ally 1 may lose confidence in the United States (because it suspects that the United States may not be able to protect it either). Thus, if the United States fails to save Ally 2, then Ally 1 may desire more arms to increase its chances of defeating the enemy on its own. As a result, it will be more likely to concede to the United States in arms transfer negotiations and agree to purchase arms.

A loss in reputation causes more profound damage to U.S. credibility than the simple diminishing of military superiority over the enemy. Once the United States is defeated, it is difficult for it to reestablish its reputation, unless it wins another conflict with the enemy. However, it is quite easy for the United States to maintain or even to increase its military superiority over the enemy by developing new technology or boosting the size of its forces. Thus, the ratio of arms sales to military aid may fluctuate as the military balance between the United States and the enemy changes. On the other hand, the ratio of arms sales to military aid may rise and remain at a high level if the ally expects the United States to lose a war.

D. U.S. Strategy and the Aid/Sale Transformation

This section argues that even if the ally has complete confidence that the United States will win a conflict, U.S. strategic planning may create different costs of fighting for the United States and the ally. The party that expects to incur a larger portion of the costs in the event of a conflict will be more likely to concede to its partner in arms transfer negotiations.

U.S. commitment includes a strategic plan that defines how the it will act in a conflict. This plan specifies the type of warfare that the United States will employ to protect the ally (for example, Massive Retaliation *versus* Flexible Response). The plan may also include releasing information about when and under what conditions the United States will fight (for example, the Nixon Doctrine). As assumed earlier, when the enemy confronts the United States, it only uses the strategy of tit-for-tat. Thus, different strategies chosen by the United States will cause the enemy to retaliate differently. Even if the United

States wins, the cost of the victory will be distributed differently between the United States and the ally, depending on the strategy the United States chose to use. Therefore, the ratio of arms sale to military aid will change when the United States changes its strategy.

When the U.S. adopts a strategy that will bring extreme costs to the ally but not to the United States,[19] the ally will not be in a good position to request military aid. In this situation, even though the ally believes that the United States will win the war, it expects to incur severe costs, which is a much worse outcome than that of defeating the enemy on its own. The United States can tell the ally that even if the United States keeps its promise and successfully defends the ally, the ally will still bear most of the cost of the conflict. The ally must decide 1) to pay for its own weapons, or 2) to insist on military aid. If the ally agrees to pay, the United States will have no objection. In this case, the ally can increase its chances of defeating the enemy, which also benefits the United States. If the ally insists on military aid, it risks the arms transfer negotiations failing because the United States prefers sales to aid. Thus, no arms will be transferred to increase the ally's military capability. This outcome will hurt both the United States and the ally, although the ally's cost will be higher than that for the United States. Therefore, in such as situation, the ally is more likely to concede to the United States and to agree to purchase arms.

Furthermore, in this situation, even if the United States is uncertain of its choice in an actual conflict, it does not expect to suffer an extreme a cost as the ally will. Thus, the United States may insist on arms sale to maximize its interests. Obviously, this outcome will benefit the United States more than the ally because it not only enhances the ally's military capability (which reduces the chances that the United States will have to confront the enemy), but also brings economic benefits to the United States. On the other hand, when the United States shows through its choice of strategy that it is willing to incur extreme costs, the ally will be in a good bargaining position to ask for military aid. The United States will no longer have enough bargaining power to insist that the ally pay for weapons. Thus, military aid is likely to be the predominant method of arms transfer in such a situation. In the previous case, the main reason the ally will concede to the United States is that even if the United States wins the conflict, the cost will be extreme to the ally but not to the United States. However, when the United States adopts a strategy that will bring an extreme cost to itself (for example, massive retaliation),[20] it can no longer use the cost of winning as a source of bargaining power, since it already anticipates a high cost for fighting, and the ally knows it. As assumed earlier, the United States will not intimidate its ally with the threat that it will not carry out its commitment or the scenario that it will lose the conflict. Thus, the United States has much less bargaining power when it anticipates a high cost for fighting. The ally knows that the United States is willing to sustain a high cost for fighting and that the United States is uncertain about its choice in an actual conflict.[21] Thus, the ally is in a better position to ask for military aid. If the United States offers military aid, the ally has no reason to reject it. If the United States insists on selling arms, negotiations may end without an agreement to transfer arms because the ally prefers aid to sales. To avoid the possibility of fighting a costly war, the United States is likely to concede and offer the ally a good deal.

In general, U.S. strategy can affect both the U.S. and the ally's cost of winning. Thus, when the United States changes its strategy, the ratio of arms sales to military aid will change accordingly. In summary, military aid will be the predominant method of arms transfer when 1) the ally has little economic ability to pay for its own weapons, 2) U.S. commitment to defeat the enemy is credible, and 3) the United States is willing to incur extreme costs for carrying out its commitment. However, arms sales are likely to increase when 1) the ally improves its economic capability, 2) U.S. commitment becomes less credible, or 3) the United States adopts a strategy that leads the ally to expect a high cost for not defeating the enemy on its own. The next section tests whether these factors can actually explain U.S. arms transfer behaviour in Asia during the Cold War period.

EMPIRICAL EVIDENCE FROM ASIA

During the Cold War, East Asia was one of the largest regions importing U.S. weapons. As shown in Figure 5.2, Asian states[22] had two noticeable variations on the ratio of arms sales. The first occurred in 1964, and the second around 1971, providing this study with empirical data to test the explanation developed in the previous two sections.

A. East Asian States in 1964

From 1950 to early 1963, the ratio of arms sales to military aid to East Asian states never exceeded 3 per cent. In 1964, this ratio suddenly increased to about 10 per cent. However, for the next six years (1965 to 1970), it dropped to between 2 and 4 per cent. This study argues that the sudden increase in this ratio occurred because China made significant progress in its military technology. Throughout the 1950s and 1960s, the military threat that faced U.S. allies in East Asia was not only from the Soviet Union, but also from

FIGURE 5.2
Ratio of Arms Sales to East Asia 1950–2001

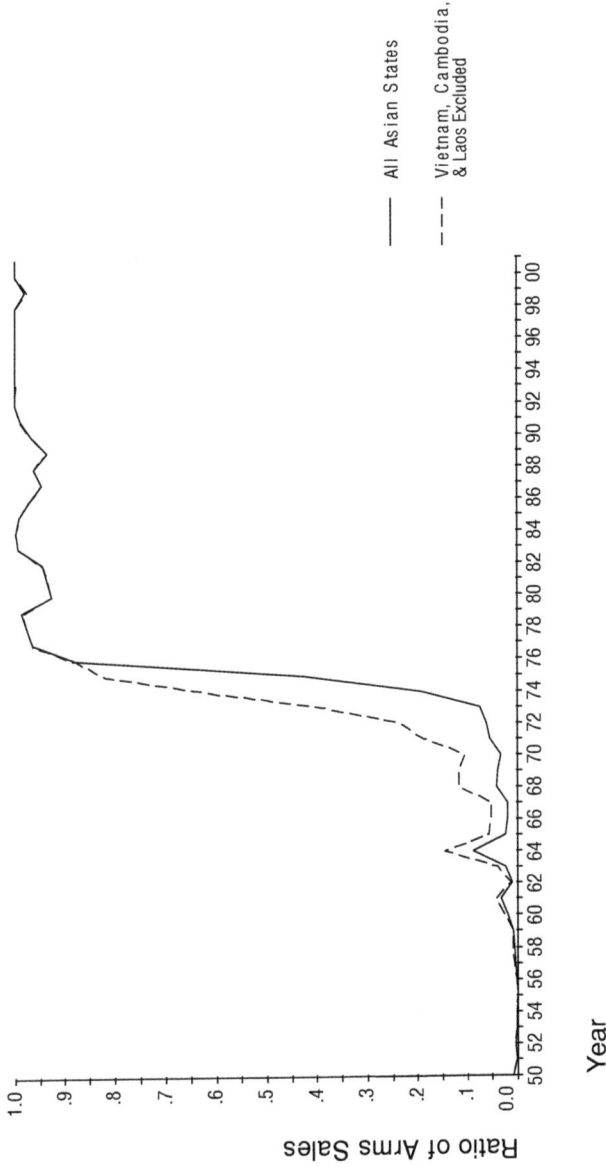

Source: DSAA Fiscal Series 1991 and DSCA Foreign Military Sales, Foreign Military Construction Sales and Military Assistance Facts: As of 30 September 2001.

China. During this period, there were several overt confrontations in this area directly involving U.S. allies, China, and the United States itself, such as the Korean War, and two Taiwan Straits crises in 1955 and 1958. Unlike the Soviet Union, China lagged far behind in military technology, and had a weak navy and air force. It also had no nuclear weapons or nuclear strike capability in the 1950s and early 1960s. The United States had also shown strong willingness to confront China in overt conflicts, such as in the Korean War. Thus, U.S. allies in the region considered U.S. commitment credible.

However, in 1964, China made a significant breakthrough in its military technology. In June, it successfully tested its Dongfeng-2 medium-range missile. This 1,450-kilometre-range missile had a single stage fuelled by non-storable alcohol and liquid oxygen and was road-mobile, which meant it could target U.S. bases in Japan, Korea, Taiwan, and the Philippines.[23] In October, China tested a nuclear weapon for the first time. These two events significantly changed the balance of military power in this region, and made the allies question U.S. commitment. Though China was not able to strike at the U.S. homeland with nuclear warheads, it could hit most U.S. military bases in East Asia. U.S. allies now suspected that the United States was becoming less willing to carry out its commitment against China in a crisis or an overt conflict, since the expected cost of fighting for the United States had increased. As a result, the ratio of arms sales suddenly jumped.

Later developments showed that the Chinese "threat" to the U.S. allies had in fact not significantly increased, and that they could still trust the commitment of the United States. First, there was no sign that China intended to produce a great number of nuclear weapons or had made significant progress in its nuclear technology. From 1964 to 1970, China only conducted eleven nuclear device tests. During that same period, 238 tests were conducted by the United States, and 93 by the Soviet Union. If the number of tests of nuclear weapons was a measure of progress in nuclear capability, Chinese nuclear capacity lagged far behind that of the United States and the Soviet Union. Furthermore, the United States began to send more troops in Vietnam. As proposed by McNamara, the United States planned to increase its presence in Vietnam from 75,000 in 1964 to 200,000 in 1965 and to 300,000 in 1966. This demonstrated to U.S. allies that the United States was willing to fulfill its commitment, even if it faced a close ally of China or the Soviet Union. In other words, the escalation of the Vietnam War boosted the United States' reputation for carrying out its commitment in the region. In time, the Sino-Soviet split became more evident. The dispute between them began in the late 1950s due to different interpretations of communist ideology. In the later half of the 1960s, their relationship worsened. There was an overt conflict between these two countries in 1969 in border regions, which reduced Chinese military threats toward U.S. allies in this area.[24] These developments suggested that U.S. commitment was still reliable. As a result, the ratio of arms sales went down.

B. East Asian States between 1970 and 1975

In 1971, the ratio of arms sales at the aggregate level went up. This increase can primarily be attributed to Third World states[25] such as U.S. allies in East Asia. The broken line in Figure 5.2 shows the ratio of arms sales for East Asian states.[26] This ratio was never higher than 12 per cent before 1970. However, a steep upward trend started in 1971. The sales ratio increased from 11 per cent in 1970 to 82 per cent in 1975.[27] As mentioned in the introduction, many scholars argue that the upward trend in arms sales in the 1970s was because of the oil crisis in 1973. The problem with this explanation is that the upward trend of arms sales agreements started two years earlier than the oil crisis. Therefore, it was unlikely that the oil crisis was the direct cause of the arms sales increase. This study argues that the increase was mainly due to the new direction that U.S. foreign policy had taken, through the Nixon Doctrine, and U.S. withdrawal from Vietnam. These two factors made U.S. commitment less credible; therefore, U.S. allies expected a greater cost than before for not defeating an invasion all by themselves. As a result, they were more willing to pay for their own weapons.

In July 1969, President Nixon made an *ad hoc* foreign policy announcement on Guam. There were three major themes of this announcement:

> First, the US will keep all of its treaty commitments ... Second, we shall provide a shield if a nuclear power threatens the freedom of a nation allied with us or of a nation whose survival we consider vital to our security ... Third, in cases involving other types of aggression we shall furnish military and economic assistance when requested in accordance with our treaty commitments. But we shall look to the nation directly threatened to assume the primary responsibility of providing the manpower for its defense.[28]

The form of this announcement was *ad hoc* indeed. There were no formal discussions in the Washington community nor were there prior consultations with allies. It emerged at a background briefing for the news media on Nixon's trip to Asia. Thus, it was not immediately obvious to U.S. allies what U.S. foreign policy changes would be made.[29] The Nixon Doctrine evolved along the line of four Reports to Congress made by President Nixon from 1970 to 1973. Some important parts of the doctrine were never clear, which further confused the U.S. allies. For example, the three major themes announced in Guam reappeared in different contexts on each Report to Congress. This confused the allies about the scope and purposes of this doctrine. In the 1970 Report to Congress, these three themes appeared in the section on Asia and the Pacific in the second part of the report under the title "Partnership and the Nixon Doctrine". This suggested that these three themes would only apply to U.S. allies in Asia and the Pacific. However, in the 1971 report, these three themes reappeared in the first part of the report, which was entitled "The Nixon Doctrine". This seemed to suggest that the Nixon Doctrine would apply to all allies of the United States. Furthermore, the three major themes seemed to contradict each other. For example, in the 1971 Report to Congress, President Nixon elaborated the third theme by saying that

> No president can guarantee that future conflicts will never involve American personnel — but in some theaters the threshold of involvement will be raised and in some instances involvement will be much more unlikely. The defense and progress of other countries must be first their responsibility and second, a regional responsibility. Without the foundations of self-help and regional help, American help will not succeed.[30]

If U.S. involvement in a conflict were unlikely, how would the United States fulfil its treaty commitments? If self-help and regional help were the necessary conditions for U.S. help, how much self-help or regional contribution would be enough to safeguard the continuity of U.S. commitment? Nixon did not provide answers to any of these questions.

The direct goal of the Nixon Doctrine was for the Americans to withdraw honorably from Vietnam, an engagement that had absorbed more than a half million U.S. military personnel, and required US$2,500 million a month to maintain. Indeed, one major course for achieving the Nixon Doctrine was "Vietnamization", which intended to strengthen the military ability of South Vietnam to defend itself and to provide an opportunity for the United States to withdraw without suffering a defeat. Within four years (from 1969 to 1972), the United States reduced its force level in South Vietnam by 95 per cent (from more than 540,000 in April 1969 to less than 30,000 in December 1972). It was obvious to U.S. allies around the world that the United States was about to abandon South Vietnam. Thus, U.S. reputation for keeping its commitment was damaged. Moreover, as indicated by the 1971 Report to Congress, the United States planned a global reduction of U.S. military presence. The United States would not only withdraw from Vietnam but also lower its military personnel by 20,000 in Korea, 12,000 in Japan, 5,000 in Okinawa, 16,000 in Thailand, 9,000 in the Philippines, and 86,000 elsewhere.[31] East Asian states feared that the United States would not be able to keep its existing commitments if the level of combat forces were reduced in the region. Most allies interpreted these words and actions as a diminishing of U.S. resolve to use force to maintain the security of its allies. In this situation, they would have to manage their own security by increasing military power. This meant that the expected cost for not reaching an arms transfer agreement increased for the ally, which put the United States in a better position to sell arms. After the Vietnam War, the ratio of U.S. arms sales to this region has never fallen lower than 80 per cent. This suggests that most U.S. allies in Asia have not been expecting the United States to keep its promise to protect its allies in an overt conflict.

CONCLUSION

This chapter explains why the United States changed its method of arms transfer from military aid to military sales during the Cold War. The core of the explanation is that the party — the United States or the ally — that has more to lose if no transfer of arms is agreed upon is likely to concede to its partner in negotiations. Empirical data of East Asian states seem to support the explanation developed in this chapter. The context of arms transfers changed at the end of the Cold War. It is necessary to make some adjustments and more observations if this explanation to predict the ratio of arms sales can continue being used in the post Cold War period. The major difference between these two eras is the military power of the enemy. The most powerful enemy of the Cold War — the Soviet Union — no longer exists. However, there are still many less powerful "enemies" threatening the security interests of the United States and its allies, such as North Korea, Iraq, and some terrorist groups. Thus, arms transfers between the United States and its allies are likely to continue, especially after the 9/11 terrorist attack. Since the degree of threat to allies has decreased, the volume of arms transfers is also likely to be smaller than that of the Cold War years. As indicated by the Defence Security Assistant Agency (DSCA), U.S. arms transfers have decreased significantly since 1990. In 1997, the United States only exported about US$10 billion of arms, which was the lowest in twenty-three years. More importantly, the major importing area for U.S. weapons has changed from East Asia to the Middle East. This suggests that the United States is still transferring arms to areas that threaten U.S. security.

TABLE 5.2
U.S. Arms Transfers 1992–2001

Year	Total U.S. Arms Export	Total U.S. Sale	Sale ratio	U.S. arms export to East Asia	Arms sales to East Asia	Sale ratio to East Asia
92	15323830	10933085	.71	4667642	4638781	.99
93	33091235	28415620	.86	8802118	8775318	1.00
94	16423674	12185571	.74	4050007	4049257	1.00
95	11852193	8022947	.68	2990028	2988728	1.00
96	11288388	7121705	.63	3159064	3153413	1.00
97	10265780	6663863	.65	2897421	2896421	1.00
98	11028552	7513842	.68	2360349	2360349	1.00
99	12522037	8884097	.71	2782081	2725581	.98
00	11948078	7530678	.63	2118637	2116500	1.00
01	13996870	10420440	.74	2528773	2521457	1.00

Source: DSCA Foreign Military Sales, Foreign Military Construction Sales and Military Assistance Facts, 30 September 2001.

What then, is the major method of arms transfer in the post-Cold War period? Three aspects may be important in answering this question. First, after the collapse of the Soviet Union, the United States became the sole "super power". There is no question that the United States can defeat any one of its less powerful enemies. At the same time, these smaller foes are unlikely to impose significant cost to the United States in an overt conflict. Since the cost of fighting for the United States has become much smaller than during Cold War era, the ally may expect the United States to be more willing to keep its commitment. More importantly, after the attack of 9/11, the United States obviously expects a greater cost from failed arms transfer negotiations. Third, U.S. security interests in the post-Cold War period are not clearly defined. The United States has shown a strong resolution to fight when its own interests are at stake, as in the Gulf War. However, it has been reluctant to fight for its allies' interests, as in Bosnia and Kosovo. Based upon the first and second conditions, the ratio of arms sale should continue to decrease in the post-Cold War period. However, the third condition suggests that the sale ration should increase. According to the DSCA, the ratio of arms sales fluctuated between 63 and 86 per cent between 1992 and 2001, as shown in Table 5.2. Thus, until we have more information about how the United States and its allies share security interests, predicting the trend for arms transfer will remain difficult.

Notes

*   Part of this research is funded by the National Science Council, No. 92-2414-H-431-001- "*Compromise or Allying — on Strategic Choices for the Small State*".

1   The term "aid/sale transformation" in this chapter refers to the United States changing its arms transfer method from military aid to military sales during this period.

2   U.S. Security Cooperation Agency, *Fiscal Year Series: As of September 30, 2002*, pp. 2–3.

3   U.S. Arms Control and Disarmament Agency, *World Military Expenditures and Arms Transfers 1985*, Washington, D.C.: Government Printing Office, 1985, p. 143.

4   In the late 1980s, the ratio of arms sales to total arms transfers did decrease. However, it was never lower than 65 per cent, as the case in the 1950s and 1960s.

5   For the ally, losing a conflict means being conquered, while the United States only loses an ally.

6   The "credibility" of U.S. commitment is defined as the probability that the United States will win a conflict against a common enemy.

7   For example, the United States may fight a conventional war against the enemy in the ally's territory.

8   In fact, during the Cold War, the United States did not enter any conflict before the ally was defeated. Several conflicts were fought by an ally alone with American support behind it, such as in the Kinmen crises in 1954 and 1958. In the Korean War and the Vietnam War, the United States decided to get involved only after the ally had suffered a major defeat.

9   "Firebreak" is a situation in which the ally fails to stop the enemy and continues to suffer damages while the enemy continues advancing until it finally meets U.S. resistance.

10 These include the possibility of being conquered by the enemy and the cost of continued fighting between the United States and the enemy.

11 The enemy may attack if the United States cannot offer deterrence, as discussed earlier.

12 It is assumed that the ally cannot produce enough military equipment by itself and is not able or willing to import arms from other suppliers.

13 It is assumed that the enemy only uses the strategy of tit-for-tat. Thus, the cost imposed by the enemy depends upon how much cost the United States has imposed upon the enemy in a previous move.

14 The ally may suffer an even higher cost because of the continuation of the conflict between the United States and the enemy in its territory.

15 This can occur for example if the enemy increases its conventional forces, or makes a breakthrough in its military technology (for example, a nuclear bomb, a long range bomber, or an ICBM).

16 A credible commitment is the major reason why the ally is willing to maintain

a coalition to prevent the expansion of the enemy. If the ally knows that the United States will lose a conflict, there will be no grounds for collaboration, and the ally may pursue a more independent foreign policy, which may cause the alliance formed with the United States to collapse. Thus, if the ally is important to U.S. security, the United States will have a strong desire to keep its commitment as credible as possible.

[17] A good example of this was the relationship between the United States and Taiwan. When the United States tried to improve its relationship with China, the strategic position of Taiwan was no longer of importance to the United States. However, Taiwan and the United States maintained an "alliance relationship" until 1979.

[18] This study only considers the interaction of three actors — the United States, the enemy, and the ally. However, to discuss U.S. reputation, it is necessary to mention a second ally that became a victim due to U.S. behaviour in the context of another conflict. For more discussion on the issue of reputation see R. Harrison Wagner "Rationality and Misperception in Deterrence Theory" *Journal of Theoretical Politics* 4, no. 2 (1992): 115–41.

[19] For example, from 1967 to the end of the Cold War, the "flexible response" was the official strategy adopted by the United States to protect NATO allies. Since the flexible response relied heavily on conventional forces and technical nuclear weapons to defeat an attack, European allies expected an extremely high cost for conflict because the major battleground would be in their territories.

[20] Powell points out that although there is no advantage in striking first and no situation in which a state can rationally launch an unlimited first strike, a state may still be able to use the sanction of massive nuclear attack to protect its interests by manipulating the risk that a crisis will get out of control and escalate into a general nuclear exchange (see Powell 1990, pp. 16–17). This is generally known as "brinkmanship" or a "threat that leaves something to chance" (Schelling 1963), which offers a conceptual solution to the credibility problem of Massive Retaliation in the situation of MAD (see Powell 1989, p. 505). The unique character of this strategy is that when the ally fails to defend itself in a conflict, the United States will not immediately launch an all-out nuclear attack as it might do if the enemy was not capable of fighting back. Rather, the United States will only take action to create a "recognizable" risk of general nuclear war by deliberately letting the situation get somewhat out of hand to convince the enemy to back down. When the United States escalates the conflict by letting the situation gradually get out of hand, the United States itself may not be able to control the chances of a massive nuclear strike. A nuclear attack may be "unintentionally" launched at any stage of the conflict because of human or mechanical error (see Schelling 1963, pp. 201–03).

[21] In other words, the ally knows that the United States expects to suffer extremely high costs for fighting.

22 "East Asian states" include Myanmar, Taiwan, Indonesia, Japan, Cambodia, South Korea, Laos, Malaysia, Philippines, Singapore, Thailand, and Vietnam.

23 John Wilson Lewis and Xue Litai, *China Builds the Bomb*, Stanford, California: Stanford University Press, 1986, p. 212.

24 In 1969, the Beijing government ordered its strategic forces to implement a new plan with a new adversary in mind — the Soviet Union — and started targeting Soviet cities. Two years later, newly developed DF-4 missiles were moved to Northwest China, which was closer to key Soviet targets. For more discussion on this issue see Lewis and Xue, pp. 210–18.

25 By 1971, most developed countries were already paying for weapons imported from the United States, and their demand for U.S. weapons remained stable. Thus, there was no room for this ratio to increase.

26 Vietnam, Cambodia, and Laos were not included.

27 Even if Vietnam, Cambodia, and Laos are included among East Asian States, this ratio still increased — from 5 per cent to 42 per cent during the period between 1971 and 1975.

28 Richard Nixon, *U.S. Foreign Policy For the 1970s: A New Strategy for Peace, a Report to the Congress*, Washington, D.C.: Government Printing Office, 1970, p. 55.

29 See Joo-hong Nam, *America's Commitment to South Korea — The First Decade of the Nixon Doctrine*, Cambridge: Cambridge University Press, 1986, pp. 64–65.

30 Richard Nixon, *U.S. Foreign Policy For the 1970s: Building For Peace, A Report To The Congress*, Washington, D.C.: Government Printing Office, 1971, p. 14.

31 Nixon (1971) p. 18.

References

Chan, Steve. "The Consequences of Expensive Oil on Arms Transfers". *Journal of Peace Research* 17, no. 3 (1980): 235–46.

Daffron, Stephen C. "U.S. Arms Transfers: New Rules, New Reasons". *Parameters U.S. Army War College Quarterly* 21, no. 1 (1991).

Klare, Michael T. *American Arms Supermarket*. Austin, Texas: University of Texas Press, 1984.

Lewis, John W. and Xue, Litai. *China Builds the Bomb*. Stanford, California: Stanford University Press, 1986.

Louscher, David J. and Michael D. Solomon. *Marketing Security Assistance: New Perspectives on Arms Sales*. Lexington, Massachusetts: Lexington Books, 1988.

Nam Joo-hong. *America's Commitment to South Korea — The First Decade of the Nixon Doctrine*. Cambridge: Cambridge University Press, 1986.

Nixon, Richard. *U.S Foreign Policy for the 1970s: A New Strategy for Peace, a Report to the Congress*. Washington, D.C.: U.S. Government Printing Office, 1970.

————. *U.S Foreign Policy for the 1970s: Building for Peace, a Report to the Congress.* Washington, D.C.: U.S. Government Printing Office, 1971.

Powell, Robert. *Nuclear Deterrence Theory: The Search for Credibility.* New York: Cambridge University Press, 1990.

Sanjian, Gregory S. *Arms Transfers to the Third World — Probability Models of Superpower Decision Making.* Boulder: The University of Denver, 1988.

Schelling, Thomas C. *Arms and Influence.* New Haven: Yale University Press, 1966.

————. *The Strategy of Conflict.* New York: Oxford University Press, 1963.

Smith, Ron, Anthony Humm and Jacques Fontanel. "The Economics of Exporting Arms". *Journal of Peace Research* 22, no. 3 (1985): 230–47.

U.S. Arms Control and Disarmament Agency. *World Military Expenditures and Arms Transfers 1985.* Washington, D.C.: Government Printing Office, 1985.

————. *World Military Expenditures and Arms Transfers.* Washington, D.C.: Government Printing Office, 1995.

U.S. Department of Defence Security Assistance Agency (DSAA) [now Defence Security Cooperation Agency (DSCA). *Fiscal Year Series: As of September 30, 1991.*

————. 1993. *Fiscal Year Series: As of September 30, 1993.*

————. 1991. *Foreign Military Sales, Foreign Military Construction Sales and Military Assistance Facts: As of September 30, 1991.*

————. 2001. *Foreign Military Sales, Foreign Military Construction Sales and Military Assistance Facts: As of September 30, 2001.*

Wagner, R. Harrison. Rationality and Misperception in Deterrence Theory. *Journal of Theoretical Politics* 4, no. 2 (1991): 115–41.

6

A MULTICULTURAL EUROPEAN UNION AND ITS IMPLICATIONS FOR ASIA

Klaus C. Hsu

THE CHARACTER OF EUROPE

Europe is the cradle of Western civilization. Ancient Greece is normally considered to have laid the foundations of European civilization. Later on, the Roman Empire and its Christianized civil society exercised a strong influence on all European peoples. Despite experiencing the thousand-year long Dark Ages, Europe still emerged by the time of the Renaissance as the most advanced civilization in the world. With the Enlightenment, Neo-Platonism and industrialization, the West took shape. European cultures grew in confidence and came to display unprecedented hegemonic power throughout the world.

However, in the aftermath of World War I, European societies entered a negative trend, as its citizens became more and more distrustful of inherited values and beliefs. Oswald Spengler labelled this the "Decline of the West". Nevertheless, after 1945, Western Europe gradually rebuilt itself into a highly integrated and cohesive grouping of economies and peoples.

PEACE AND EUROPEAN UNION

For centuries, Europe was the scene of frequent and bloody wars. Between 1870 and 1945, France and Germany went to war against each other three times, with terrible loss of life. After World War II, some visionary European leaders became convinced that the only way to secure lasting peace between their countries was to unite them economically and politically. The French Foreign Minister, Robert Schuman, proposed integrating the coal and steel industries of Western Europe. As a result, in 1951, the European Coal and Steel Community (ECSC) was set up with six members: Belgium, West Germany, Luxembourg, France, Italy and the Netherlands. The power to make decisions about the coal and steel industry in these countries was placed in the hands of an independent, supranational body called the "High Authority".[1] Jean Monnet was its first president.

The ECSC was such a success that, within a few years, these same six countries decided to integrate other sectors of their economies. In 1957 they signed the Treaty of Rome, creating the European Atomic Energy Community (EURATOM) and the European Economic Community (EEC) in the process. The member states set about removing trade barriers between themselves and forming a "common market". In 1967 the three European communities were merged into one. From that point on, there was one single Commission and one single Council of Ministers with a directly elected European Parliament.[2] From then on, it was called the "European Community" or "European Communities" (EC). The Treaty of Maastricht (1992) introduced new forms of co-operation between member governments, for example in defence and in "justice and home affairs". By adding this inter-governmental cooperation to the existing "Community" system, the Maastricht Treaty created the European Union (EU).[3] This consists of five institutions, each given a specific role.[4]

The EU has grown in size with successive waves of accessions. Denmark, Ireland and the United Kingdom joined in 1973, followed by Greece in 1981, Spain and Portugal in 1986 and Austria, Finland and Sweden in 1995. Encouraged by the growth from six to fifteen members, the European Union took its greatest leap in June 2004 by allowing ten countries in eastern and southern Europe to join. These were Cyprus, the Czech Republic, Estonia, Hungary, Latvia, Lithuania, Malta, Poland, Slovakia and Slovenia.[5] Bulgaria and Romania expect to follow suit in a few years' time. Turkey is also a candidate country.

EUROPEAN CULTURAL IDENTITY

Economic and political integration within the European Union means that member states have to make joint decisions in many areas. They have thus developed common policies in a wide range of fields — from agriculture to culture, from consumer affairs to rules of competition, and from the environment and energy to transport and trade.[6] During the 1990s it became increasingly easy for people to move around in Europe within the Single Market.[7] Passport and customs checks were abolished at most of the EU's internal borders. One consequence is greater mobility for EU citizens. Since 1987, more than a million young Europeans have taken study courses abroad.[8] As for cultural integration, the EU has many "cultural programmes" and "cultural actions" for publishing, libraries, language training, city rebuilding, etc. The gradual use of terms such as "European awareness", "European feeling" and "European identity", seek to form a new unified European culture.

It is still a matter of much controversy whether one should speak about "European culture" or "European cultures". The Europeans are now faced with the prospect of a multicultural society in a real and thorough way. A careful study of the two forces of integration and disintegration in Europe during the twentieth century can reveal how the Europeans adapted to the movement towards multi-culturalism. While individuals may be proud of their nationality, they apparently feel that they are also European citizens at the same time. They may love their own country and their own culture, but today they are also supposed to feel for the whole of Europe and know and recognize different cultures within the Union. The following table seeks to describe European identity today. Many individuals seem to identify with their fatherland while admitting themselves to be Europeans at the same time (See Table 6.1).

Indeed, in appealing to a common historical background and cultural heritage, in the common experiencing of movements of transformation and integration, and in entertaining notions such as decentralization and multi-culturalism, Europeans seem willing to move ahead together. Cooperation and co-existence seem to be replacing conflict orientation as the political agenda of contemporary Europe.

EVALUATION OF EU POLICIES

Nowadays, it is unwise for policymakers to ignore public opinion and the general attitudes of the people. Public opinion, both in current and future member states, is clearly a key factor in the EU's "communication strategy on enlargement".[9] This strategy is designed to be responsive to the needs of the general public, and it is therefore important that the commission pays attention to the key concerns of Europe's citizens. According to the official announcement of the commission, the Eurobarometer remains its main source of information. As a complement to this, and in order to provide as much information as

TABLE 6.1
Identification with Europe and/or Nation

unit %

	Europe only	Europe, then Nation	Nation, then Europe	Nation only
Italy	5	7	55	28
France	6	9	49	31
Luxembourg	13	7	43	31
Spain	3	4	49	39
Netherlands	3	6	46	45
Belgium	7	8	38	43
Denmark	2	3	45	48
Germany	5	7	35	49
Austria	2	7	37	50
Ireland	3	4	37	53
Greece	1	3	39	56
Finland	2	4	37	56
Sweden	2	3	35	59
UK	5	5	25	60
Portugal	2	2	28	62
EU15	5	6	41	44

Source: European Commission, *Eurobarometer*, Report Number 49 (Bruxelles: September 1998), p. 42. Incomplete statistics are due to answers such as "I don't know".

possible on any specific issue, a section of the website presents opinion polls conducted by other agencies. These may have been carried out on the initiative of governments, of the local commission delegation, or by others, but they all offer an insight into public opinion.[10]

The Eurobarometer survey for Spring 2002 was conducted in all the fifteen member states between 29 March and 1 May 2002. It questioned approximately 16,000 EU citizens on their attitudes towards issues of current political and social interest. Highlights from this survey were published in June 2002.[11] The main issues covered included the enlargement of the European Union and the introduction of the Euro. The public's attitudes towards and knowledge about other issues such as the convention on the future of Europe and EU priorities for action were also polled.

The Eurobarometer showed that the majority of respondents (52 per cent) inside the Euro zone agreed the Euro was a success. Outside the Euro zone, the Euro was least popular in the UK, where 47 per cent thought it a bad thing. People in Denmark and Sweden were more positive towards the idea of adopting the Euro instead of their national currency (47 per cent for the Euro in Denmark; 42 per cent in Sweden).[12] The survey found that half of all respondents in the EU (50 per cent) supported enlargement. More than half of all respondents thought that enlargement would guarantee peace and security in Europe (53 per cent), and increase the importance of the European Union in the world (63 per cent).[13] Only one in five respondents (21 per cent) felt well informed about the enlargement.[14] Many respondents (51 per cent) were worried about the costs of the enlargement, while almost as many (49 per cent) thought that their country, as a result of the EU, would lose out on financial aid.[15]

A majority of respondents (65 per cent) agreed that following enlargement, it would be more difficult to make decisions on a European scale. The most favoured option (41 per cent) was for decisions to be taken by a majority of member states, although half of all respondents (50 per cent) said that each member state should retain its national right of veto in order to safeguard national interests. Over 60 per cent of respondents indicated support for a constitution for the EU.[16] There were also some results from Eurobarometer in 2002 that may work against the EU's further enlargement. More than two in three respondents, for example, thought that foreign policy, terrorism, crime and human trafficking should be tackled through joint EU decision-making rather than through national decision-making.[17] Respondents were more evenly divided on responsibility for issues such as defence, asylum and immigration.[18] On the other hand, domestic issues such as unemployment, food safety, drug trafficking, poverty and social exclusion continued to concern the public. More than four out of five of those questioned named these as the chief priorities for action by the EU.[19]

However, the most recent studies of public opinion show that over half of European citizens support European integration. These polls are certainly one of the strongest references that the EU Commission can avail itself of in accessing its own progress.

IMPLICATIONS FOR ASIA

There is no "nation-state" today. At most, some aspire to create a "state-nation". In whichever case, nationalism and racism are the prevalent problems. For the present and in the future, both localization and globalization are issues that must be attended to. "Overlapping loyalty" may be a fruitful idea for Asians and their governments to consider. As one of the prime civilizations constituting the globalized world system, Europe, with its technology and enthusiasm, is now realizing that it is time to counteract deeply rooted problems such as racism, nationalism, xenophobia, secessionism, ethnocentrism and Eurocentrism that are always the catalyst for hostility and conflict. Whether the "Community of European Cultures" proposed by the European Union will change a newly self-centred continent into one that celebrates cultural diversity has yet to seen. On the other hand, many questions have been raised about the diversity of European culture at the local, regional, national, and supranational levels: how does the European Union deal with complicated internal cultural ties? How will it handle cultural diversity, and in accordance with which choice of characteristics? What are the main issues where cultural integration is concerned?

If Asians also pay early attention to these issues, they will be able to contribute more towards the creation of an Asian citizen.

CONCLUSION

In the early years, cooperation between EU countries was in trade and the economy. Today, the EU deals with many other matters of direct importance to everyday life, such as citizen rights, protection of social freedom, security and justice, job creation, regional development, environmental protection and making globalization work for as wide a population as possible. The European Union has delivered half a century of stability, peace and prosperity. It has helped to raise living standards, built a single Europe-wide market, launched a single European currency, the Euro, and strengthened Europe's voice in the world.

Europe is a continent with many different traditions and languages, but also with shared values. The EU, though potentially a homogenizing force, appears to defend these values. It fosters cooperation between the peoples of Europe, promoting unity while preserving diversity and ensuring that decisions are taken at a level that is as close as possible to the citizens. In the increasingly inter-dependent world of the twenty-first century, it will be even more necessary for every European citizen to cooperate with peoples from other countries in a spirit of respect, tolerance and solidarity.[20]

European integration has been successful for over forty years where politics and economics are concerned. However, the EU finds it difficult to handle cultural integration, given the existent diversity. In fact, the economic and political progress of the 1970s made it painfully clear to EU member states that a lot has yet to be done in the field of culture.

Notes

1   <http://europa.eu.int/abc/history/index_en.htm>.
2   Originally, members of the European Parliament were chosen by the national parliaments, but in 1979 the first direct elections were held, allowing citizens of member states to vote for the candidate of their choice. Since then, direct elections have been held every five years.
3   <http://europa.eu.int/abc/history/index_en.htm>.
4   The five institutions are the European Parliament, the Council of the European Union, the European Commission, the Court of Justice and the Court of Auditors. See <http://europa.eu.int/abc/index_en.htm>.
5   These countries need to fulfil economic and political conditions known as the "Copenhagen criteria", according to which a prospective member must: (1) be a stable democracy, respecting human rights, the rule of law, and the protection of minorities, (2) have a functioning market economy, and (3) adopt the rules, standards and policies that make up the body of EU law. See <http://www.europa.eu.int/comm/enlargement/opinion/index.htm>.
6   In the early days, the focus was on a common commercial policy for coal and steel and a common agricultural policy. Other policies were added as time went by, and when the need arose. Some key policy aims have changed as circumstances changed. For example, the aim of the agricultural policy is no longer to produce as much food as cheaply as possible but to support farming methods that produce healthy, high-quality food and to protect the environment. The need for environmental protection is now taken into account across the whole range of EU policies. The European Union's relations with the rest of the world have also become important. The EU negotiates major trade and aid agreements with other countries and is developing a Common Foreign and Security Policy (CFSP).
7   The Single Market was formally completed at the end of 1992. It took some time for member states to remove all barriers to trade between them and to turn their "common market" into a genuine single market in which goods, services, people and capital could move freely.
8   <http://europa.eu.int/abc/index_en.htm>.
9   The European Commission adopted its Communication Strategy for Enlargement in May 2000. Up to that point, preparations for enlargement were based on two tracks: the pre-accession strategy (the reform process in the candidate countries) and the accession negotiations. The Communication Strategy for Enlargement is now the third track in preparations for enlargement.
10   Klaus C. Hsu. "The Public Opinion for Enlargement in Both Current and Future Member States of the EU", The International Conference of Tamkang University, Taipei, November 2003, p. 5.
11   The full survey report provides more detail on the preliminary results. The report is published in two formats. The full report covering all fifteen member-

states is published at the commission, in English and in French. Each of the representations of member states simultaneously publishes a report on its national survey results. The executive summaries of all fifteen national reports are also available from the commission.

[12]   <http://europa.eu.int/comm/public_opinion>.

[13]   Ibid.

[14]   Ibid. The self-administered questionnaire on Europarl gave a different result: 50 per cent of respondents in the member states were "very well informed or quite well informed", 49 per cent were not well informed or not informed at all.

[15]   Ibid.

[16]   Ibid.

[17]   Ibid.

[18]   Ibid.

[19]   Ibid.

[20]   <http://europa.eu.int/abc/index_en.htm>.

References

European Commission. *Eurobarometer Report Number* 49, 1998.

Hsu, Klaus C. *European Culture vs. Cultural Policy of the European Union*, Taipei, 1999.

———. *The Public Opinion for Enlargement in both Current and Future Member States of the EU.* Taipei: The International Conference of Tamkang University, 2003.

<http://europa.eu.int/abc/history/index_en.htm>.

<http://europa.eu.int/abc/index_en.htm>.

<http://europa.eu.int/comm/public_opinion>.

7

THE FUTURE PROSPECTS OF MULTILATERALISM IN SOUTHEAST AND EAST ASIA

N. Ganesan

Multilateralism, both as an approach and policy position, falls within the liberal tradition in international relations. It emphasizes the utility of states acting in concert to achieve a common purpose. Alternatively, individual issues or areas may be isolated for transnational cooperation. International norms and regimes that are classic expressions of multilateralism are meant to support and augment national interests in the creation of what Hedley Bull would call international society.[1] While multilateralism may function alongside a realism that typically construes international relations in statist terms, liberal variants of multilateralism are intended to broaden transnational cooperation and in the process, weaken realist-styled state interests. Accordingly, regime theory and neo-liberal institutionalism fall well within the multilateral enterprise.[2]

The liberal approach to international relations was played down after World War II in favour of realism. The Cold War that defined international relations from 1950 onwards was premised on arch-realist principles that emphasized the centrality of states. Additionally, state interests were defined and articulated in terms of the retention and acquisition of state power in a variety of forms. Hence, over time, the liberal tradition came to be called "idealist", with all the attendant negative connotations. However, the 1991 collapse of the Soviet Union, long regarded as the fountainhead of communism and as being antithetical to liberal-democracy and capitalism, altered the bipolar structure of international relations. The decompression effect associated with this structural transformation turned convergent conceptions of international norms and society into a real possibility, and was aided and abetted by the increasing popularity of constructivism in international relations inspired by the liberal tradition.

Constructivists, unlike realists, argued that norms and practices associated with collective identity formation could serve as a catalyst in international relations just as well as the realist state-centric model that had acquired paradigmatic status after 1950.[3] The fundamental assumption, made well within the liberal tradition, was that mutual gains rather than mutual fear could equally well underpin state motivations in international relations. The dissipation of bipolarity afforded constructivists the structural possibilities for making their case. Greater transnational cooperation and the strengthening of international regimes throughout the 1990s did indeed give cause for such optimism. Although the United States has recently elevated its own national interests or conceptions thereof as overriding considerations in international relations, this position was not always the case. In this regard, the 9/11 terrorist attacks in the United States have altered the tone and texture of international relations, at least for the time being. It remains unclear whether the United States will continue acting in a unilateral fashion. Such a possibility is in turn contingent on a variety of factors that include the calibration of domestic politics and international structural opportunities and constraints. Nonetheless, constructivism and general conceptions of an international society with convergent norms have acquired greater currency in the post-Cold War period.

The Association of Southeast Asian Nations (ASEAN) fulfils the classic characteristics of multilateralism. It comprises a group of states with a reasonably cohesive regional and cultural identity that has endured since the time of its formation in 1967 — a feat rather uncommon in many parts of the world outside the industrialized West. This chapter traces the evolution of ASEAN within a multilateral perspective, identifying periods when the organization exhibited lesser and greater multilateral convergence. Fortunately or otherwise for ASEAN, the best period of multilateralism when policy coordination and identity formation were strongest, happened within the structural imperatives of the Cold War, or the Sino-Soviet strategic competition in the Asia-Pacific.[4] However, since ASEAN has continued into the post-Cold War period and has in fact extended its membership to include all countries in Southeast Asia, it is probable that multilateralism was not solely dictated by external structural considerations. Additionally, ASEAN is now in the process of formalizing its culture of regular consultations and accommodation of differing national interests and priorities onto a widening community that includes Northeast Asia. This extended embryonic community is referred to as "ASEAN+3" in the literature. Simultaneously, ASEAN is also inducing a number of large Asian powers to become signatories of the Treaty of Amity and Cooperation (TAC) first signed in 1976 to stabilize ASEAN's immediate external environment. It needs to be noted, however, that both these initiatives, in form and substance, are a function of the political will of the states concerned as well as a result of favourable systemic attributes. After all, history is replete with examples of large powers attending to their own agendas and leaving the international system in turmoil.

This chapter is divided into four broad sections. The first section is in turn sub-divided into four sub-sections, and deals with the evolution of ASEAN. The second major section deals with the promises of multilateralism in ASEAN and East Asia, while the third examines some perils of or obstacles to multilateralism. The fourth and final section identifies lessons learnt from the ASEAN experience with regards to the practice of multilateralism in international relations. The focus of this chapter is only on multilateral security initiatives. The final caveat that needs to be noted is that the issue of cross-straits relations between Taiwan and China, and the North Korean nuclear issue are not dealt with in this chapter. Suffice it to note however, that both issues retain serious potential for a deteriorated security, environment in Asia, including the possibility of armed conflict and external intervention reminiscent of the Cold War.

SOUTHEAST ASIA BEFORE ASEAN

Southeast Asia in the 1960s, prior to the formation of ASEAN, recorded a fair amount of turbulence in its international relations.[5] While mainland Southeast Asia was mired in the Second Indochina War that dovetailed from the First following the conclusion of the Geneva Accords in 1954 that severed Vietnam into two, and involved new external powers, maritime Southeast Asia experienced turbulence as a function of decolonization. ASEAN's precursor multilateral organization, the Association of Southeast Asia (ASA) that collectively grouped Malaya, the Philippines and Thailand, ended abruptly in 1963. The major reason for its sudden demise was the formation of the Federation of Malaysia — a British-inspired federation that sought to unite the colonial territories of Sabah and Sarawak on the island of Borneo, and Singapore, with the Federation of Malaya that had achieved independence in 1957.

When the newly enlarged federation was declared in September 1963, Indonesia launched a policy of military confrontation against Malaysia that lasted from 1963 to 1966.[6] There were both internal and external motivations for such a policy. Internally, President Sukarno of Indonesia was rapidly losing control of the three main factions — the nationalists, the Islamic constituency and the communists — that competed for power in domestic politics. His grand strategy, encapsulated in the acronym *NASAKOM* (*Nasionalis, Agama dan Kommunis* — Nationalists, Religious Groups and Communists) was failing as Indonesian domestic politics drifted leftwards. Hence, there was a case for a diversionary foreign policy to sustain national unity and to maintain a common sense of purpose.

Equally important were external and foreign policy considerations. Indonesia was unhappy about the British carving away the two states of Sabah and Sarawak from Borneo and tagging it onto Malaya. Except for Brunei, the remaining territory in the vast island constituted Indonesian Kalimantan. As a result, from as early as the 1950s, Indonesia supported the concept of a North Kalimantan Federation that would include these British-occupied territories. Sukarno was not enthusiastic about the fact that he was neither consulted nor informed about the new federation, which in the event was announced only as a *fait accompli*. By this time, Indonesia regarded itself a champion of the Third World, having convened the Afro-Asian Bandung Summit in 1955. Sukarno also regarded himself a revolutionary against OLDEFOES (Old Decaying Forces) and in support of NEFOES (Newly Emerging Forces). This revolutionary proclamation was decidedly anti-imperialist and anti-Western, in line with a foreign policy identified as active and neutral (*aktif dan bebas*).

The formation of the Malaysian Federation also angered the Philippines, which severed diplomatic ties with Malaysia and laid claim to the state of Sabah.[7] The Filipino argument was that the Sulu Sultanate had leased Sabah out to the British for trade and as a consequence, the Philippines retained residual sovereignty over the state. In light of the Indonesian and Philippine objections, ASA naturally collapsed. It was revived for a brief period in 1967 but was subsequently replaced by ASEAN.

The second major source of turbulence in maritime Southeast Asia was the fissure of the Malaysian Federation in 1965, when Singapore became an independent state. The state's two-year merger with Malaysia was fraught with sensitive conflicts that led to it being eventually expelled in August 1965.[8] For the next two years, Singapore's relations with both Malaysia and Indonesia were turbulent. As a result of these developments in the 1960s, Southeast Asia was hardly suited for multi-lateralism.

The establishment of ASEAN in August 1967 was due largely to the cessation of Indonesian hostilities against Malaysia and Filipino accommodation of the latter. These developments were, however, inspired in turn by dramatic changes in Indonesian domestic politics. A failed coup attributed to the Indonesian Communist Party (PKI — *Partai Kommunis Indonesia*) and the resulting violence afterwards unseated Sukarno. His successor, Suharto, inaugurated a New Order (*Order Baru*) government two years later in 1967 and announced a pro-Western developmentalist policy. Equally, he sought reconciliation with Malaysia and, to a lesser extent, Singapore.[9] It was on the back of this regime change in Indonesia and the country's willingness to join ASEAN that the organization was launched with the Bangkok Declaration in 1967. At the time of its formation, the declaration vaguely promised economic and cultural cooperation, although unstated political reconciliation was the major motivation.

THE LETHARGIC YEARS OF
MULTILATERALISM IN ASEAN (1967–75)

ASEAN's inauguration in 1967 following the regime change in Indonesia clearly started the process of political reconciliation in maritime Southeast Asia. However, suspicions and anxieties, particularly between the countries located in the Malay archipelago — Brunei, Indonesia, Malaysia and Singapore — continued for almost a decade before serious political reconciliation began to take hold. Tensions arising from ASEAN's pre-formation years had a significant impact on the organization at the outset — a situation that lasted for almost a decade. Naturally, it was worsened by anxieties associated with newly independent statehood, domestic challenges that included communism and communalism, political contestations, and developmental concerns. As a result of these, national interests took precedence over regional reconciliation.

The turn in ASEAN's favour was externally motivated, and derived from structural changes associated with the winding down of the Cold War in Europe by the late 1960s and the American decision to engage China in the early 1970s. The latter decision was especially important for ASEAN since it in turn led to the recalibration of great power interests and alignments within the broader Asia-Pacific region. Worsening hostilities between China and the Soviet Union that culminated in conflicts at the Amur-Ussuri river border and the Soviet decision to cultivate Vietnam as a "Third Force" to counter growing Chinese influence in Asia molded the strategic environment.[10] Following these were the CIA-sponsored coup in Cambodia that ousted the Sihanouk government, and the Chinese cultivation in turn of the Khmer

Rouge. It would, however, take some time for Sino-Vietnamese relations to worsen. In this regard, the 1970s heralded intense competition between China and the Soviet Union for regional influence in the Asia-Pacific — a situation continuing well into the 1980s that in turn influenced ASEAN's regional considerations and priorities.[11]

It was in response to these broader changes that ASEAN issued its first substantive political declaration in 1971, calling for Southeast Asia to be declared a Zone of Peace, Freedom and Neutrality (ZOPFAN).[12] However, the declaration had little impact on the regional environment since it only had declaratory intent and carried with it no substantive obligations. The Philippines and Thailand had pre-existing security arrangements with the United States while Malaysia and Singapore were part of a security pact inspired by and anchored around the British.[13] Only Indonesia, among the five ASEAN member states, retained a measure of neutrality in foreign policy.

In the meantime, ASEAN's general drift towards the West and the United States in particular, meant that it held ranks against what was increasingly becoming a reconstituted communist French Indochinese Union. The victory of North Vietnam over the South in 1975 sealed that reconstitution. Owing to Vietnam's political consolidation in communist terms and insurgencies in Laos and Cambodia, Southeast Asia became divided into two halves.[14] The half that compromised maritime Southeast Asia and Thailand was collectively grouped in ASEAN, while mainland Southeast Asia where revolutionary communism had been victorious, displayed not only different but antithetical structural characteristics and worldviews. Long before these developments, Burma, which had been subjected to a military coup led by Ne Win, had in 1962 declared a policy of neutrality obtained through self-imposed isolationism. In light of the how the cards had been dealt in Southeast Asia and the broader Asia-Pacific region by 1975, the stage was set for a confrontation between Vietnam and ASEAN.

THE BOOM YEARS OF MULTILATERALISM
IN ASEAN (1976–88)

The conclusion of the Second Indochina War in 1975 did not lead to stability on mainland Southeast Asia. On the contrary, Sino-Soviet rivalry in the broader Asia-Pacific theatre was re-enacted in Southeast Asia. From 1975, unified and communist Vietnam gradually gravitated towards the Soviet Union, which culminated in a bilateral Treaty of Friendship and Cooperation in 1978. Simultaneously, the Khmer Rouge came into power in Cambodia, with China as benefactor. The xenophobic anti-Vietnamese policies of the

Khmer Rouge and cross-border tensions between Vietnam and Cambodia, supported by different and competitive patrons were the harbinger of conflict. Accordingly, in December 1978, Vietnam invaded Cambodia and occupied it until 1989. In response, China launched a short-lived "punitive expedition" against Vietnam in February 1980.

Developments associated with Sino-Soviet rivalry and the resultant conflict in mainland Southeast Asia naturally galvanized ASEAN into action. Such action began in the first instance with an altered philosophical predisposition that it should assume a measure of responsibility for regional security.[15] Such a re-orientation in turn implied that ASEAN's centre of gravity had to move from maritime Southeast Asia to the mainland. Such an accommodation involved relegating the Malay Archipelago Security Complex to the background in deference to the Indochina Security Complex.[16] This change was easily absorbed by ASEAN, since a decade of interactions had yielded positive spillover effects in the international relations of maritime Southeast Asia.

It was therefore in response to Thai security considerations that ASEAN chose to involve itself in the politics of mainland Southeast Asia. ASEAN's strategy was primarily diplomatic and was meant to deny the Vietnamese occupation forces in Cambodia legal recognition in international fora, particularly the United Nations. Thailand, on the other hand, pursued a second strategy in defence of its own national security. Following American withdrawal from Vietnam in 1975 and in recognition of its inability to deal with Vietnam independently, Thailand secured an informal strategic alignment with China between 1975 and 1988.[17] It was in part to ease the burden on Thailand and assuage its security concerns that China attacked Vietnam in 1980. Separately, China and Thailand also created border sanctuaries along the Thai-Cambodian border for Cambodian resistance fighters to attack Vietnamese occupation forces. This strategy was not without some cost to Thailand in terms of border incursions by Vietnamese troops in hot pursuit of Cambodian fighters.

In order to involve itself in the evolving political situation on the mainland, ASEAN undertook a number of initiatives. The first of these was the creation of a Central Secretariat in Jakarta in 1976 — a tacit acknowledgement of Indonesia's *primus inter pares* status within the association. Following the formal introduction of a secretariat, ASEAN members signed two explicitly political treaties. The first of these, the Treaty of Amity and Cooperation (TAC) required signatories to resolve inter-state disputes peacefully and not through conflict. The second, the Treaty of ASEAN Concord, provided expressly for ASEAN member states to consult and assist one another when in difficulty. In other words, it was meant to be a gesture of political solidarity. TAC was specifically invoked in the 1990s as a signing precondition for the admittance of Vietnam, Laos, Myanmar and Cambodia. By 1976, ASEAN had therefore clearly developed a political agenda and sought to act in concert within the framework of multilateralism.

Initiatives to deny Vietnam diplomatic recognition for the occupation of Cambodia unfolded in the 1970s and the 1980s. The first such initiative was the installation of the Democratic Kampuchea (DK, read Khmer Rouge) regime in the United Nations in 1979. By 1982, Khmer Rouge genocidal policies received widespread international media coverage, making the DK Government unacceptable for diplomatic lobbying. Consequently, in 1982, ASEAN was instrumental in enlarging the DK Government by inducting two other nationalist resistance groups headed by Son Sann and Sihanouk.[18] The enlarged coalition was renamed the Coalition Government of Democratic Kampuchea (CGDK) and held the Cambodian seat at the United Nations until 1989 when international mediation efforts to resolve the Cambodian impasse were undertaken. Finally, in 1988, prior to the involvement of the international community, Indonesia hosted two rounds of informal talks — Jakarta Informal Meetings 1 and 2 — to attempt reconciliation between the factions in the CGDK and Hun Sen's Cambodian Peoples' Party (CPP).[19] Unfortunately, both ended in failure.

The multilateralism that obtained in ASEAN from the mid-1970s to the late 1980s was born out of Cold War dynamics. ASEAN's efforts were aimed at bolstering Thai security and involving itself in regional security. In a sense, it represented ASEAN's first and perhaps most effective demonstration of regional solidarity and multilateralism. In fact, it was ASEAN's diplomatic involvement in the Cambodian situation that earned it the visible and positive international profile that it continues to enjoy today.[20] ASEAN's efforts at multilateralism in the 1990s was again executed in relation to a new and altered security environment — the cessation of conflict in mainland Southeast Asia and the collapse of the Soviet Union shortly afterwards. Additionally, there was a clear attempt at replicating the apparent success of multilateral efforts onto the broader Asia-Pacific region.

RE-NEGOTIATED LIBERAL MULTILATERALISM IN ASEAN AND BEYOND (1989–)

By the late 1980s there were signs of impending structural changes in the Asia-Pacific region. "Velvet revolutions" were sweeping Eastern Europe and the Berlin Wall had collapsed. The Soviet Union was clearly beginning to show signs of being overstretched while communism commanded little enthusiasm in international society. In Southeast Asia, the earliest signs of change came from domestic political developments in Thailand. By April 1988, the government of General Prem Tinsulanonda had collapsed and in August 1988, the newly elected Thai Prime Minister, Chatichai Choonhavan, launched the Indochina Initiative with the avowed aim of transforming the battlefields of Indochina into market places.[21] This new initiative significantly downgraded Vietnam as a source of threat to Thai national interests and to regional security, signaling the collapse of the Indochina Security Complex. Approximately a year later, Vietnam withdrew its occupation forces from Cambodia while the latter prepared for domestic political reconciliation and stability through international mediation efforts. Not to be outdone, China assisted with the disbandment of the Communist Party of Malaya (CPM) and the Communist Party of Thailand (CPT) in December 1989. The Chinese goodwill gesture was reciprocated in turn by Indonesia's normalization of diplomatic ties with China in August 1990 and a similar initiative by Singapore in November of that same year.[22] The combination of these developments appeared to signal that Southeast Asia was ready to reap the peace dividend of the post-Cold War period. Consequently, ASEAN's multilateral initiatives in the 1990s were primarily motivated by liberal considerations rather than as responses to the external security situation — a characteristic feature of its *modus operandi* during the Cold War period and the Sino-Soviet strategic competition.[23]

The earliest of such multilateral initiatives was the constitution of an ASEAN caucus within the Asia-Pacific Economic Cooperation (APEC) forum. Arising from this were the delivery of block votes on important matters and the convening of APEC meetings in ASEAN countries every other year. Membership in APEC was the first of a series of multilateral initiatives taken by ASEAN to expand into a broader security environment. The second such initiative was the formation of the ASEAN Regional Forum (ARF) in Bangkok in 1994.[24] Again, this was an attempt to extend ASEAN-style consensual and informal security architecture. Finally, in 2000, ASEAN endorsed the new "ASEAN+3" regional grouping that combined ASEAN with China, Japan and South Korea. Among all ASEAN members, Malaysia was the most keen about the grouping's establishment, after having earlier been rebuffed for the East Asian Economic Grouping.[25] In bringing together great powers and regular dialogue partners, this new arrangement was meant to diffuse the ASEAN approach to security in the wider Asia-Pacific region and in particular throughout East Asia.

Besides the externalization of its agenda and approach to security that characterized ASEAN initiatives in the 1990s, there was also an attempt to enlarge the membership of the association itself. After all, both in terms of declaratory intent and policy output, ASEAN had aspired to induct all Southeast Asian countries into its fold. Accordingly, ASEAN accepted Brunei in 1984, and then extended membership to Vietnam in 1995 and Laos and Myanmar in 1997. It was both ASEAN's and Malaysian Prime Minister Mahathir's intention to embrace Cambodia as well at the Association's Thirtieth Anniversary Summit Meeting in Kuala Lumpur. However, factional fighting between Hun Sen and Norodom Ranarridh led to the postponement of Cambodian membership until April 1999. While the inclusion of all Southeast Asian countries strengthened ASEAN's regional representation, new problems arose. Especially problematic was the inclusion of Myanmar, much to the chagrin of the international community, in particular the United States and the European Union, which imposed economic and diplomatic sanctions on Myanmar and cancelled a number of bilateral meetings. This difficulty has continued into the present since both the United States and the EU expect Myanmar opposition leader Aung San Suu Kyi and the National League for Democracy (NLD) that she leads to be incorporated into any future government in the country. Unfortunately, Suu Kyi, who has been under house arrest since May 2003, is not included in the military junta's plans for restructuring the politics of the country. In fact, she was even excluded from the Constitutional Convention that the junta hosted in May 2004.

Shortly after the induction of Cambodia in 1999, ASEAN continued to expand outwards to engage countries in Northeast Asia. This was by no means ASEAN's first attempt to do so. In fact, from about the time the APEC forum was inaugurated in 1989, Malaysia had lobbied hard for the establishment of an East Asian Community. However, such efforts were rebuffed by the United States and to a lesser extent, Japan. Within ASEAN, Indonesia was not particularly comfortable with Malaysian attempts at regional leadership. It was also fairly well known that President Suharto of Indonesia and Prime Minister Mahathir of Malaysia did not see eye-to-eye on many matters. Nonetheless, such efforts at regionalization bore fruit after the Asian Financial Crisis of 1997 led to a greater willingness for independent management of regional affairs. Although the much-touted Asian Monetary Fund initially mooted by Japan was stillborn as a result of American resistance, Asian finance ministers began to meet regularly after 1998 to better the management of the regional economic environment. This embryonic meeting eventually culminated in the formation of the "ASEAN+3" grouping. Indonesian resistance to the idea was stymied after a domestic regime transition in 1998 and ASEAN was itself prepared to establish greater latitude from the United States in the aftermath of the financial crisis and in the expansion of its own membership to include Myanmar in 1997, in the face of United States and European Union resistance.

PROMISES OF MULTILATERALISM IN SOUTHEAST AND EAST ASIA

Perhaps the greatest promise that multilateralism holds, judging from the ASEAN experience, is the achievement of inter-state accommodation and familiarity. From what used to be a grouping of squabbling and newly independent states, ASEAN has allowed for the evolution of regular consultation and for attempts at achieving a measure of policy consensus on important regional matters, particularly in foreign and defence policies. Such regular consultation has instilled a common habit of allowing for the sensitivities of member states and for their accommodation. Elite accommodation has also percolated into the policy-making communities. In the early years of post-independence statehood, such accommodation lessened anxieties within the immediate regional environment and afforded member states the opportunity to work towards nation-building and economic development. This familiarity among the regional elite has been institutionalized to the point that it is now common practice for new elites as well as retiring ones to pay courtesy calls on their ASEAN counterparts on assuming office or on retirement. Additionally, the alphabetical rotation of the ASEAN secretary-general's position has provided for the interest of smaller member states.

ASEAN also provides for group status by individual member states in furtherance of specific national interests. Hence, individual countries, and in particular the smaller ones, are able to lobby for national positions from an ASEAN platform. Such representation performs the useful task of enhancing an individual country's leverage internationally. The international goodwill that ASEAN has accrued throughout its existence can therefore be appropriated by individual member states. Such name recognition has been utilized for everything from political posturing and nucleic membership in larger multilateral organizations, to tariff and trade benefits and even tourism.

ASEAN's common sense of purpose and sometimes destiny has imbued the region with a cohesive and collective identity. This identity has led to the evolution of a consciousness as well as method that have come to be called "The ASEAN Way".[26] Characterized by informal dialogue and conflict avoidance rather than by a large organization and procedural restraints, there have been attempts to project this form of engagement outwards. The "ASEAN+3" grouping is a classic example of such an attempt. This consciousness and sense of community, it has been argued, also form the basis for a common security culture. The culture of conflict avoidance, informal dialogue, regular consultation and accommodation is thought to aid the emergence of a security community. While such a community may not have yet eventuated, given the prevalence of intra-regional threat perceptions and tensions, some analysts have argued that such identity formation falls well within the constructivist tradition that is in turn underpinned by the liberal value of mutual gain. In seeming recognition of the utility of this approach, China and India acceded as signatories to TAC in late 2003, while Japan has indicated its willingness to do likewise. What such gestures effectively mean is that Southeast Asian countries are succeeding in encouraging larger regional powers to resolve inter-state differences peacefully.

PERILS OF MULTILATERALISM IN ASEAN

The perils of multilateralism that can be discerned from the ASEAN and East Asian experience may be broadly divided into common perils attendant on all multilateral organizations on the one hand, and those specific to the region on the other. To begin with, there still exists a tendency for the national interests of individual member states to bear disproportionately on multi-lateral initiatives. Indonesia's *primus inter pares* status in ASEAN is of course significant. Besides that, we still have to consider, for example, the Thai decision to launch the Indochina Initiative in 1988, or the decision by Indonesia and Malaysia to announce the Kuantan Declaration in 1980, which noted legitimate Vietnamese security interests *vis-à-vis* China, and brought traditional threat perceptions of individual member states into play. Most recently, the Asian Financial Crisis of 1997 also led to ASEAN member countries becoming introverted. They preferred to attend to domestic problems rather than further collective regional interests. It is entirely possible that a much longer gestation period is required for a regional identity to evolve. For now, the fact remains that national interests sometimes take precedence over or exist uneasily alongside multilateral initiatives. Hence, a tendency for member states to revert to a national agenda in the first or final instance exists.

The second major peril associated with ASEAN is that its best and most coordinated international initiatives obtained from external rather than internal motivations. It therefore comes as no surprise that ASEAN's evolution and maturation were closely correlated to the Indochinese conflicts in general, and Vietnam in particular. Hence, ASEAN initiatives have tended to be responsive rather than proactive. Correlated to this responsive tendency is ASEAN's inability to deal, even collectively, with the great powers that exercise strong leverage in international relations and possess an incomparably wider range of instruments for achieving their agenda. As a result, ASEAN and East Asian initiatives such as the ARF and "ASEAN+3" are in turn subjected to the tacit goodwill or agreement of the large powers. This situation is perhaps inevitable but needs to be noted as an operational constraint. It remains unclear if greater cohesion and a less realist international security architecture will yield more positive regional outcomes. Structurally, there is also the tendency for Japanese and South Korean policy initiatives to be closely aligned with that of the United States — a legacy of World War II and the Cold War. This alignment allows the United States, as the only remaining super power, to bring to bear disproportionate influence on the region. Such influence has in the past detracted countries in the region from articulating an independent policy. The failure of the Asian Monetary Fund was such an example.

The next major operational constraint is the importance of Indonesian leadership to the effective functioning of ASEAN.[27] The collapse of Suharto's New Order government following the 1997 Asian Financial Crisis meant that Indonesia became preoccupied with its domestic situation. It may be remembered how critical the regime change in Indonesia in 1967 was to the formation and subsequent sustenance of ASEAN in the first instance. Hence the importance of Indonesian leadership to ASEAN cannot be exaggerated. Equally important is the willingness of larger regional powers such as China and Japan to participate voluntarily in multilateral fora. Thus, Chinese participation in regional multilateral efforts is contingent on the agenda and membership not being hijacked by the United States or its regional allies. Such a position, while both fair and objective, is sometimes not congruent with structural realities as they exist.

ASEAN's decision-making style and culture of informal consultations can also prove problematic from time to time. The twin approaches of consultation and consensus (*musyawarah* dan *mufakat*) that are central to "The ASEAN Way" pose some constraints.[28] Informal consultation rather than clearly established procedural norms work against cumulative gains since there are neither sanctions nor enforcement mechanisms for compliance. Similarly, consensual decision-making regularly implies acceding to the lowest common denominator, to borrow a mathematical formula. Under the circumstances, policy coordination among ten members since 1999 has yielded significantly lower levels of convergence.

Finally, in recent times, ASEAN has demonstrated internal weakness in dealing with domestic problems among member states.[29] The political violence that characterized Burmese domestic politics since 1988, the violence associated with the Timorese referendum in 1998 and subsequent independence in 2000, and the conflict between Hun Sen and Norodom Ranarridh in 1997 all required external assistance and intervention. Such conditions have considerably lessened ASEAN's clout in recent years. Likewise, ASEAN also continues to be subjected to a high level of tension between member states that detracts from the formation of a security community.[30] Although no wide-scale open military conflict has broken out, there have been periodic skirmishes, particularly between Thailand and Myanmar.[31] Consequently, the post-Cold War period has witnessed the resurfacing of tensions between geographically proximate ASEAN member states as well as new and often non-traditional threats and tensions such as environmental degradation (euphemistically referred to as haze), illegal fishing, migration and refugees. While certain types of intervention in the domestic politics of a country may be regarded as unacceptable (with respect to the sovereignty principle), the world has also progressed to the point where general or broad-based life-threatening situations provide sufficient justification for multilateral humanitarian intervention. The situation in Cambodia, Somalia and Timor clearly fell under this category.

CONCLUSION

Since its formation in 1967, ASEAN has evolved significantly in favour of collaborative multilateralism. Such efforts began slowly as a result of mutual anxieties and suspicions. However, from 1976 onwards, and in close correlation with the Indochinese security situation, ASEAN has harvested much greater success in policy coordination. Especially significant in this regard was ASEAN's attempt to deny legitimacy to the Vietnamese occupation of Cambodia. Throughout the 1990s, ASEAN sought both to incorporate and to represent all the countries of Southeast Asia. Simultaneously, it also attempted to extend its influence and organizational norms to the broader Asia-Pacific region, and in particular to East Asia. Apparently, there is encouraging enthusiasm among the countries of East Asia to be part of such a larger community.

The ASEAN and East Asian experience with multilateralism is a mixed bag. Perhaps the most positive outcome is familiarity between and accommodation among member states. This outcome has further entrenched the regular consultations that appear to have percolated from the political elite to the policy-making community. Whether this common constructivist identity will eventually yield the Deutschian equivalent of a security community is still hard to tell. As for difficulties associated with pursuing a multilateral agenda, the responsive nature of decision-making and the overwhelming influence of the great powers on the broader security architecture are important constraints. ASEAN and East Asian countries are also hampered by the continuing importance attributed to the national interests of individual member states, an apparent inability to manage their internal environment, and the need to cope with structural alignments previously associated with bipolarity in international relations. Finally, the informal and consensual decision-making model also leads to minimalist policy output and to the easy availability of a non-compliance stand towards common positions.

Notes

[1]   See Hedley Bull, *The Anarchical Society: A Study of Order in World Politics*, London: Macmillan, 1977, p. 7. For an excellent introduction to early theories of international relations, see Robert Lieber, *Theory and World Politics*, London: Allen and Unwin, 1973.

[2]   For a treatment of regime theory see Stephen D. Krasser, ed., *International Regimes*, Ithaca: Cornell University Press, 1995. Liberalism and its variants are studied in David A. Baldwin, ed., *Neorealism and Neoliberalism: The Contemporary Debate*, New York: Columbia University Press, 1993.

[3]   The classic reference on constructivism is Alexander Wendt, "Anarchy is What States Make of It: The Social Construction of Power Politics", *International Organization* 46, no. 2 (1992): 391–425. Also see Wendt's later piece, "Collective Identity Formation and the International State", *American Political Science Review* 88 (1994): 384–96.

[4]   For an assessment of ASEAN both within the realist and constructivist tradition, see N. Ganesan, "Mirror, Mirror on the Wall: Misplaced Polarities in the Study of Southeast Asian Security", *International Relations of the Asia-Pacific* 3, no. 2 (August 2003): 221–40.

[5]   A good treatment of the political climate in Southeast Asia in the 1960s can be found in Bernard K. Gordon, *The Dimensions of Conflict in Southeast Asia*, New Jersey: Prentice Hall, 1966.

[6]   See Donald Hindley, "Indonesia's Confrontation with Malaysia: A Search for Motives", *Asian Survey* 4, no. 6 (June 1964): 904–13. A detailed account of the actual military campaign can be found in Jamie Mackie, *Konfrontasi: The Indonesian-Malaysian Dispute, 1963–1966*, Kuala Lumpur: Oxford University Press, 1974. Also see Michael Leifer, *Indonesia's Foreign Policy*, London: Allen and Unwin, 1983.

[7]   Michael Leifer, *The Philippine Claim to Sabah*, Hull: Hull Monographs on Southeast Asia, 1968.

[8]   See R.S. Milne, "Singapore's Exit from Malaysia: The Consequences of

Ambiguity," *Asian Survey* 4, no. 3 (March 1966): 175–84 and Lau Teik Soon, "Malaysia-Singapore Relations: Crisis of Adjustment, 1965–68", *Journal of Southeast Asian History* 11 (March 1969): 155–76.

[9] Relations between Indonesia and Singapore did not normalize until 1973 owing to Singapore's hanging of two Indonesian marines in 1968 for sabotage. See Lee Khoon Choy, *An Ambassador's Journey*, Singapore: Scientific International, 1982.

[10] The classic study of this conflict is Donald Zagoria, *The Sino-Soviet Conflict, 1956–1961*, New Jersey: Princeton University Press, 1962.

[11] See Muthiah Alagappa, "The Major Powers and Southeast Asia", *International Journal* 44 (Summer 1989): 541–97.

[12] ZOPFAN is studied in Heiner Hanggi, *ASEAN and the ZOPFAN Concept*, Singapore: Institute of Southeast Asian Studies, 1992.

[13] This pact is a reference to the Anglo-Malayan Defence Agreements (AMDA) that lapsed in 1971 and was replaced by the Five Power Defence Arrangements. See Chin Kin Wah, *The Five Power Defence Arrangements and AMDA*, Singapore: Institute of Southeast Asian Studies, 1972.

[14] Donald Weatherbee, *Southeast Asia Divided*, Boulder, Colorado: Westview Press, 1985.

[15] See Muthiah Alagappa, "Regionalism and the Quest for Security, ASEAN and the Cambodian Conflict", *Journal of International Affairs* 46, no. 2 (Winter 1993): 439–67 and Michael Leifer, *ASEAN and the Security of Southeast Asia*, London: Routledge, 1989.

[16] A Security Complex refers to a traditional pattern of interaction among states that reveals a hierarchical ordering of power. Threat perceptions derive from such a relatively self-contained patterning process. The Indochina Security Complex refers to such a patterning process between Vietnam, Thailand, Laos, Burma and Cambodia while the Malay Archipelago Complex groups the countries of maritime Southeast Asia. Vietnam was the dominant hegemonic power in the former and Indonesia in the latter. See Barry Buzan, "The Southeast Asian Security Complex", *Contemporary Southeast Asia* 10, no. 1 (June 1988): 1–16. For a refinement of the concept, see Muthiah Alagappa, "The Dynamics of International Security in Southeast Asia: Change and Continuity", *Australian Journal of International Affairs* 45, no. 1 (May 1991): 17–22.

[17] Sukhumphand Paribatra, *From Enmity to Alignment: Thailand's Evolving Relations with China*, Bangkok: Chulalongkorn University, 1987.

[18] The broadened coalition included Son Sann's Khmer Peoples' National Liberation Front (KPNLF) and Sihanouk's *Front de Union Nationale Pour un Cambodge Independent, Neutrale, Pacifique et Co-Operatif* (FUNCINPEC).

[19] See Justus van der Kroef, "Cambodia: The Vagaries of 'Cocktail' Diplomacy", *Contemporary Southeast Asia* 9, no. 4 (March 1988): 301–15.

[20] N. Ganesan, "Testing Neoliberal Institutionalism in Southeast Asia", *International Journal* 50, no. 4 (Autumn 1995): 779–804.

[21] See Katharya Um, "Thailand and the Dynamics of Economic and Security

Complex in mainland Southeast Asia", *Contemporary Southeast Asia* 13, no. 3 (December 1991): 245–70.

22 On the Indonesian decision to normalize ties with China, see Leo Suryadinata, "Indonesia-China Relations: A Recent Breakthrough", *Asian Survey* 30, no. 7 (July 1990): 682–96.

23 This observation was made by Michael Leifer almost two decades ago.

24 See Michael Leifer, *The ASEAN Regional Forum*, London: Royal Institute of International Affairs, Adelphi Paper, 1996.

25 The original Malaysian proposal for an East Asian Economic Grouping (EAEG) was meant to bring together Northeast and Southeast Asia in defence of Asian interests in the late 1980s at a time when the world seemed to be drifting into trading blocs such as NAFTA and the EU. However, the U.S.-inspired and Australian and Indonesian-endorsed APEC gained precedence and institutionalization. Subsequently the EAEG was downgraded to the East Asian Economic Caucus (EAEC) in ASEAN deliberations and was cynically referred to as East Asia without Caucasians. "ASEAN+3" emerged in the later 1990s following the Asian Financial Crisis in 1997.

26 Amitav Acharya, "From the 'ASEAN Way' to the 'Asia-Pacific Way'?" *The Pacific Review* 10, no. 3 (1997): 319–46.

27 See Anthony Smith, *Strategic Centrality: Indonesia's Changing Role in ASEAN*, Singapore: Institute of Southeast Asian Studies, 2000.

28 ASEAN's decision-making style is examined in Pushpa Thambipillai and Johan Saravanamuttu, *ASEAN Negotiations: Two Insights*, Singapore: Institute of Southeast Asian Studies, 1985.

29 Jürgen Haacke, "The Concept of Flexible Engagement and the Practice of Enhanced Interaction: Intramural Challenges to the 'ASEAN Way' ", *The Pacific Review* 12, no. 4 (1999): 581–611 and Kay Möller, "Cambodia and Burma: The ASEAN Way Ends Here", *Asian Survey* 38, no. 12 (1998): 1087–104.

30 N. Ganesan, "Taking Stock of Post-Cold War Developments in ASEAN", *Security Dialogue* 25, no. 4 (December 1994): 457–68 and Bilateral Tensions in Post-Cold War ASEAN (Singapore: Institute of Southeast Asian Studies, 1999).

31 N. Ganesan, "Thailand's Relations with Malaysia and Myanmar in Post-Cold War Southeast Asia", *Japanese Journal of Political Science* 2, no. 1 (May 2001): 127–46.

8

THE HISTORICAL AND CULTURAL LEGACY OF RELATIONS BETWEEN SOUTHEAST ASIA AND EAST ASIA, WITH SPECIAL REFERENCE TO MALAYSIA

Khoo Kay Kim

INTRODUCTION

It should be mentioned from the outset that the discussion here is slanted more towards a Southeast Asian perception than an East Asian one. Understandably, if the discussion were to be led by someone from East Asia, it would probably be the other way round. But that is putting it very generally. Neither Southeast Asia nor East Asia is a homogeneous entity. The need to generalize in intellectual discussions, while unavoidable, is also full of pitfalls. Scholarship is quite often, for one reason or another, coloured by sentimentalism that can result in more being seen than there is to see. On the other hand, if the distant past is almost faded from memory or is clouded by contemporary prejudices, its significance may be underplayed. It is difficult at any rate to deny that even the remote past is never really obliterated. Bali, for example, one of Indonesia's over 17,000 islands, has retained its Hindu culture and religion within a country with an overwhelmingly Muslim population. Inversely, in contemporary Javanese culture, a thick layer of Hinduism is still recognizable. Historical and cultural links have greater lasting impact if they are authentic rather than mythical, and if each succeeding generation is able to consciously cherish them.

The discipline of history is concerned with the total past — from as far back as it is possible to imagine up to the recent moment. However, no single historian can hope to cope with the total past. To help simplify matters, a broad distinction is often made between "proto-history" and "pre-history" on the one hand, and "history" on the other. The historical period begins when scholars can rely on sound documentary evidence. The period prior to that is by and large the domain of archaeologists who primarily conduct studies based on artefacts, relics, buildings and monuments. It is also common when discussing history to use categories such as the distant/remote past and the recent past, or ancient and contemporary/current history.

Neither Southeast Asia nor East Asia (especially China) lacks ancient artefacts and sites. However, documents are not easily available for the pre-fifteenth century period with regard to relations between the two regions. Based on what is available and what is still perceivable of the cultural scenario today, one cannot but surmise that there was, in the distant past, profound cultural links between South Asia and Southeast Asia. Furthermore, evidence shows that the Chinese made their presence felt here earlier than the Indians did. The difference between India and China, the world's two largest countries, and also two of the oldest civilizations, is that while there were Indians in the remote past who became settlers and, in due course, blended with peoples in Southeast Asia, the Chinese, even when they had settled and become partially assimilated, as in the case of the Straits-born Chinese (popularly known as *Baba* and *Nyonya*), continued to maintain a separate identity. In the case of Indonesia, for example, it was remarked by the Minority Rights Group many years ago that:

> Despite the length and pervasiveness of Chinese contact, Indonesian culture was little influenced. Little attention has been paid to why this was so when under similar circumstances Indian and Islamic cultures made a deep impact. Whatever the reasons, and allowing for occasional assimilation and integration, the Chinese as a whole remained distinct, and this distinctiveness was strengthened in colonial times when the Chinese held a legal and social position between the Dutch rulers and the indigenous people.[1]

Much of Southeast Asia in more modern times continues to reveal evidence of strong Indian religious and cultural influences, a significant portion of which was not eradicated even with the coming of Islam and the subsequent

Islamization of maritime Southeast Asia since at least the eleventh and twelfth centuries.

It is important to note that India played a major part even in the spread of Islam in the Malay Archipelago. This occurred after the thirteenth century. With the decline of the Caliphate of Baghdad in the latter half of that century, Arab commercial activity in the Indian Ocean decreased. It was taken over by Muslims from Gujerat and other centres on the Indian continent. Hindu merchants who did not travel exported their merchandise in Muslim-owned vessels. Thriving centres of commercial activity studded the Indian coastline.[2] These traders swarmed the Indian Ocean and the Bay of Bengal, playing a dominant part in trading on behalf of indigenous rulers. Indeed, until the mid-eighteenth century, when the Dutch were already in Melaka, Indian Muslim merchants continued to play a major commercial role in the Malay Archipelago.

COMMERCIAL ACTIVITIES

Trade in the distant past was undoubtedly the main motive for Indian and Chinese voyages to foreign lands. There was a period in the early part of the fifteenth century, however, when the Chinese had other motives in mind. They established tributary relations with many polities, Melaka among them. Moreover, many of the voyages during the Ming dynasty were undertaken in pursuit of enemies.[3] It was also trade considerations that drove the Europeans to North America and Asia, beginning in the fifteenth century. The Portuguese and the Spaniards arrived in Southeast Asia from different directions during the first quarter of the sixteenth century. Both came in search of spices. Spain was more ambitious. Also on its agenda was the conversion of China and Japan. This, as D.G.E. Hall remarks, was "a chimera".[4] The Spaniards were quick to realize this and when it was clear that even spices were beyond their reach because the Philippines had little of such products, they moved to establish trading relations with China and Japan to make the Philippine colony pay its way. This turned out to be a success. Manila became the resort of traders from China, Japan, Siam, Cambodia and the Spice Islands. By the end of the sixteenth century, the China trade was prospering.

Spain's religious mission in the Philippines was partially successful. The northern part of modern Philippines was converted to Catholicism, but Islam, which had arrived earlier, continued to hold sway in the southern islands. To this day, the situation has remained unchanged, American (1898–1941) and Japanese (1941–45) rule notwithstanding. In general, Christian proselytizers were less active in this region compared to their Muslim counterparts.[5]

In dealing with East Asia's foreign relations in the distant past (especially its links with Southeast Asia), the focus has primarily to be on China, which held sway over Korea and Taiwan until they were ceded to Japan through the Treaty of Shimonoseki. This treaty brought the Sino-Japanese War of 1894–95 to an end. China never succeeded in establishing control over Japan. The first naval confrontations between China and Japan had occurred in AD 662 during the Tang period. After Kublai Khan had conquered China, he attempted to invade Japan, but failed. In 1281, he made another attempt from bases in China and Korea, but was defeated by the Japanese. In short, the Yuan Dynasty did not succeed in its efforts to rule Japan. Japan, on the other hand, did not make any concerted effort to establish close economic ties with Southeast Asia until the later part of the nineteenth century.[6]

Much has been said recently about China's voyages of exploration (the name of Cheng Ho, or Zheng He, has gained a very high profile), which pre-dated those of Vasco da Gama, Magellan and Christopher Columbus. Indeed China's earliest contact with Southeast Asia is believed to have occurred during the period of the Western Han Empire (206 BC–AD 9), which reached the zenith of its influence under Emperor Wu Di (140–87 BC), when commercial and cultural links were established with Central as well as Southeast Asia. Han control of the southern coast of China opened up the sea route to maritime Southeast Asia. Chinese annals recorded that a Chinese fleet was sent to the southern seas (Nanyang) between 116 and 110 BC and the countries of the south had been sending tribute to China after that.[7]

There is further evidence from Southeast Asia of direct contact with China in the form of numerous specimens of Han pottery found in eastern Borneo, western Java and in southern Sumatra. It is therefore likely that Chinese trade with and settlement in Southeast Asia had already begun by the first century BC, or perhaps even as early as the Vietnam's Dong Son period (400–100 BC).[8] While China did establish diplomatic relations with many polities in Southeast Asia, it did not attempt to colonize them. This contrasts with the case of the West, which sent out expeditions much later. In the later case, the story was played out very much to the refrain of "I came, I saw, I conquered".

China's historical links with Southeast Asia were understandably influenced by geography. Mainland Southeast Asia was more subjected to intrusion from China than maritime Southeast Asia. Vietnam, in particular, could not avoid absorbing strong elements of Chinese culture. Alastair Lamb remarked many years ago:

In the centuries immediately before the opening of the Christian era, Chinese influence, both political and cultural, began to penetrate into what is now Vietnam. In Tongking and along the Annamese coast, Chinese colonies emerged and Chinese culture blended with that of the indigenous people in regions beyond the direct political control of the Chinese dynasties.[9]

Nevertheless, India's religious influence on mainland Southeast Asia was, to say the least, overwhelming. Buddhism had long penetrated the entire area. Neither Confucian teaching nor Taoist philosophy has had any significant impact on the people of most parts of Southeast Asia, especially its maritime regions. Making a similar point, Ronald Hill says:

> By contrast Sinic influences are mostly later and sporadic except along China's borderlands, mostly notably in Viet Nam, where the whole structure of government, even the architecture and layout of the ninth–tenth-century capital at Hue, were based upon Chinese models, not surprisingly since northern Viet Nam was essentially a colony of China from about the second century BC until AD 938. The Vietnamese language ... was written in Chinese characters until well into colonial times when the French ... replaced Chinese writing with a specially devised Roman script called *quoc nu*.[10]

Within the same context, Burma's case is also noteworthy. Those who inhabited the hilly north were racially not very different from the Chinese who lived on the other side of the border. The movement of people from China into Burma was unavoidable, though small. Access between India and Burma was also easy. Purcell made the interesting remark that "Burma's racial affinities were with China, but its cultural ties were with India."[11]

It is quite well known that the greater part of Southeast Asia is dependent on agriculture. Indonesia itself, despite having over 17,000 islands, has most of its population concentrated at Java, which is more agrarian than maritime. Indonesia's commercial links with China, however, are believed to date back to at least the beginning of the fifth century. D.G.E. Hall remarks:[12]

> From as early as 441 [AD] *Kan-t'o-li* [the chief port of Sumatra] had adopted the policy of sending tribute to China. The evidence does not show whether it was situated at either Jambi or Palembang, but [O.W. Wolters who published his study of the history of Srivijaya in 1968] is convinced that it alone of the "tributary" kingdoms of Indonesia during the fifth and sixth centuries was the predecessor of Srivijaya as overlord of the "favoured court", attracting to its service the roaming Malay

shippers of this coast and of the offshore islands. The international communications, leading to and from it, sustained its maritime trade with China.

Chinese settlements emerged long before the advent of the West in Southeast Asia. For instance, when the Dutch were taking effective control of Java in the late seventeenth century, they found that the Chinese had arrived there even before the Portuguese, and were securely entrenched in the local economy. The Chinese were so appreciated for their industry and diligence that the Dutch encouraged them to settle in Batavia. By the year 1700, there were approximately 10,000 of them living in or around the city. Among them were mainly craftsmen, tea traders and sugar cultivators. Many also acted as middlemen between the Dutch and the Javanese. Some became extremely wealthy. In the early eighteenth century, however, Indonesia faced a problem that Malaya was to encounter much later. The junks plying regularly from China increasingly brought along individuals without means of subsistence. These became a social problem.[13]

There is evidence that the Chinese were probably in Palembang even earlier. After the decline of Srivijaya, Palembang fell into Chinese hands and remained so for the next 200 years. It was probably one of the earliest places in Southeast Asia where the Chinese settled in any numbers. Most were Hokkien or Cantonese.[14] For centuries, Southeast Asia, especially the Malay Archipelago, was a commercial centre. It was not just a market where merchants from South and West Asia could exchange goods with those from East Asia; it was also a very productive area. Spices apart, there were other major products such as rattan, birds' nest, *attap*, camphor, ivory and coral, and various kinds of wood that were in demand in countries outside the region. There was a time when the British East India Company based in India sought Southeast Asian products to help reduce the cost of their trade with China. Until the early eighteenth century, even after the arrival of the European powers, the coastal areas of Southeast Asia continued to be visited and settled by the Chinese.

After the fall of Melaka to the Portuguese in 1511, and following the commercial decline in the Straits of Melaka, especially after the Dutch ousted the Portuguese and robbed Aceh of its vitality, the east coast of the Malay Peninsula began to attract foreign traders. In the eighteenth century, Chinese settlements were established in Kuala Kelantan, Kuala Terengganu and Kuala Pahang. Chinese traders were appointed agents to local rulers. Kuala Terengganu, in particular, like Riau, which was then a part of ancient Johor, was an international port. The Chinese population grew steadily in the early nineteenth century despite the existence of the ports of Penang, Melaka and Singapore. The situation was to change radically from about the mid-nineteenth century, owing to technological progress in the West.[15]

THE INDUSTRIAL REVOLUTION IN THE WEST

While it is true that contact between East Asia (primarily China and Japan) and Southeast Asia began long before the nineteenth century, sustained and massive population movements from East Asia (largely China) to Southeast Asia began after the West had gained firm control over the region. It is well known that even Siam (Thailand), which succeeded in retaining its independence, lost territories to Western powers in the late nineteenth century and had to Westernize its administrative and economic systems in order to convince these powers that its state structure was in healthy condition. To an important extent, it succeeded in maintaining its integrity because it served as a geographical buffer between the British in Burma (Myanmar) and the French in what used to be called Indochina.

Until the turn of the nineteenth century, statistical records were based on estimates that were often highly inaccurate. By the time of the 1930 slump, the system of population enumeration in the region had attained a much higher level of reliability. The figures below show the demographic presence of the Chinese in Southeast Asia during the global economic depression (the figures for 1947 are also given to provide a better perspective on the subject).[16]

Country	Chinese Population 1930	Chinese Population 1947	Total Population 1947
Burma (Myanmar):	194,000	300,000	17,000,000
Siam (Thailand)	445,000	2,500,000	17,459,000
French Indochina	418,000	850,000	27,000,000
Malaya (with Singapore)	1,704,000	2,615,000	5,840,000
Sarawak, North Borneo and Brunei	n.a.	220,000	878,000
Indonesia	1,233,000	1,900,000	69,000,000
Philippines	72,000	120,000	19,511,000

It is pertinent to note that Malaya alone of all the countries in the region had a Chinese population that formed about 50 per cent of the total. Numerically, it also exceeded that of Chinese present in any of the other countries in the region. Continual political and economic instability was partly responsible for migration from the southeastern parts of China. This was especially true of the mid-nineteenth century, which was the period of the Opium Wars as well as the Taiping Rebellion. Nevertheless, until the turn of the nineteenth century, trade continued to be the main pull factor in the migration of Chinese to the west coast of the Malay Peninsula.

Between 1786 and 1824, the British took complete control of Penang, Singapore and Melaka. All three ports played a leading role in the coastal trade of the archipelago. Most of the traders were Hokkien and until today, in all the port towns in Malaysia (except Sabah), Hokkien is the main dialect spoken. After the Dutch departed from Melaka in 1824, thus putting an end to the monopoly they had imposed on tin export from the Malay sultanates, tin mining activities picked up steam. By the mid-nineteenth century, with the tin-plate industry of Britain starved for raw material after the decline of the Cornwall mines, tin mining in the Malay Peninsula grew greatly in importance.

Chinese workers were primarily used in the mines. As the tin sector peaked, the number of Chinese entering the Malay states also increased radically. So large were their numbers that they formed the large majority of the population in new urban areas established near mining centres. Kuala Lumpur was one of them. While the Hokkiens supplied the capital — sometimes borrowed from the Chettiar (Indian money lenders from the province of Madras, now better known as Tamil Nadu) — the Hakkas worked in the mines. In later years, some Hakkas were able to accumulate sufficient wealth to finance tin mining on their own. The establishment of British administration in the tin-mining states in the 1870s and 1880s helped to stabilize the areas where the Chinese population continued to increase.

Most standard works on Malaysian history highlight tin mining to the exclusion of agriculture as the primary factor that induced Chinese to come to the Malay Peninsula in the nineteenth century. In fact, while Chinese miners flocked to western Malay territories (Larut, the Klang valley and Sungai Ujong) and later the Kinta district, Chinese agriculturalists (mostly Teochew) moved into Province Wellesley (opposite Penang), to plant sugar, and Johor (opposite Singapore) to plant gambier and pepper. Sometime in the 1860s, Chinese, mainly from Melaka, were planting tapioca in the neighbouring territory of Negri Sembilan. It is worth noting that, like tin mining, commercial agriculture was initially undertaken by the Chinese before the advent of the British. However, unlike tin mining, where the Chinese held sway until the advent of the dredge in the twentieth century, plantation agriculture came under European control by the close of the nineteenth century. The Chinese, like the Malays, were mainly smallholders.[17]

The Chinese moved into yet another sector with the expansion of trade, namely shipping. A major change occurred in the second half of the nineteenth century, however. This was the advent of steamships. The Chinese, who by then controlled coastal shipping, quickly shifted from sail to steam. By the last quarter of the nineteenth century, there were close to 200 Chinese companies operating ships over the entire archipelago, and between the archipelago and China.

The opening of the Suez Canal in 1869 diverted traffic from Europe away from the Cape of Good Hope to the Straits of Melaka, thereby boosting the commercial importance of Singapore, and later Port Swettenham (opened in 1901) on the west coast of the peninsula. The opening of the canal more or less coincided with the growth of steam communication in this region. By the turn of the twentieth century, the telegraph too had become an important instrument for commercial transaction in Malaya, helping to boost trading activities.[18]

Western technological development as a whole had a significant impact on the region. Some of course benefited more than others. Singapore and the Malay Peninsula were particular beneficiaries. The existing Chinese population played a part in inducing other Chinese to come to Southeast Asia to partake of the economic opportunities to be found within the social and political order of the Western powers, and which was enhanced by the development of an infrastructure. The increase in the foreign population in any society must give rise to tensions between the long-domiciled and the newcomers. While vertical separation among ethnic groups in the region was caused by cultural differences, conflict was aggravated mainly by the contest for political supremacy.

THE CULTURAL PERSPECTIVE

It has been mentioned earlier that Chinese cultural influence on indigenous societies in Southeast Asia has been quite inconsequential. It must be said, however, that in most countries in the region, the gradual absorption of the Chinese into local societies has made it difficult today to distinguish between the indigenes and the Chinese. Unlike countries such as Thailand, the Philippines, and even Indonesia to a lesser extent, where substantial ethnic fusion between the indigenous people and the Chinese had taken place by the post-World War II period, there was little integration, much less assimilation, in Malaya between the indigenous people and the newcomers. The Chinese who had settled at Melaka and Penang since the eighteenth century did, however, come close to assimilation. Since Chinese women then did not accompany male migrants, those whom Chinese male migrants married or consummated with were local women, not necessarily Malays but also non-Muslim Sumatrans, Siamese and, to a lesser extent, Burmese. Hence was formed the group of Chinese known as *Baba* and *Nyonya,* more often referred to now as *Peranakan* or local-born Chinese.[19]

There is a mistaken notion even among the Chinese outside the group that the *Peranakan,* now a dwindling group, had discarded Chinese traditions. On the contrary, despite having partially assimilated indigenous culture, they were zealous custodians of Chinese culture. Surprisingly, while the community stemmed from marriages between male Chinese and women of other ethnic groups, once it had reached a sizeable proportion, it began to frown on marriages between their own members and those outside the group irrespective of whether these were Chinese or not. The situation, however, changed after World War II for reasons that need not be discussed here. The socio-cultural transformation of Malaysian Chinese throughout the twentieth century deserves an in-depth study of its own.

Compared to Chinese in other parts of the region — Singapore being an exception since it is very much a Chinese city-state — those in Malaya have been able to maintain their cultural identity. This has been possible because of the existence, since the days of the British, of Chinese schools, Chinese newspapers (nowadays, news in Chinese is also available *via* the radio and television), surname as well as clan associations, temples, churches where sermons are delivered entirely in Chinese and, not least of all, Chinese or Chinese-based political parties since 1949. Even the Malayan Communist Party, formed in 1930, was looked upon locally as a Chinese organization since the majority of its members were Chinese.

Until 1949, Malayan Chinese links with China were practically inextricable. Although not all were able to keep in close touch with the villages from which they originated, they tried to preserve memories through the numerous associations that they formed. Various cultural and political movements in China found support among Malayan Chinese, who were always in a position to contribute handsomely to them. The Kuomintang was a powerful organization in Malaya after about 1912, and worked closely with major secret societies. Despite the state of emergency between 1948–60, declared in the face of the communist insurrection, at no time did the Malayan Communist Party gain greater influence within the Chinese community than the Kuomintang did, whose leaders were instrumental to the founding of the Malayan Chinese Association in 1949.

There is a common understanding that the British played a crucial role in the creation of Malaysia's plural society. Historical evidence does not support this. The British were not the first to encourage Chinese migration to Malaya and although they brought in the Indians and Jaffnese to work in both the private and public sectors, they were not responsible for the numerous cultural and ethnic associations that multiplied during the late nineteenth and early twentieth century. The existence of Chinese schools owed nothing to the British who, however, did compel the estates to provide Tamil education. It would be more accurate to say that Malaya's plural society existed — and continues to exist — because the various ethnic groups desired it.

The cultural, as distinct from the political, relationship between "overseas Chinese" and China differed from country to country. During the time when Chinese nationalism was strong, inflamed by events such as Japan's invasion of Manchuria (1931) or the outbreak of the Second Sino-Japanese War (1937), there were concerted anti-Japanese activities in some Southeast Asian countries. Malaya and Singapore were by far the most prominent on that score. Chinese schools were hotbeds of political activities aimed at directly or indirectly assisting China. This was unavoidable since these schools used textbooks imported from China, many of which were entirely Sino-centric. These helped to create a sense of nostalgia even among those who had never seen China. Teachers imported from China, many of whom were highly politicized, were also very effective in encouraging this state of things.

CONCLUDING REMARKS

It makes greater sense to study history by moving from the present back into the past than to begin from the past and then examine the endless ramifications of historical development without giving priority to matters that are of current interest. History cannot be totally rewritten unless deliberate and concerted attempts are made to achieve that, and even then, it is dubious if such an agenda can succeed. Interest in the history of Southeast Asia–East Asia relations is today clearly prompted by the desire to effectuate closer economic ties between the two regions. While there are those who believe that much can be discerned from historical experiences, it is not always the case that the very distant past exerts any significant influence on the present.

Culture itself cannot always persist, since technological change can have a major effect on it. The advent of cinematography, in particular the "Talkies", for instance, affected much of Chinese society in Malaya. Girls began to "bob" their hair, wear Western dresses, learn ballroom dancing, and go out on dates. The highly inventive West has constantly affected both Southeast Asia and East Asia. Today more than in the past, East Asia (including Japan, South Korea and Taiwan) is of considerable importance to Southeast Asia because of the former's growing economies. No doubt, Southeast Asia is also important to East Asia. But, like the West, each East Asian state prefers to treat Southeast Asia as one single economic entity since sustained economic growth is what primarily concerns the developed countries of the world.

Japan has not been discussed at any length here because its economic interests in Southeast Asia began mainly around the turn of the twentieth century and its direct cultural impact is inconsequential. There are very few people in the region who claim descent from the Japanese. In terms of economic impact, however, Japan was able to carve itself such an important niche in British Malaya that by the eve of World War II, there was fear among the business community in Malaya that Japan might emerge as the leading economic power.

The war that was to gain Japan political and, as a consequence, economic control of Southeast Asia brought instead destruction to the region and, in the immediate post-World War II period, extensive rehabilitation work had to be undertaken. Japan suffered as much at home as the countries that it had invaded, with the dropping of the devastative atom bombs on Hiroshima and Nagasaki in 1945. But, by the early 1950s, through the assistance of the United States, Japan's economy had recovered. Between 1952 and 1976, about 30 per cent of its trade was with only one nation — the United States. While no single Southeast Asian nation accounted for more than 3 per cent of Japan's international trade, the trade of all the Southeast Asian countries (including Vietnam) that experienced serious war between 1965–75 was at the same time dependent on Japan, which ranked within the top three trading positions for each of these countries.[20]

Whether in the past or in the present, and despite their deep involvement in Southeast Asian economies, the Japanese have made few attempts to become part of the local social scene. Before World War II, apart from Singapore, there were only two places — Melaka and Seremban — where Japanese quite actively participated in social activities. They were particularly fond of tennis. The only Japan club formed before World War II on the peninsula was in Seremban. However, this does not mean that they lived a life of total seclusion. They were conspicuously present in the business sector. Malaysians who lived through the pre-World War II period remember them. They were very visible as dentists and photographers. Not many, however, are aware that the Japanese also controlled fishing, the textile sector, iron mining, and the trade in rubber goods.[21] Southeast Asia also depended, and depends, heavily on Japan for assistance in many other forms. For example, Japanese foundations have for decades now, funded most of the research done on the region by Southeast Asian scholars themselves. The Toyota Foundation, for example, has been especially generous.

Southeast Asia–East Asia relations are not thoroughly studied and thus tend to be understood mainly in economic terms. The cultural gap between East Asians and the indigenous peoples of Southeast Asia remains glaringly wide. Even in Malaysia, where Malaysians are in a better position than the nationals of other Asian countries to cross cultural barriers, ethnic enclaves of various East Asian groups are easily discernible. Because of the large number of persons of Chinese descent in Malaysia (about 27 per cent of the total population of approximately twenty-three million), visitors from China and, to some extent, Taiwan, who are here for economic or educational purposes, are bound to relate more easily to Chinese Malaysians than do expatriates from Japan and Korea.

Since 1974, when Malaysia's Prime Minister Tun Abdul Razak visited China and the two countries established official diplomatic ties, the relationship between the two states has progressively improved. While obvious efforts are made in Malaysia to draw even closer to China, there is a tendency to over-emphasize economics to the exclusion of culture. Economics involves transactions between human beings, not systems *per se*. Culture is often treated as a common denominator among people from a particular territory. While this may be generally true, every nation-state is an aggregation of people that do not necessarily share identical cultures.

Divergence of culture must always be considered before any form of transaction between two groups can meaningfully take place. It is ironic that the majority of Southeast Asian peoples (including those of Chinese descent) today are likely to find people from China more difficult to comprehend than those from Korea and Japan who have been successfully doing business here for so many years, considering that migration from China to Southeast Asia began such a long time ago while migration from Japan and Korea has been negligible. Since 1945, while the political climate in both Japan and (South) Korea has been able to harmonize with that of most Southeast Asian states, China until more recently was regarded with mistrust and suspicion. Assuming that the Chinese in the near future will progressively change, resulting in the narrowing of the cultural gap between China and Southeast Asian nations, it will still take a while before the peoples of Southeast Asia can acquire a more consummate knowledge about the people in China, and *vice-versa*.

Notes

[1] Minority Rights Group, *The Chinese in Indonesia, the Philippines and Malaysia*, London, 1972, p. 4. For a general discussion on the subject of Chinese and Indian contacts with Southeast Asia, see Brian Harrison, *South-East Asia: A Short History*, 3rd edition, New York, 1968.

[2] See Kamalik Pierie, "The Muslims in Sri Lanka", <http://www.geocities.com/forumsl/msl.htm>.

[3] See "China to Honour Ancient Navigator who Came to India in 1405–07", <http://ushome.rediff.com/news/2003/dec./10china.htm>.

[4] *A History of South-east Asia*, 3rd edition, New York, 1968, p. 274.

[5] Ibid.

[6] See Hall Gardner, "China and International Relations in the New Millennium", <http://members.aol.com/wignesh/3gardner.htm>.

[7] Harrison, op. cit., p. 10.

[8] Ibid.

[9] "Early History" in Wang Gungwu, *Malaysia A Survey*, London: Pall Mall Press, 1965, p. 101.

[10] Ronald Hill, *Southeast Asia People, Land and Economy*, Crows Nest, N.S.W., Allen & Unwin, 2002, p. 9.

[11] Victor Purcell, *The Chinese in Southeast Asia*, 2nd edition, London, 1965, p. 49.

[12] Ibid., p. 47.

[13] Ibid., p. 356.

[14] Ibid. For an interesting account of Palembang, see Peter J.M.Nas, "Palembang The Venice of the East" <http://www.leidenuniv.nl/fsw/nas/pub_palembang.htm>, originally published in Dutch in *Orion*, jng. 1, no. 4 (1984).

[15] See Khoo Kay Kim, "Kuala Terengganu: International Training Centre", in *Malaysia in History* 17, no. 2 (1974).

[16] Purcell, op. cit., p. 2.

[17] J.C. Jackson, *Planters and Speculators*, Oxford: Oxford University Press, 1968.

[18] For a perspective of Chinese economic activities in Peninsular Malaysia from the nineteenth century to 1941, see Khoo Kay Kim, *The Western Malay States: The Political Effects of Commercial Development in the Malay States 1850–1873*, Kuala Lumpur, 1972, and Khoo Kay Kim, "Chinese Economic Activities in Malaya: A Historical Perspective" in *Economic Performance in Malaysia: The Insiders' View*, edited by Manning Nash, New York: Professor's World Peace Academy, 1988.

[19] See Khoo Kay Kim, "Malaysia: Immigration and the Growth of a Plural Society" in *Journal of the Royal Asiatic Society*, Malaysian Branch LXXI, part 1, 1998.

[20] See Pagewise: "Japan and Southeast Asia History 1952–1976", <http://njnj.essortment.com/southeastasiah_rljc.htm>.

[21] This is dealt with in some detail in my paper presently being revised for publication, "Japanese Economic Activities in Malaya: the Inter-War Years".

PART FOUR

New Knowledge, New Problems, New Solutions

9

REINVENTING TRADITIONAL VALUES FOR OUR FUTURE
A Malaysian Organizational Response

Shamsul A.B.

Dedication: This humble effort of mine is dedicated to the late Professor Norazit Selat, a very dear childhood friend and Director of the Academy of Malay Studies, University of Malaya, Kuala Lumpur, who passed away on 27 January 2004.

INTRODUCTION

In contemporary international politics, the phrase "reinventing traditional values" can be misconstrued as an effort to reintroduce "fundamentalism" of sorts, such as Muslims and Islam have been accused by the West of doing. So the tradition of wearing turban and beard, head scarf and all sorts of head covers, whether in traditional or reinvented forms, is being prohibited by law, for example in France. Important as it is for those in the East to observe, preserve and reinvent traditions and traditional values, the globalized world has other plans for us. As such, our efforts at reinvention must take cognizance of the world beyond the East. In other words, not all reinventions of traditional values are welcomed by all parties at all times. However, there is one particular "traditional value", if we may refer to it as such, that is continually reinvented because of its cumulative nature and its critical role in our intellectual life. This refers to the "traditional value" of knowledge-seeking and of being involved in knowledge-generating activities, which is the focus of this chapter.

Terms such as "East Asia", "Southeast Asia", "traditions" and "traditional values" signify both abstract and real entities. They are "forms of knowledge" in that each is reconstituted over time either in the form of academic or non-academic texts (paper-based and digital-based), images or memories. Because they are forms of knowledge, they are not only subjected to reinvention but reconstruction through new findings, and have often to be repackaged in response to changing use. The experiences at the Institute of the Malay World and Civilization (better known by its Malay acronym ATMA, at Universiti Kebangsaan Malaysia) gained through what may be categorized as an organizational response to the call for the "reinvention of traditional values", are briefly presented in this chapter. The "traditional value" highlighted here is not directly behavioural in nature and does not involve symbolic and ritualistic activities. It is not the epistemology or ontology of a particular "traditional value" but rather, the method of knowledge production and reproduction involved in the reinvention of traditional values itself. This matter also needs to be addressed.

The ATMA experiences mentioned above refer to three concrete projects that it has implemented, with encouraging results. The need to complement analyses of the "reinvention of traditional values" with results that are concrete, such as the ones that ATMA have achieved. Of course, there are alternative methods that are perhaps more effective than what ATMA has used, but let us meanwhile take a peek at what ATMA's attempts have brought about.

"EAST ASIA" AND "SOUTHEAST ASIA" AS FORMS OF KNOWLEDGE

Society is both real and imagined. It is real through face-to-face contact, and imagined when the idea of its existence is mediated through mediums such as printed materials and electronic images, and, in particular, Information Communication Technology (ICT). So, it refers simultaneously to a micro-unit that is observable, and to a macro-unit that we can only partially engage. We therefore have empirical "societies" within macro-units of imagined "societies", so to speak. East Asia and Southeast Asia, like other regions of the world, are both these things. However, it is the way that both have been weaved into an enduring complex whole that seems to have taught East Asians and Southeast Asians how to thrive and survive under conditions as adverse as those of the recent financial crisis.

Thus East Asian studies and Southeast Asian studies, dominated by the humanities and the social sciences, have been about the study of "society" as such, and of "societies" in their various dimensions, in the past and in the present. The plurality of these "societies", of these societal forms that indeed co-exist, endures and enjoys some functional stability. This has made it necessary for researchers to apply an equally diverse set of approaches, some discipline-based (anthropology, sociology, geography, history, political science, etc.) and others theme-oriented (development studies, gender studies, cultural studies, etc.). In some cases, even methods from the natural and applied sciences have been adopted.

The greatest challenge in East Asian and Southeast Asian studies has been to keep pace with major changes that affect "society" and "societies", and describe, explain and analyse these changes in ways generally accessible to readers from within and outside the region. How knowledge is presented is critical. Framing an analysis is very important in aiding comprehension of what East Asian and Southeast Asian studies are about and how knowledge in the field is reproduced.

The "knowledge baseline" approach is useful in making sense of this framing process. Social scientific knowledge (the humanities included) about East Asia and Southeast Asia has a clear knowledge baseline, meaning a continuous and inter-related intellectual-cum-conceptual ground, that is founded on its own history. The two popular concepts used frequently to characterize East Asia and Southeast Asia are "plurality" and "plural society", both of which are socio-scientific constructs that emerged from empirical studies conducted within East Asia and Southeast Asia by scholars from outside the region. In historical terms, or during the "proto-globalization" era, "plurality" characterized East Asia and Southeast Asia before the coming of the Europeans, who subsequently divided the region into "plural societies". Plurality here signifies free-flowing, natural processes beyond mere migration, and includes cultural borrowings and adaptations. The polities of the time expressed a flexible non-bureaucratic structure focusing on management and ceremony by demonstrative rulers. States, governments and nation states that rely on an elaborate bureaucratic system did not really exist until the Europeans arrived. The colonialists dismantled the traditional polities of Southeast Asia and evolved their own systems of governance based on "colonial knowledge", giving rise to "plural societies". The Japanese later reconstructed and deconstructed major structures in the European colonies they invaded, and the "knowledge" used to construct Japanese colonies, especially Taiwan and Korea, was different from that used by the Europeans.

Historically, therefore, plural society signifies both "coercion" and "separation". It evolved after the introduction of knowledge, social constructs, vocabulary, idioms and institutions hitherto unknown to the indigenous population (such as maps, census, museums and ethnic categories), the assimilation of local economies into a colonial market-oriented economy, and the installation of systematized hegemonic politics as well new techniques of presentation (read print capitalism). The modern nation-states or state-nations in East Asia and Southeast Asia emerged from this complex of plural societies. It is not difficult to show that social scientific knowledge on East Asia and Southeast Asia has moved along this plurality–plural society continuum. When scholars conduct research on pre-European East Asia and Southeast Asia, they are compelled to respond to the reality of the "proto-globalization" East Asian and Southeast Asian plurality of that period. The region was then a meeting place of civilizations and cultures, where converging winds and currents brought people together from all over the world who were interested in "God, gold and glory", and where groups of indigenes moved in various circuits to seek their fortunes. Whether or not an Orientalist approach is employed, one cannot avoid writing about that period within a plurality framework, and one cannot ignore the region's diversity and traditions. In other words, this social reality to a large extent configures analytical frameworks for the study of that period.

However, for the period after colonial rule had been established and plural societies created, to be followed later by nation states, analytical frameworks were forced to change. Not only did the reality of the plural society have to be addressed, the complex of plural societies in the region exerted influences too obvious to be denied. To handle this, analytical frameworks narrowed to studies of the nation state, the ethnic group, inter-nation-state relations, intra-nation-state problems, nationalism and so on. This gave rise to what may be called "methodological nationalism", a construction and usage of knowledge based mainly on the "territoriality" of the nation state and not on the notion that social life is a universal and geographically fluid phenomenon. Hence appeared disciplines such as "Japanese studies", "Indonesian studies", "Korean studies", "Malaysian studies", "Thai studies" and so on.

With the advent of the Cold War and the modernization efforts of newly independent nations, analysts further narrowed their frames of reference. They began to talk of poverty and basic needs in the rural areas of a particular nation, also focusing on resistance and warfare, slums in urban areas, economic growth of smallholder farmers, etc. The interests of particular disciplines, such as anthropology, became even narrower when focus was put on particular communities in remote areas, some particular battle in a mountain area, a failed irrigation project in a delta, or the gender identity of an ethnic minority in a market town.

In truth, the number of studies produced on East Asia and Southeast Asia in the plural society context surpasses by many times those produced on East Asia and Southeast Asia in the plurality context. Although social scientific studies about East Asia and Southeast Asia developed rapidly after World War II, the focus became increasingly narrow not only within academic disciplines but also in order to conform to the boundaries of modern post-colonial nations. Hence, social scientific knowledge on East Asia and Southeast Asia became, to borrow a Javanese term, *kraton*ized (compartmentalized). It is inevitable that a substantial amount of social scientific knowledge about East Asia or Southeast Asia should have been paradigmatically generated and contextualized within the plural society framework since the "nation state" as an analytical category has a higher academic and political status, than, say, the plurality perception of the Penans of Central Borneo. These Penans, like their ancestors centuries ago, move freely between Indonesia and Malaysia to eke out a living alongside other tribal groups and foreign traders, ignoring the existence of political boundaries. In fact, anthropologists seem to have found it expedient analytically, scientifically and academically to separate Penans in Indonesia from those in Malaysia when, in reality, they are one and the same people.

Thus, the plurality–plural society continuum is not only a "knowledge baseline" but also configures the social reality within which people exist day-to-day. The presence of ICT does not alter this fact. Instead, ICT enhances the plurality–plural society conceptual-cum-analytic divide when new digital databases uncritically accept the existing knowledge grid as a given fact. The voluminous empirical material, published and unpublished, that are now accessible in digital form, either online or offline, continue to be classified and catalogued according to the logic of this grid.

THE REINVENTION OF TRADITIONAL VALUES: SHARING THE ATMA EXPERIENCE

The case study presented here demonstrates where the methodological application goes beyond the particular case. No doubt similar efforts that we are not aware of are being made in other countries in East Asia, especially in local languages. The case study of ATMA will both provide explanations and raise questions regarding the project's conceptualization and operationalization.

THE CONCEPT AND THE INSTITUTION

ATMA has an interesting history. Established in 1970 as the Department of Malay Language and Literature, it was upgraded in December 1972 to an academic institute and renamed The Institute of Malay Language, Literature and Culture, known by its Malay acronym, IBKKM. In 1993 IBKKM was again renamed, this time as the Institute of the Malay World and Civilization (ATMA). ATMA's declared core concern is the promotion of "Malay studies", for both "academic analysis" and "public advocacy". "Malay studies" has roots in the colonial epoch and is another instance of the colonial invasion of epistemological space. Syed Naguib Al-Attas, the founding director of IBKKM, held the view that Malay studies began with Stamford Raffles, a merchant-scholar and "Agent to the Governor-General with the Malay States", who in the first decade of 1800 visited Malacca to collect old Malay manuscripts and who subsequently mooted the idea that an educational institution for the natives of the Malay world should be established. In Raffles' words, as quoted by Al-Attas (see *Buku Panduan* 1972, p. 14):

> (An educational) institution of the nature of a Native College which shall embrace not only the object of educating the higher classes of the native population, but at the same time that of affording instruction to the officers of the Company in native languages and of facilitating our more general researches into the history, condition and resources of these countries. It is from the banks of the Ganges to the utmost limits of China and Japan and to New-Holland that the influence of our proposed Institution is calculated to extend.

Raffles even suggested the appointment of "native professors" to teach Malay, Bugis and Siamese, with supporting staff to teach Chinese, Javanese, Burmese, Pali and Arabic. The idea of Malay studies thus exercised a strong influence over a considerable length of time on Raffles' mind. It was, however, not until a hundred years later, in 1919, that such a college was established. This institution was, however, not similar to that envisaged by Raffles. Appropriately, it was named after him — "Raffles College". It functioned as a "University College", such as those affiliated to the University of London, running a three-year undergraduate degree course, teaching English, geography, history, economics, mathematics, physics and chemistry. A notable absence was "Malay studies", a field dear to Raffles.

It was not until 1949 that Raffles College, together with the King Edward VII College of Medicine, was jointly upgraded to "University College of Malaya". Within this new organization, Malay studies finally found a space. A Department of Malay Studies, alongside a Department of Chinese Studies and a Department of Tamil Studies, was set up. Za'aba, or Zainal Abidin Ahmad, an eminent scholar, was its first Head of Department. About a decade later, in 1957, the year of independence for the Federation of Malaya, the Faculty of Arts at the University of Malaya (UM), was shifted to Kuala Lumpur from Singapore. The Department of Malay Studies then expanded its scope to include the study of culture, modern and classical Malay literature, and also modern linguistics. In 1970, when the Malay language became the sole medium of instruction in government-funded national schools, and UKM (Universiti Kebangsaan Malaysia) was established, scholars at the Malay Department that was to become ATMA were already critical of the furtherance of the Malay-oriented "nationalist/ethnic cause". It thus started with a political agenda that was quite different from that of the Department of Malay Studies at UM.

The institution at UM was clearly founded as part of a colonial project, and because "nationalist" Malay academics from that body were involved in the setting up of UKM at large, a political-historical connection between the two institutions has always existed. Because of this, it is sometimes argued that ATMA has nevertheless been a post-independence Malay ethnic project promoting Malay language-based knowledge and consolidating "Malayness". Thus, "Malay studies", though a colonial epistemology, quickly became an integral part of the post-independence project, and was central to the epistemology of nation-building in Malaysia, particularly in the defining of a Malay-based "national culture", "national language", "national education system", "national identity", "national integration", and so on. This last concern was not unrelated to the launching of the pro-Malay affirmative action policy called the New Economic Policy of 1971–1990, a long-term economic strategy for building the Malaysian nation.

ATMA's participation in the post-independence project intensified when it became involved in a number of programmes initiated together with Malay literary NGOs such as GAPENA (*Gabungan Penulis Nasional* or the National Writers Union, a loosely organized, nationality-based writers' association) and quasi-government bodies in charge of the Malay language and its development (such as Dewan Bahasa and Pustaka). ATMA's major role was to be the academic platform for international conferences and meetings about the Malay world, the organizer of overseas "educational and study" trips to visit "Malays" in various parts of the world (the "Malay diaspora"), and the publisher of material for enhancing both popular and academic knowledge about the Malays as an ethnic group. Slowly, "Malay studies" in the 1970s and 1980s became the study of the "ethnic Malays" instead of the "Malay world", more specifically Malays in Peninsular Malaysia and not so much Malays in East Malaysia, Brunei, Indonesia or Singapore. The topic of Malays in Singapore was under the purview, so to speak, of the Department of Malay Studies, National University of Singapore, while the study of Malays in Brunei constituted the academic and research domain of the Academy of Brunei Studies, Universiti Brunei Darussalam.

Such parcelling of knowledge was an expression of the afore-mentioned "methodological nationalism" as well as the "ethnicization of knowledge" that narrowed Malay studies to the subject of the "Malay ethnic". It soon became apparent, especially to the UKM academic leadership, that a widening of ATMA's focus from "Malay studies as an ethnic study" to "Malay world studies as area studies" was needed if the richness, diversity and pluralism of the Malay world were to be properly acknowledged. In the latter construction, the word "Malay" refers to a historical, geo-political reality inhabited by locals and foreigners and not to a particular ethnic group. This applies even though an ethnic group known by that name does exist in the region, whose language has become the regional *lingua franca* and who has furnished the major cultural elements that give the region conceptual unity. The scientific unity of the Malay world as a "biological geo-body", it should be remembered, was established by the famous British naturalist, Alfred Russel Wallace, in his famous book *Malay Archipelago* (1869).

For a long time, the colonial understanding of "Malay studies" has been influential, not only in academic circles around the world but also in Malaysia's own political arena. Indeed, even in post-colonial Malaysia, "Malay studies" has always been associated with Malaysia's ethnic Malay-centred post-independence ideology. As noted above, this association narrowed the empirical focus to Malays living in Peninsular Malaysia. While it can be argued that such a focus has been important for political reasons, it nevertheless limits the scope and activity of the academic enterprise. Nevertheless, the view that "Malay studies" should concentrate on the ethnic Malay remains alive today, especially among academics who proclaim themselves "Malay nationalists" or "defenders of the Malays".

For instance, even though ATMA has been actively promoting the concept of the "Malay diaspora" since the late 1980s (for example, through works on "lost cousins" in Sri Lanka, Vietnam, Champa, South Africa, Madagascar, Western Australia, Saudi Arabia and elsewhere), there is nonetheless a clear absence of a rigorous academic debate on the theme of the "Malay diaspora" despite the publications that resulted from trips to those places. Findings from these trips have been dominated by, and therefore limited to, what may be called a pseudo-scientific "litmus test" approach in which each journey had the mission of determining, as it were, the level of "Malayness" of the people studied, as compared to Malays in Malaysia. Some of the findings may have shored up a notional benchmark for Malayness that was useful in political and academic exercises, and may even have led to an increase in publications on Malays around the world. This approach, however, does not further serious academic study of the Malay world and its civilization. This shortcoming is particularly glaring when found within the precincts of a university-based research institute bearing the name, "Institute of the Malay World and Civilization".

THE PARADIGM SHIFT

In April 1999, ATMA decided to re-embrace the original concept of Malay studies as an orientation around "the Malay world" rather than the "Malay ethnic". Perhaps it is useful to note that the scholars promoting this change have different ethnic origins — Malay, Chinese, Indian, Japanese and European — and specialize in different disciplines within the natural and social sciences and the humanities. Indeed, their expertise on various aspects of the Malay world is recognized internationally, largely through their research and publications.

Although the analogy may not be a perfect fit, it is still useful, as Wolters points out, to perceive the Malay world as a "Mediterranean" in the sense that it is a physical as well as a cultural space where civilizations have met throughout the ages. The Malay world has indeed been the location where the Chinese, Indian, Arabian, European and other world civilizations have come together and interacted. Similarly, the dialogues between these civilizations have produced a diverse yet integrated network that typified pluralism long before the term came into fashion. For this reason, the Malay world, like the Mediterranean, has been a significant contributor to developments in both the physical and the social sciences. Among examples that readily come to mind are the contribution of Alfred Wallace and his letters to Charles Darwin before Darwin's *Origin of Species* was published in 1859; the theory of "economic dualism" by the Dutch economist Boeke; the theory of the "plural society" by Furnivall; the "interpretation of culture" paradigm made famous by anthropologist Clifford Geertz; and a critique on Orientalism by Syed Hussein Alatas, author of the famous book, *Myth of the Lazy Native* (1977), and his brother, Syed Naguib al-Attas, who wrote about "Islam and secularism" in the Malay world.

Knowing the importance of the Malay world conceived as a "Mediterranean" and knowing its contribution to the global tradition of knowledge production, ATMA thought it time to take stock of how the corpus of knowledge about the Malay world, or "Malay world studies", has been constituted and disseminated throughout the world in so many different languages and within equally many language-communities: firstly, in Europe in English, French, German, Dutch, Nordic, Spanish, Russian, Italian, Polish and others, and, secondly, in Asia in Arabic, Chinese, Hindi, Urdu, Japanese, Persian, Armenian, Turkish, Thai, Vietnamese and so on. This effort at stock-taking has of course involved subsequent dissemination of collected materials, and has happily generated, since April 1999, three major inter-related projects at ATMA.

The first took the form of international colloquia, the second the construction of a digital database, and the third the production of interactive CDs on classical Malay texts (or *hikayat*) and other Malay world traditions for the younger audience. Each is envisaged eventually to generate further academic and non-academic spin-offs. From the international colloquia, for example, we expect the formation of new local and foreign networks that may lead to joint publications, research projects, seminars and the like. The digital database is just the beginning of bigger things such as the establishment of an e-commerce portal that incorporates materials of an academic and non-academic nature accessible to a wider market-oriented audience. The interactive CDs will hopefully revive interest, or at least increase the inquisitiveness of the younger generation, in important classical texts, and provide glimpses into the historical thought systems and lifestyles of peoples in the Malay world.

Project 1

Encouraged by the inspiration that studies of the Malay world has exercised on various fields of knowledge, ATMA researchers and associates from various academic fields came to realize that it was time to investigate further the processes of theory construction relevant to the Malay world. To that end, ATMA has launched a long-term project called "The Construction of the Malay World by Others", aimed at examining closely the writings from as far back in time as possible by non-Southeast Asian writers, academics and others, about this region. The project also seeks to examine the way relevant writers came to view and analyse their own societies in the course of their experiences of the Malay world. The presence at ATMA of the "Grand Old Man" Professor Syed Hussein Alatas, the author of the much quoted and referenced classic study, *The Myth of the Lazy Native* (1977), has been a source of inspiration for this project. His critique on European Orientalism, which preceded that of Edward Said's, provided the blueprint for ATMA to conceptualize and operationalize the international colloquia project and its spin-offs.

ATMA's series of international colloquia began in November 2000, and has so far examined "Dutch scholarship and the Malay World" (November 2000), "French scholarship and the Malay World" (April 2001), "Nordic scholarship and the Malay World" (November 2001), "German-speaking scholarship and the Malay World" (March 2002) and "Chinese scholarship and the Malay world" (September 2002). Plans for the future include "Japanese scholarship and the Malay world", "Indian scholarship and the Malay world", "Arab-speaking scholarship and the Malay world", "British scholarship and the Malay world" and "Natural Science and the Malay world". Intensive efforts are presently being made to realize these meetings with the help of various individual academics, academic institutions and funding bodies throughout the world. The series aims at demonstrating the significant global contribution to knowledge construction in numerous fields inspired by studies done in and of the Malay world. More importantly, it seeks to stimulate scholars in the Malay world itself to match the outstanding research done by "others". This is a crucial and not impossible task. It demands a great deal of rethinking, self-reflection and self-criticism about the development and maintenance of high quality scholarship and research.

A number of proceedings from the colloquia have been published in different forms and are publicly available. Selected contributions from the colloquium on the "Chinese Scholarship and the Malay World" was published as a book in September 2003, edited jointly by Ding Choo Ming of ATMA and Ooi Kee Beng of Stockholm University (*Chinese Studies of the Malay World*. Singapore: Times Media Publishers, Marshall Cavendish). The KITLV in Leiden and ATMA have come to a preliminary agreement to publish jointly a series called "The Malay World Studies Series" that shall consist of volumes of selected essays from the various colloquia, dealing separately with Dutch, French, Germanic and Nordic contributions to knowledge about the Malay world. It has been no easy task getting these scholars together and soliciting their contributions. However, with the presence at ATMA of Jim Collins, a world-renowned scholar on Malay dialectology, this project has been made possible.

The international colloquia have not only led to publications but also to new scholarly networks being formed across the globe. ATMA also began to receive more foreign students, either enrolled in our research-based M.Litt.

and Ph.D. courses or as non-graduating students. We have also begun to receive donations from foreign foundations interested in funding our projects, and scholarships and fellowships have been offered to our students or researchers.

Project 2

In 2000, a "Malay World Database", simply called PADAT (*Pangkalan Data Alam dan Tamadun Melayu*), was established by ATMA. It consists of a collection of single-article texts (in Malay and English) indexed and catalogued according to author, title, source and keywords, and was created by world-class Malay world studies scholars from ATMA, with the assistance of local ICT graduates. This collection is now available both in print (photocopy) form and also online. There are also plans to make it available offline, perhaps in a CD-ROM version. The biggest challenge for ATMA now is the obtaining of permission for each article or text from the copyright holders. It has been successful in some cases but failed in others, and is currently awaiting permission for the public use of the rest of the material in the database. As of December 2003, the collection consisted of about 35,000 articles. The aim was to reach at least 50,000 articles by the end of 2005. Making such a large and growing collection accessible on the Internet has brought status and fame to ATMA, despite the fact that the project was initially received with much scepticism. It will undoubtedly become the single largest database on the Malay world accessible electronically from anywhere in the world <URL: www.atma.ukm.my>.

In 2003, the "Malaycivilization.com Project" began in earnest, the aim of which was to construct an interactive portal. The main platform for this portal is already in place, and contains several databases, some of which are built around images and sounds, while most are in textual form. There is still much that needs to be done to make the portal professionally useful and effective. Access to the portal is still free, but registration is required. In the near future, a fee will be charged to cover maintenance costs. Substantial funds for this project were granted by the Malaysian Government, and by private funding bodies. The whole exercise involved cooperation from the private, the community and the public sector for the comprehensive and wide range of subjects and contents to be made available. This Malay language portal is one of a kind in the world today, with "Malay world studies" as the core. Just as the Malay region historically interacted with the rest of the world through trade in the fifteenth century, it is hoped that continuing contacts and exchanges will take place between the Malay world and the rest of the globe with the help of the Internet in the twenty-first century.

Project 3

One of the major records of the values and practices of different communities and polities in the pre-European Malay world are classical Malay texts known as *hikayat*. These are *istana-sentrik* (palace-centric) documents recording official functions, protocols, genealogies and even stories of conspiracies and scandals. They are publicly available, and were originally salvaged by scholars and colonial officers from all sorts of sources. Some of them have become standard texts in the teaching of Malay literature at all levels of education. These texts and their commentaries are thus largely available in paper-based form, such as books, newspaper cuttings, magazine articles and schoolbooks, which makes the need all the stronger for them to be made available in digital form.

In 2002, ATMA embarked on a project to digitize different forms of classical Malay literature — such as proverbs, adages, pantuns, poems, hikayat and the like — for public consumption in the form of interactive CDs. For its first attempt, it chose to transform the famous classical Malay literary text *Sejarah Melayu*, or Malay Annals. Even though the technology used for this had been available on the market for more than a decade, no attempt had been made to turn *Sejarah Melayu* into an interactive CD. After much painstaking effort, it was launched in 2003, in Malay. The English version came out in January 2004. This CD tries to meet the need of the younger generation to know and understand traditional values, but does not take a stand as to whether these values should be reinvented or not. At the end of the day, the users have to decide what they would like to do with their new knowledge. For ATMA, this is but a small beginning, and much remains to be done.

CONCLUSION

One of the unspoken aims of these projects is of course to revive and maintain general interest in the traditions and cultures of the peoples of the Malay world, not only amongst the peoples from Southeast Asia themselves but also beyond. The discovery of one's heritage can take place through contacts with an oral tradition or a written text. ATMA's projects intend to accumulate sources — texts, digitized images and sounds — and provide channels for such discoveries.

Indeed, one has to know what traditional values are and how their meanings and articulations varied in different historical epochs before one can ponder what to do about them. ATMA is hopeful that its projects can help provide the initial critical knowledge that is needed before the journey towards reinventing traditional values for future use can start.

References

Abdel Malik, Anouar. *Civilization and Social Theory*. London: Macmillan, 1983.

Alatas, Syed Hussein. *The Myth of the Lazy Native*. London: Frank Cass, 1977.

Al-Attas, Syed Naguib. *Preliminary Statement on the General Theory of the Islamization of the Malay-Indonesia Archipelago*. Kuala Lumpur: Dewan Bahasa and Pustaka, 1969.

Buku Panduan: Jabatan Bahasa dan Kesusasteraan Melayu, Universiti Kebangsaan Malaysia, Kuala Lumpur, 1972.

Chelliah, D.D. *A History of the Educational Policy of the Straits Settlements with Recommendations for a New System Based on Vernaculars*. Ph.D. thesis, University of London, 1940.

Cohn, Bernard. *Colonialism and its Forms of Knowledge: The British in India*. Princeton (New Jersey): Princeton University Press, 1996.

———. *An Anthropologist among the Historians and Other Essays*. Delhi: Oxford University Press, 1986.

Mohd Taib Osman. *Pengajian Melayu Sebagai Bidang Ilmu di Universiti,* Inaugural Lecture for the Chair of Malay Studies, Kuala Lumpur: University of Malaya Press, 1991.

Said, Edward. *Orientalism*. Hammondsworth: Penguin, 1978.

———. *Covering Islam*. New York: Pantheon, 1981.

———. *Culture and Imperialism*. London: Chatto, 1993.

Shamsul A.B. *Antropologi dan Modenisasi: Mengungkapkan Pengalaman Malaysia,* Professorial Inaugural Lecture, Bangi: Penerbit UKM, 1993.

———. Ethnicity, Class, Culture or Identity? Competing Paradigms in Malaysian Studies *Akademika* 53 (1998): 33–59.

———. Colonial Knowledge and Identity Formation: Literature and the Construction of Malay and Malayness. *Asian Culture Quarterly* 28, no. 1 (2000): 49–64.

———. "Malay" and "Malayness" in Malaysia Reconsidered: A Critical Review", *Communal/Plural* 9, no. 1 (2001): 69–80.

Shamsul, A.B. and Rumaizah Mohamed. "Globalization, ICT and Islam after September 11: A Brief Commentary". A paper for a seminar on "Islam, Globalization and the Knowledge Economy: Issues and Challenges", organized by International Institute of Public Policy and Management (INPUMA), Universiti Malaya, at Shah Alam, on 26 March 2002.

Shamsul, A.B., Rumaizah Mohamed and Haslindawati Hamzah. Pengajian Alam

Melayu di Pentas Global: Teknologi Maklumat dan Penstrukturan Ilmu di ATMA, UKM. A paper for a national seminar on "Language and Malay Thought: Malay Excellence in the ICT Era", organized by Akademi Pengajian Melayu, Universiti Malaya, Kuala Lumpur, 18–19 June 2002.

Shamsul, A.B., Rumaizah Mohamed and Haslindawati Hamzah. "Knowledge Production and Globalization: Is ICT really Critical?" A paper for the international conference on "Globalisation, Culture and Inequalities — In Honour of the Work of the Late Professor Ishak Shari", organized by IKMAS, Universiti Kebangsaan Malaysia, Bangi, Malaysia, held on 19–21 August 2002.

Wilkinson, R.J. *Papers on Malay Subjects*. Selected and Introduced by P.L. Burns, Kuala Lumpur: Oxford University Press, 1971.

Winstedt, R.W. *The Malays: A Cultural History,* Revised and updated by Tham Seong Chee, Singapore: Graham Brash, 1988.

Wolters, O.W. *History, Culture, and Region in Southeast Asian Perspectives,* Revised edition, Singapore: Institute of Southeast Asian Studies, 1999.

Wallace, Alfred Russell. *The Malay Archipelago, the Land of the Orang-Utan and the Bird of Paradise: A Narrative of Travel with Studies of Man and Nature.* London: Macmillan, 1869.

10

THE DYNAMIC GROWTH ORDER IN EAST AND SOUTHEAST ASIA
Strategic Challenges and Prospects in the Post-9/11 Era

K.S. Nathan

INTRODUCTION: GLOBALIZATION AND POLITICAL STABILITY IN EAST AND SOUTHEAST ASIA

The East Asian region as a whole (both Northeast and Southeast Asia) has evidenced a remarkable growth pattern since the late 1980s and early 1990s — a trend that was somewhat deflected by the Asian Financial Crisis in the late 1990s. Economic recovery and growth appear to have come back on track after the turn of the century. However, this most recent period of growth has being punctuated by the SARS epidemic (2003), and most recently, by the outbreak of bird flu in East Asia. Will these negative developments in the health sector affect overall economic growth and political stability as well as regional security? There is no doubt that the 11 September 2001 (9/11) terrorist attacks in the United States did and continues to have an impact on external and regional perceptions and policies regarding Asia-Pacific security. In any case, the more interesting feature of the post-9/11 scenario lies along two dimensions: First, the nature of initiatives and responses by East Asian (especially ASEAN) governments to the terrorist threat, and second, the glaring inability of international terrorism to overthrow or significantly alter the political, social, and territorial *status quo* in the region.

Globalization understood in terms of its totalizing economic, political, social and cultural impact on human civilization is a fairly recent phenomenon that commenced with the advance of Western imperialism and territorial conquest in the latter half of the nineteenth and early twentieth centuries. The non-Western world was arguably globalized by the imperial activities of Western powers and also Japan, whose emergence as a military-industrial power under the Meiji restoration gave the "Land of the Rising Sun" the same imperial energy and drive that had characterized the Europeans. Nevertheless, in the aftermath of the two world wars, the world community essentially accepted the nation-state process of globalization, and symbolized the post-World War II *status quo* by establishing the United Nations in 1945. Henceforth, unilateral ambitions were to be moderated by multi-lateral impulses through the machinery of international organization, and pacific settlements of disputes achieved through the medium of international law. Multi-lateralism in trade and economic matters was also endorsed under the General Agreement on Tariffs and Trade (GATT) system, whilst the 1944 Bretton-Woods agreement attempted to stabilize the international monetary system. Despite all human efforts to create a more humane international order, the struggle for political dominance and the search for security through "realist" rather than "institutionalist" approaches still remain largely embedded in the foreign policies of states.

Faith in multilateralism and the United Nations was dealt a heavy blow in the crisis over Iraq and the subsequent invasion (19 March–9 April 2003) and occupation of that country by the United States and Britain. The United Nations could only be a mere observer in that brief conflict — and even the five custodians of international security (Britain, France, United States, Russia and China) failed to avert crisis and war over Iraq's presumed possession of weapons of mass destruction (WMD). To date, evidence unearthed by both the American and international authorities tends virtually to conclude that Saddam Hussein's Iraq did not possess WMD. Nevertheless, the apparent paralysis of the United Nations has not deterred regional organizations such as ASEAN from devising methods and strategies to address issues of regional and international security within their competence. Indeed, East and Southeast Asia are cohering even more in the economic, political and security fields. Finding regional solutions to regional problems through collective action, and through cooperation with external powers, appears to be the strategy adopted by ASEAN in dealing with strategic challenges in the post-9/11 era.

THE POLITICAL/IDEOLOGICAL DIMENSION OF GLOBALIZATION: ISLAMIC MILITANCY IN SOUTHEAST ASIA

Globalization understood as an integrative process in terms of the pace and volume of political, economic, military, social, intellectual, technological and cultural transactions and exchanges, invariably produces an uneven impact on the global community. This community is after all, politically divided into 191 extremely heterogeneous Nation-States, with tremendous diversity in all the indices stated above. Cultural globalism is necessarily modified by local conditions that in turn stem from geography, history, ideology, and the capability of humans to transact their needs and address challenges at various levels. In this regard, one may even evaluate this phenomenon in terms of "subjects" or initiators, and "objects" or recipients, of global processes. Individuals, communities and states that are more adapt at coping with, and benefiting from, globalization will welcome it as a process that enhances their material condition, while those lacking the necessary skills may not only fear its impact, but also react negatively to its manifestations. An NGO activist from Thailand has even claimed that "globalization is endangering every part of society, and perhaps economic globalization is the most powerful cause of many social illnesses".[1] Is terrorism therefore a negative response to globalization or cultural globalism?

The terrorism unleashed in Southeast Asia, and more specifically, on Bali in Indonesia on 12 October 2002 and at the J.W. Marriott Hotel in Jakarta on 5 August 2003 needs further analysis if we are to understand why a generally peace-loving and tolerant people with a rich tradition of cultural pluralism would allow a few misguided individuals to unleash such violence on innocent people. Nevertheless, some answers do exist as to how cultural globalism impacts upon local (individual/group), or even national identity.

Islamic revivalism and resurgence since the Khomeini Revolution in 1979 is becoming a more visible as well as salient factor in the politics and security considerations of several countries in the region, including Muslim-majority Indonesia and Malaysia, and also the Philippines and Thailand (the latter two being ASEAN countries with vocal Muslim minorities). Extremist ideologies, be they religious or otherwise, tend to feed more easily on the failure of governments on the socio-economic front, take advantage of poor governance and ineffective legal systems, and thrive on rampant corruption. Additionally, secular globalization is viewed by radical Muslims as un-Islamic and contrary to the teachings of the Quran. They would like to see the emergence of a local, national, regional, and if possible, global world order that is truly based on Islamic principles. They consider existing Islamic legal, political, economic and social systems to be at best incomplete, and therefore ineffective in promoting or achieving justice, development and prosperity. More assertive or radical Muslims are frustrated by the powerlessness of the Muslim world *vis-à-vis* the Western industrialized, capitalist and secular world. Professor Azyumardi Azra, a well-known Indonesian expert on political Islam, notes that while Islamic revivalism is continually gaining momentum, there are signs that many secular nation states in the Muslim world have failed to keep their promises, with the result that the centre stage is being hijacked by Islamic movements and leaders offering more radical solutions that can empower Muslims, such as the establishment of an "Islamic state" [*al-khilafah*].[2] Being unable to change the power equation through existing channels and structures that they would claim to be stacked against Islam, certain ideologues such as Osama bin Laden and his disciples the world over have decided that the only weapon for change available to them is "terror". They are fully convinced that Muslim identities can never flourish in a West-dominated international system — hence the option is to wreck it in the rather faint hope that the changes brought about will favour the Islamic world.

The existing nation-state system in the non-Western world, which Muslim discontents would argue is the product of Western imperialism and colonialism, is the cause of the continuing disproportional balance of power between Islam and the West. Yet, it must be noted that Islamists are actually attempting to craft the "Islamic state" onto an originally secular political entity whose attributes are fairly finite — territoriality, sovereignty, municipal government and legal system — and which has a capacity to transact business with other nation states with similar politico-legal attributes. There is thus a conflation of "Islamic identity" with "national identity", resulting therefore in confusion about what is desirable and what is possible. As Azra himself notes, the caliphate of yesteryears was itself an undemocratic concept, and any attempt to reconstruct an Islamic national identity through the model of an "Islamic state" within Indonesia's present national borders, for example, would be unrealizable.

Since the 1990s, Islamic organizations such as Hizb al-Tahir and Jamaah Tarbiyah, which entertain such dreams and which were suppressed during the Suharto era, have been using their new-found freedom under democratization to rekindle support.[3] By extension, certain Jemaah Islamiyah (JI) elements are also advocating the creation of an "Islamic nation" encompassing southern Thailand, Malaysia, Indonesia, Singapore and southern Philippines. Such grandiose designs run counter to the UN-endorsed principles of international relations and inter-state cooperation through bodies such as ASEAN in Southeast Asia, and the EAEC and ASEAN+3 encompassing all of East Asia. In the event, it is unclear how East Asia will deal with a security scenario where transnational religious terrorism threatens regional stability and security.

ASEAN'S COUNTER-TERROR STRATEGIES AS RESPONSE TO THE MILITANT DIMENSION OF ISLAMIC GLOBALIZATION — THE INSTITUTIONAL APPROACH

ASEAN responded to 9/11 through official declarations at summit level by strongly condemning the attacks, and pledging to work very closely with the United Nations and also the United States in organizing a Global Coalition Against Terror. Malaysia, as a strong advocate of ASEAN-based regional cooperation, joined in the collective condemnation at the Seventh ASEAN Summit (Brunei 2001), and the Eighth ASEAN Summit (Phnom Penh 2002). The Brunei Summit issued a strong statement that the 9/11 attack on the United States "was a direct challenge to the attainment of peace, progress and prosperity of ASEAN and the realization of ASEAN Vision 2020".[4] Besides, the APEC Forum was another platform for ASEAN members to join forces with global players such as the United States, China and Japan in condemning terrorism. The members of both fora attempted to implement UNSC Resolution 1373, which was unanimously adopted on 28 September 2001. Resolution 1373 *inter alia* obliges all UN member states to: (a) prevent and suppress the financing of terrorist acts, (b) criminalize the wilful provision or collection by their nationals of terrorist-related funds, (c) freeze without delay terrorist-related funds and other financial assets, economic resources or property that can be used for the commission of terror, (d) prohibit their nationals from making available funds, resources and facilities for the benefit of potential terrorists, and (e) engage in bilateral, regional, and multilateral cooperation to suppress international terrorism.[5]

Pursuant to UNSC Resolution 1373, the regional grouping held the ASEAN Ad Hoc Experts Group meeting in Bali, Indonesia in January 2002 to implement the ASEAN Plan of Action to Combat Transnational Crime. Eight task forces were established aimed at combating: (1) terrorism, (2) trafficking in persons, (3) arms smuggling, (4) sea piracy, (5) money laundering, (6) illicit drug trafficking, (7) international economic crime, and (8) cyber crime. At another institutional forum, that is, the ASEAN Regional Forum (ARF), the twenty-three-member regional security consultative group held a workshop in April 2002 under the auspices of the Thai and Australian governments. Malaysia took a further step in hosting the Special ASEAN Ministerial Meeting on Transnational Crime in May 2002, in furtherance of Resolution 1373. Being also a leading member of the fifty-seven-nation Organization of Islamic Conference (OIC), Kuala Lumpur hosted an Extraordinary Meeting of OIC Foreign Ministers on Terrorism in April 2002. However, Malaysia argued that state-based strategies and policies to combat terror must necessarily be premised on an internationally agreed definition of terrorism. Prime Minister Mahathir proposed that anyone who attacks civilians is a terrorist, and that acts of terror must include the attack on the World Trade Centre in New York in September 2001, suicide bomb attacks by Palestinians and the Tamil Tigers, attacks on civilians by Israeli security forces, and the killing of Bosnian Muslims.[6] Nevertheless, the failure of the OIC meeting in Kuala Lumpur to reach a consensus on an acceptable definition of terrorism is highly suggestive of the problematique itself. The more one tries to universalize its definition, the more likely it is to remain undefined for policy purposes, thereby forestalling collective action against terrorists. Arab and Middle Eastern OIC members withheld support for Mahathir's definition since it also branded the Palestinians as terrorists. They disagreed with Mahathir's concept on the grounds that the Palestinian struggle was aimed at regaining land taken by Israel since the 1967 Arab-Israeli war.[7] It is for these political-ideological reasons that Malaysia as an OIC member is now attempting to step out of the political agenda and instead focus the organization's energies on the economic and educational improvement of the one-third of poor people in the world who are Muslims.

For most ASEAN members, cooperation with the United States should not be confined purely to the military dimension, since the root causes of terrorism are multiple, and do not stem from religious compunctions alone. Malaysia concurred with the view presented by Sultan Hassanal Bolkiah on the U.S.-ASEAN Accord to Combat Global Terror, that terrorism could not be wiped out with military might alone. It was also necessary to remove the frustration and resentment that made people join or associate themselves with groups that promoted terrorism. Economic factors are very important in U.S.-ASEAN cooperation against terrorism, hence trade and economic issues continue to stay high on the agenda of the multi-faceted relationship that Washington has with the region.[8]

The effectiveness of regional cooperation is subject to national security perceptions and pressure from domestic politics and interests. In the case of Malaysia, a fundamental concern of national security managers in the wake of 9/11 is control over Islamic extremism within its borders. This goal became all the more urgent after disclosures of possible al-Qaeda links with local and regional extremist/terrorist groups. The government moved swiftly to arrest and detain over seventy suspected militants as a pre-emptive measure — to deter terrorist activities such as those in Bali on 12 October 2002. While Australia and the United States posit an external dimension to the doctrine of pre-emption, Malaysia, and arguably Singapore as well, emphasize its internal import. This form of pre-emptive strategy can limit the scope for legitimate action available to civil society in curbing governmental abuse. Yet, national security managers assert, perhaps rightfully, that the protection of the freedom and liberties of the overwhelming majority should take priority over the freedom and fundamental liberties of the few who, given the opportunity, would deprive the whole society of its right to live free from terror.

Indeed, the agenda of the "Islamic state" in Malaysia has thrown up innumerable opportunities for Islamists of different orientations from near and far to link up and consolidate their plan of action to attain their cherished goal of an "Islamic nation". The point of coherence in the ASEAN region for this grandiose design is the Jemaah Islamiah (JI), whose operational structures in Malaysia, Singapore, Indonesia and the Philippines have been seriously disrupted by governmental anti-terror action. As mentioned earlier, regional al-Qaeda operatives (JI and KMM or Kumpulan Militan Malaysia, initially known as Kumpulan Mujahideen Malaysia) have thus far failed "to destroy the precarious work of post-colonial nation building in Southeast Asia with an Islamic arrangement".[9] Other than the arms heist carried out by the religious sect of Al-Ma'unah in Perak, Malaysia in July 2000, the country has been relatively safe from religious terrorists — largely due to pre-emptive action and police and intelligence cooperation with ASEAN neighbours, that is, Malaysia's FPDA partners (Singapore, Australia, New Zealand and Britain), and also the United States through the bilateral U.S.-Malaysia Anti-Terrorism Pact signed in May 2002.

ADDRESSING COLLECTIVELY THE TRANSNATIONAL CHALLENGE OF RADICAL ISLAM

Radical Islam's transnational nature invariably requires governments to resist by adopting regional strategies with a clear multi-lateral dimension. ASEAN has been moving quite steadily in that direction since 9/11. However, the efficacy of this approach is necessarily diluted by the rather strict adherence by member states to the principle of national sovereignty. A few years ago, Thai Foreign Minister Surin Pitsuwan attempted to circumvent this problem by proposing a formula for "flexible engagement", but encountered resistance from the majority. The objective was to build and strengthen ASEAN's capacity to tackle internal problems in member countries that posed a threat to regional security.[10] Only Bangkok and Manila were agreeable to the idea while the other eight members, including the two Muslim-majority states — Malaysia and Indonesia — preferred to stick to the non-interference principle, thus scuttling a radical new approach to ASEAN regional cooperation. Arguably, this new form of capacity-building to deal with transnational terrorism manifested through local and regional networks of Osama bin Laden's al-Qaeda organization requires heightened vigilance at the domestic level. Malaysia, in particular, in response to the pressures and prospects of the global Islamic revivalism that it had experienced since the 1970s, has adopted in the last decade a rather lax immigration policy towards the Muslim world. This created a space for many to identify closely with Islam and the Muslim world. Fundamentalist and radical groups quickly seized the opportunities for international movement that this offered. Eventually, they were able to consolidate to a point where they could establish local cells harbouring transnational agendas. In the process, as terrorism expert Rohan Gunaratna categorically states:

> Since the early 1990s JI's regional *shura* (operational base) in Malaysia dispatched at least 100 JI recruits from the region to train in the use of firearms and explosives in Al Qaeda's Afghan training camps at Khalden, Derunta, Khost, Siddiq and Jihad Wal. The 13 people arrested in Singapore all reported to a regional *shura* in Kuala Lumpur. The units under the regional *shura* also mirror the worldwide Al Qaeda units in both structure and *modus operandi*.[11]

The revelation that Malaysia was involved in the network of al-Qaeda was undoubtedly discomforting to Kuala Lumpur. Evidence unearthed on JI operatives and al-Qaeda-type cells in Malaysia has undoubtedly emboldened the hand of the Malaysian government to strengthen the Internal Security Act to widen what activities are to be considered highly prejudicial to national security, and a major threat to a government duly elected by the people of Malaysia. Indeed, the UMNO-led Barisan Nasional government capitalized on the fear of Islamic terrorism by assuring all Malaysians and the international community that "the Malaysian state would remain on its secular, moderate and capitalist course. UMNO leaders were careful to insist, time and again, that theirs was a brand of modern, progressive, liberal and tolerant Islam that would not allow itself to be hijacked by militant and extremist elements".[12] At the structural level, a deeper analysis of the entire accelerating process of Islamization is required if valid distinctions between "moderates" and "radicals" are to be attained. A reputed Malaysian anthropologist and scholar, Shamsul

A.B., aptly notes that conscious and conspicuous Islamization amongst Malaysian Muslims since the 1970s has been conducted not only by the Malaysian Government, but also by NGOs and other social groups and individuals. He concludes therefore that the consequences of such efforts do not necessarily lead to increased militancy amongst Malaysian Muslims, hence the justification for the widespread use of the label "moderate" by a majority of observers and analysts worldwide to characterize Malaysian Islam.[13]

The significance of the Malaysian and Singapore arrests of JI suspects lies in the profile of the detainees themselves. According to Gunaratna, "the common denominator among those arrested is neither poverty nor lack of education but a shared religious ideology that depicts the United States as the enemy of Islam and a belief that Allah will reward them for waging a global *Jihad*."[14] An additional problem of combating al-Qaeda-linked JI terrorism in Southeast Asia is the fact that its "compartmentalized, loose-knit network means that breaking up individual cells may only have a limited effect on the operation of other groups or the network as a whole". According to BBC reporter Gordon Corera, "the only way to disrupt al-Qaeda is either by infiltrating its core — almost impossible since at the centre is a highly committed, ideological group — or by destroying the entire leadership."[15] Corera also makes the point that counter-terrorism strategies are compounded by the existence of "a vast pool of potential supporters, unhappy with the economic and social dysfunction of their nations, alienated by globalization and modernization, and humiliated by American power".[16] Indeed, in the wake of the 12 October 2002 Bali bombings in which over 200 people (including 88 Australians) perished, Australian Foreign Minister Alexander Downer aptly remarked at the Anti-Terror Meeting in Bali on 4 February 2004 that the threat did not end with those bombings: "Terrorist groups are cooperating across the region using one country to train in, another to raise funds in and another for safe haven. They are working together to maximize the impact of their activities."[17]

Three ASEAN members — Indonesia, the Philippines and Malaysia — underscored their determination to fight terrorism in the region by signing an Anti-Terrorism Pact on 7 May 2002 in Putra Jaya, Malaysia's new Federal Administrative Capital (replacing Kuala Lumpur since June 1999, although Kuala Lumpur remains the capital of Malaysia). The above measures may be interpreted as state-level responses to threats of a transnational character linked to militants wanting to set up a single Islamic state comprising of these three nations. The tripartite pact is aimed at (a) targeting potential terrorist threats, and (b) devising measures to tackle money laundering, smuggling, drug trafficking, hijacking, illegal trafficking of women and children, and piracy.[18] Significantly, the three ASEAN states have been demonstrating a serious commitment to ensure that terrorists flushed out of Afghanistan would not make the region their base of operations.

Malaysia, along with other ASEAN members, has coordinated counter-terrorism measures to contain the threat from al-Qaeda. The reality of this threat was manifested by simultaneous announcements in Kuala Lumpur and Singapore of arrests of militants who had plans to bomb prominent targets in Singapore, including the embassies of the leading members of the anti-terror coalition — Australia, Britain and the United States. Specifically, the Singapore government stated that a terrorist group was targetting high value commercial and strategic assets of the United States in Singapore.[19] The arrests of Islamic militants in Indonesia, the Philippines, Singapore and Malaysia are continuing despite the lack of consensus on an acceptable and operational definition of terrorism. In the event, ASEAN members concur that the absence of unanimity on definitions need not hold back the urgent need to collaborate on an ASEAN-wide basis to stamp out this menace to regional security.[20] Thus, cooperation has been ongoing to pursue and defeat the JI in Singapore, the KMM in Malaysia, the Laskar Jihad in Indonesia, and the Abu Sayyaf in southern Philippines.

It is also noteworthy in the post-9/11 regional security scenario that governmental capacity and legitimacy have not been seriously undermined in ASEAN countries, that is, terrorism has not been able to topple the existing governments or alter significantly the political, economic and territorial *status quo*. This point is particularly pertinent in our assessment of the United States as the world's only super power since the end of the Cold War. As one specialist on Middle East politics aptly observes with reference to the ideological conflict between Islam and the West symbolized by 9/11: "The power of the USA as a military, economic and political power will not be destroyed or seriously weakened in this conflict."[21] Thus, regional ASEAN-led initiatives to stamp out the menace of international terrorism significantly depends for their success on coalition-building with the world's super power. This would necessarily entail the kind of support currently given to the United States through the establishment in Malaysia of the Southeast Asia Regional Centre for Counter-Terrorism (SEARCCT)[22] on 1 July 2003. This centre may well serve as the nucleus for fostering closer regional cooperation in the following areas identified by the Special ASEAN Ministerial Meeting on Terrorism held in Kuala Lumpur on 20–21 May 2002: intelligence, extradition, law enforcement, airport security, bomb detection, formation of national anti-terrorism units, and curbing arms smugglers and drug cartels. Yet, the strong assertion of the principle of non-interference in each other's internal affairs may well be ASEAN's stumbling block for effective anti-terrorist cooperation. To be effectively addressed, the post-9/11 agenda of problems obviously require ASEAN to adopt a more proactive role — a role built on a base quite different from the one upon which the regional grouping developed the "ASEAN Way".[23]

The challenge for ASEAN in the post-9/11 era, therefore, lies in its ability or inability to engage in non-traditional cooperation to address non-traditional threats to regional security. Thus, regional statesmen are currently attempting to revitalize the organization by redefining its original goals and mission by giving them a sharper focus and more concrete operational agendas. At the October 2003 Bali Summit, the ten ASEAN heads of state endorsed the Declaration of ASEAN Concord II, thereby mandating the progress towards an ASEAN Community in three spheres: ASEAN Security Community (ASC), ASEAN Economic Community (AEC), and ASEAN Socio-Cultural Community (ASCC). The renewed approach to regional cooperation and integration clearly accepts the notion that security is a multi-dimensional concept and must be addressed through economic, political, ideological, cultural and social strategies, given the fact that traditional approaches have been found somewhat wanting by 9/11 and post-9/11 terrorism. Nevertheless, despite the best intentions of ASEAN leaders to increase security cooperation, existing constitutional and institutional constraints may impede effective cooperation even when non-traditional security threats are concerned. Bali Concord II unequivocally reinstates the political-constitutional framework for the achievement of the ASC as follows:

> The ASEAN security Community shall abide by the UN Charter and other principles of international law and uphold ASEAN's principles of non-interference, consensus-based decision-making, national and regional resilience, respect for national sovereignty, the renunciation of the threat or use of force, and peaceful settlement of differences and disputes.[24]

In light of these constraints, it is understandable that some ASEAN members have been relying more and more on security cooperation and alliances with external powers to strengthen national and regional security. The threat of terrorism to international commerce, including the vital sea lanes of communication in Southeast Asia, is not only a matter of concern for states in the area, but also for external powers whose economic lifelines are linked to the region. In view of the fact that a quarter of the world's commerce and half of the world's oil supply pass through the Straits of Malacca each year, the major Asia-Pacific economic powers — China, Japan, Korea and the United

States — would continue to take a keen interest in Southeast Asian security. Thus any realistic and pragmatic approach by ASEAN to regional security must necessarily incorporate exogenous as well as endogenous variables that influence the regional security equation at any given time. The threat of radical or militant Islam to Southeast Asia is therefore best addressed by comprehensive security approaches as well as a combination of intra-regional and extra-regional cooperation.[25] Additionally, expanding on existing modalities of security cooperation involving both regional and external powers is yet another positive reflection of the security linkages Southeast Asia has with the rest of the world. Defence ministers of the Five Power Defence Arrangements (FPDA), namely Malaysia, Singapore, Britain, Australia and New Zealand, concurred at a meeting held after the conclusion of the Third Shangri-La Dialogue on Asia-Pacific Security in Singapore that intelligence exchanges on terrorism and other common security issues should be held regularly. As underscored by Singapore's Defence Minister Teo Chee Hean, "the FPDA continues to be a very relevant element of the regional security architecture and it is valued by all its members".[26]

CONCLUSION: EAST ASIAN AND SOUTHEAST ASIAN SECURITY IN THE TWENTY-FIRST CENTURY

Any objective evaluation of the success to date of ASEAN's anti-terror strategies must consider the fact that terrorism alone does not inform the entire agenda, perspective and priorities of regional security adopted by ASEAN members. In addition to the increased threat of global terrorism, Southeast Asia faces many other security challenges, many of which are unrelated to the 9/11 episode. These are often the offshoot of increased globalization and economic integration. Globalization has sharpened the cultural dimension of international relations in the sense that it has compelled state actors to decide on the correct mix of values pertaining to governance, democracy, and human rights needed to uphold the integrity of their societies. Are authoritarian or democratic regimes better equipped to deal with the challenges of globalization in terms of managing more open political and economic systems, encouraging competition, decreasing cronyism, increasing transparency and accountability, and structuring less racially oriented political models? Is political legitimacy sourced in democratic governance rather than in economic growth alone, or is this an irrelevant issue in globalization? Does 9/11 forebode an ongoing "clash of civilizations" as claimed by Samuel Huntington in his assessment of the post-Cold War world? Whatever might be the answer, it is obvious that the end of the Cold War has left in its wake an ideological vacuum that the remaining super power has been obliged to fill through doctrines of globalization and, now, after 9/11, counter-terrorism. To be sure, Southeast Asian security approaches, strategies, policies and responses are invariably intertwined with pressures emanating from this unipolarity.

Second, other non-traditional security threats also occupy the minds of regional statesmen, such as piracy, illegal migration, drugs, religious militancy and environmental pollution, etc., accentuated as these are by globalization. They present problems beyond the capacity of any single state to solve. As noted by Andrew Tan and Kenneth Boutin, "globalization has resulted in new security threats to communities and individuals that are transnational in character and are increasingly defined in social and economic terms."[27] Indeed, globalization on the negative side increases human vulnerability and insecurity, while on the positive side, it enables countries, particularly smaller and developing ones, to achieve economic progress beyond limits imposed by domestic resources and markets.[28]

Third, the Global Coalition against Terror — in which the leading role is played by the United States and its Anglo-Saxon partners Canada, Britain, and Australia — may have difficulty sustaining itself over time, in view of new international events, conflicts and crises in international relations. Just as the United States no longer talks about the ten-year period known as the Post-Cold War Era, new developments can, and are likely to supersede the Global War on Terror. It is already evident that when it comes to logistics and specifics, many coalition partners such as Germany and other European Union members are foot-dragging. Just as European priorities differ from America's, so too will regional concerns in Southeast Asia lead to disagreements with America, as the war on terrorism becomes protracted. Indeed, the London-based International Institute for Strategic Studies observes:

> the U.S. faces an enormous challenge in keeping allies and newfound friends focused on a war that may appear to conform to a purely American agenda … The transatlantic differences in threat perceptions prevalent before September 11 began to return in early 2002, as some European capitals appeared to be relaxing counter-terrorism postures while the U.S. remained on high alert.[29]

Furthermore, Paul Kennedy, the well-known Yale Professor of History, notes with respect to the American-led campaign against terrorism that while punishing raids against terrorist bases and brutal regimes might be understandable, "imperial policing by the American democracy is something else, politically divisive, and ultimately debilitating", and thus runs "counter to a reasoned strategy for the maintenance of American power in the twenty-first century".[30] Furthermore, the ongoing U.S.–North Korean confrontation over nuclear disarmament, as well as America's preoccupation with post-war Iraq will almost certainly complicate the Global War against Terror, particularly in terms of support from Muslim and Muslim-majority states. In this regard, both Indonesia and Malaysia have certain misgivings about the U.S.-led war since it does not fully take into account Southeast Asian priorities and national sensitivities.

Fourth, the issue of leadership transition will affect regional security in the twenty-first century, and indeed the Global War against Terror. Political transition in Southeast Asia is now ongoing, with personality-driven systems being progressively replaced by institutional mechanisms for the transfer of power, especially in non-communist states such as the Philippines (since the 1990s) and more recently, Indonesia. In Malaysia, leadership change took place on 31 October 2003 when Dr Mahathir turned over the reins of power to his successor, Abdullah Badawi. Mahathir's departure from the political scene after twenty-two years in power tests the extent to which power had been institutionalized to enable a smooth transition to a younger generation of leaders. Additionally, it tests the sustainability of the Malay-dominant power-sharing formula for the forty-five-year multi-ethnic Malaysian Federation. Any major political failure in this regard may trigger a less than optimistic scenario with potential consequences for national and regional stability: power struggles, economic decline and flight of foreign investments, inter-ethnic strife, centrifugalism, and religious militancy.

Fifth, international terrorists may try to penetrate "failed states" in Asia such as Afghanistan and Pakistan in Central Asia, and Indonesia and the Philippines in Southeast Asia, and more recently, the newly created East Timor that achieved independence on 20 May 2002. States with "receptive" Islamic populations such as Malaysia will also provide targets for recruitment by religious militants unable to satisfy their aspirations and needs within the nation-state system that they consider un-Islamic, and therefore evil and corrupt. Political Islam is here to stay. The issue is not whether political Islam is or is not a threat to the political and territorial *status quo*. In Islam, politics, religion, culture, economics and society constitute a whole. The real challenge for Muslim leaders is to ensure that Muslims practise moderation in politics, and avoid militancy in achieving political goals. It is in the interest of Muslims to view globalization not purely as a Western initiative, but as a process of cross-cultural fertilization and mutual learning, and as "a multi-source, multi-recipe global scene in the new millennium".[31]

Sixth, the regional security scenario at the dawn of the "Pacific Century" will still be characterized by American strategic preponderance. The United States will still be a dominant force shaping the security architecture of Southeast Asia and Pacific Asia, though more by default than by design, since other regional and global actors are relatively weak. The rise of China will most certainly be matched by countervailing power from the United States, Russia, Japan and India. Nevertheless, there is uncertainty as to whether the Chinese government can maintain ever-increasing growth rates alongside inequitable distributions of wealth and resources over disparate regions and provinces. Recent high levels of economic growth continue to hide the fact that the Communist Party of China's mandate to rule has not been seriously put to the test. Things might change if the democratization process is allowed to pursue its natural course — as has been the case in Taiwan. Incidentally, the China–Taiwan dispute, if unresolved, can involve undesirable consequences for regional security. Only a peaceful resolution based on principles of democracy and national self-determination for the twenty-two million people of Taiwan can contribute to consolidating the security architecture of East and Southeast Asia. In any event, Southeast Asia and ASEAN will attempt to benefit from the spin-offs from a developing China through bilateral and multi-lateral economic arrangements. The Chiang Mai Initiative of May 2000 represents one such bold effort to enact measures to avert another Asian Financial Crisis by linking the foreign exchange reserves of thirteen countries [ASEAN+3, that is, China, Japan and South Korea], which amount to almost US$1 trillion.[32] The Asian Financial Crisis of 1997–98 proved how economic collapse can trigger political instability and chaos and can create conditions for local and international terrorists to advance their agendas.

Seventh, ASEAN as a regional institution, and the ARF as a broader security process, will continue to face major constraints in their ability to respond swiftly to acts of terrorism in Southeast Asia due to at least four factors that characterize the regional security environment: (1) porous borders and generally weak immigration controls, with administrative requirements being nullified by corruption; (2) long-standing economic and trade links between Southeast Asia and Middle Eastern and South Asian countries, many of which operate outside normal financial channels not readily monitored by governments, and which in turn have facilitated fund transfers from the Middle East and South Asia to radical groups in the region; (3) widespread criminal activity including drug trafficking in the region, which in turn can facilitate the movement of resources by terrorists; and (4) the availability of large supplies of indigenously produced and imported weapons in Southeast Asia.[33]

Eighth, on the economic front, ASEAN leaders have demonstrated courage in moving beyond AFTA and the ASEAN Investment Area (AIA) envisaged under the 1998 Hanoi Plan of Action, in order to seize opportunities for regional development and prosperity arising from closer economic integration with China. The establishment of the ASEAN–China Free Trade Area over a ten-year period, which created a combined market of 1.7 billion people with a GDP of US$2 trillion and two-way trade of US$1.23 trillion, is among the innovative strategies adopted by the 37-year regional organization in dealing with the growing momentum of market liberalization and integration whilst maintaining a proactive approach to globalization. Indeed an economically strong ASEAN may emerge as a more powerful and equal actor *vis-à-vis* the European Union and the United States. Expansion of Ten+1 summit meetings with dialogue partners, particularly India, is yet another inclusive approach by ASEAN to balance political, economic, and strategic power to favour its own future role in Asia-Pacific regionalism. As mentioned earlier, two new initiatives launched at the ASEAN Summit in Bali in October 2003 reflect the efforts of the association to remain relevant to the current demands and aspirations of its citizenry: the ASEAN Economic Community (AEC) spearheaded by Singapore, the ASEAN Security Community (ASC) initiated by Indonesia, and the ASEAN Socio-Cultural Community (ASCC).[34] These efforts at political, economic and security integration at the sub-regional level facilitate closer cooperation with ASEAN's Northeast Asian neighbours — China, Japan and Korea. As these collective approaches bear fruit in the next decade, they will invariably help cement the "dynamic growth order in East and Southeast Asia".

In sum, globalization itself cannot be singled out as the root cause of terrorism. Terrorism has existed ever since humans began living in communities, societies and later nation states. The technological and communications revolution has globalized the means by which we comprehend and respond to terror. Control of the mass media has highlighted the immediacy and veracity of the impact of global terror. Additionally, American dominance invariably assigns priorities to American perceptions of world order that can be seen to be insensitive to the Muslim, and even the developing world at large. A proposal made in April 2004 by Admiral Thomas Fargo, Commander of U.S. Forces in the Pacific, to send U.S. troops to patrol the Straits of Malacca to unilaterally beef up defences against terrorist attacks on marine cargo, ships, and port infrastructure, drew a negative response from the littoral states, especially Malaysia and Indonesia. Malaysian Defence Minister Najib Razak warned that foreign forces in Southeast Asia may set back the region's ideological battle against "extremism and militancy" in radical Muslim groups.[35] The answer obviously lies in constructing shared perceptions of a world order in which cultural pluralism encourages multi-lateral approaches that emphasize not only the military component in combating global terror, but also the political, social, and economic and diplomatic strategies required to harmonize local, national, regional, and global identities in the search for peace, equity, and justice for all.

Notes

1   Pipob Udomittipong, "Rethinking Education on the Verge of Globalization", in *Religion, Politics and Society in South and Southeast Asia*, edited by N.N. Vohra and J.N. Dixit. Delhi: Konark Publishers Pvt. Ltd., 1998, p. 178.

2   Azyumardi Azra, "The Challenge of Political Islam", *PANORAMA: Insights into Southeast Asian and European Affairs*, no. 1 (2002): 25.

3   Ibid, p. 26.

4   See "ASEAN Way of Fighting Terrorism", issued by the ASEAN Secretariat, Jakarta, 2002. <http://www.aseansec.org/12776.htm>.

5   For details, see Dilip Hiro, *War Without End: The Rise of Islamist Terrorism and Global Response*, London and New York: Routledge, 2002, Appendix II: 481–85.

6   *Straits Times*, 3 April 2002, p. A7.

7   Ibid.

8   *Straits Times*, 30 July 2002, p. 1.

9   David Martin Jones and Mike Lawrence Smith, "Southeast Asia and the War Against Terrorism: The Rise of Islamism and the Challenge to the Surveillance State", in *September 11 and Political Freedom: Asian Perspectives*, edited by Uwe Johannen, Alan Smith and James Gomez. Singapore: Select Publishing Pte. Ltd., 2003, p. 162.

10 Jason F. Isaacson and Colin Rubenstein, eds. Islam in Asia: Changing Political Realities, London: Transaction Publishers, 2002, p. 228.

11 Rohan Gunaratna, *Inside Al Qaeda: Global Network of Terror*, London: C. Hurst & Co. (Publishers) Ltd., 2002, p. 193.

12 Farish A. Noor, "Globalization, Resistance, and the Discursive Politics of Terror, Post-September 11", in *The New Terrorism: Anatomy, Trends and Counter-Strategies*, edited by Andrew Tan and Kumar Ramakrishna. Singapore: Eastern Universities Press, 2002, p. 171.

13 Shamsul A.B., "The Sum of All Fears: The 'New' Islam in Southeast Asia". Unpublished paper presented at the ISEAS-SSAPS (Institute of Southeast Asian Studies, Singapore and Swedish School of Advanced Asia Pacific Studies) Seminar on "Globalization and Its Counter Forces", ISEAS, Singapore, 23–27 February 2004, pp. 13–14.

14 Gunaratna, op. cit.

15 Gordon Corera, "Inside the Terror Network", in *The Day that Shook the World:*

Understanding September 11th, edited by Jenny Baxter and Malcolm Downing. London: BBC News, 2001, p. 82.

[16] Baxter and Downing, op. cit.

[17] *Straits Times*, 5 February 2004, p. 1. For more on the implications of the Bali bombing, see Kumar Ramakrishna and See Seng Tan, eds. *After Bali: The Threat of Terrorism in Southeast Asia*, Singapore: World Scientific and Institute of Defence and Strategic Studies, Nanyang Technological University, 2003.

[18] *Straits Times*, 8 May 2002, p. 1.

[19] Statement by Singapore Deputy Prime Minister and Defence Minister, Dr Tony Tan, in connection with the December 2001 arrests of fifteen people under the Internal Security Act. *Straits Times*, 7 January 2002, p. 1.

[20] See "ASEAN Building United Front Against Terror", *Straits Times*, 21 May 2002, p. 6.

[21] Fred Halliday, *Two Hours the Shook the World: September 11, 2001: Causes and Consequences*, London: Saqi Books, 2002, p. 215.

[22] *Straits Times*, 2 July 2003, p. A7.

[23] For a comprehensive discussion of the non-interference principle and "flexible engagement", See Amitav Acharya, *Constructing a Security Community in Southeast Asia: ASEAN and the Problem of Regional Order*, London: Routledge, 2001, pp. 151–57.

[24] See *Declaration of ASEAN Concord II* (*Bali Concord II*), <http://www.aseansec.org/15160.htm> (retrieved on 15 January 2004), p. 3.

[25] The most recent evidence of the value of extra-regional cooperation in the war against terrorism and other transnational crimes is the expression of support for ASEAN's anti-terror efforts by the four Asian Dialogue Partners: China, Japan, South Korea and India at the 2003 Bali Summit. See *The Jakarta Post*, 9 October 2003, p. 1.

[26] See David Boey, "Military Drills to Include Terror Threat", *The Straits Times*, 8 June 2004, p. 1.

[27] Andrew T.H. Tan and Kenneth Boutin, eds., Non-Traditional Security Issues in Southeast Asia, Singapore: Select Publishing (for Institute of Defence and Strategic Studies), 2001, p. 5.

[28] Chia Siow Yue, "ASEAN in the Age of Globalization and Information" in *Reinventing ASEAN*, edited by Simon S.C. Tay, Jesus P. Stanislao and Hadi Soesastro. Singapore: Institute of Southeast Asian Studies, 2001, pp. 122–25.

[29] *Strategic Survey 2001/2002*, London: The International Institute for Strategic Studies, 2002, p. 7.

[30] Paul Kennedy, "Maintaining American Power: From Injury to Recovery", in *The Age of Terror: America and the World After September 11*, edited by Strobe Talbott and Nayan Chanda. New York: Basic Books, 2001, p. 77.

[31] Anthony B.L. Cheung, "Globalization versus Asian Values: Alternative Paradigms in Understanding Governance and Administration", *Asian Journal of Political Science* 8, no. 2 (December 2000): 13.

32   Joseph Y.S. Cheng. "Sino-ASEAN Relations in the Early Twenty-first Century",
     Contemporary Southeast Asia 23, no. 3 (December 2001): 437.
33   See article by Frank Frost, Ann Rann and Andrew Chin, "Terrorism in Southeast
     Asia", Department of the Parliamentary Library, Parliament of Australia, Canberra,
     7 January 2003. <http://www.aph.gov.au/library/intguide/FAD/sea.htm>.
34   See *Declaration of ASEAN Concord II* (*Bali Concord II*), <http:// www.aseansec.org/
     15160.htm> (retrieved on 15 January 2004), pp. 1–7.
35   "Malaysia Opposes US Help to Protect Malacca Straits": <http://www.politinfo.
     com/articles/article_2004_06_6_57578.html>.

11

ISLAM IN ASIA
The Way Ahead

Mohamad Abu Bakar

Islam as encapsulated in Samuel Huntington's *Clash of Civilizations and the Remaking of the New World Order* is a culture very much at variance with the Christian West. In his words, "both are universalistic, claiming to be the one true faith to which all humans can adhere. Both are missionary religions believing that their adherents have an obligation to convert non-believers to that one faith" (1996: 211). By alluding to "bloody borders" arising from their juxtaposition and encounter, he considers Islam not only as incongruous, but as being at odds with other ways of life. Huntington's simplistic rendering of history and international relations has won many a follower, not least among policymakers in the West searching for a bogey-man, following the collapse of the Soviet Union and the disintegration of world communism. Some Asian leaders, especially those of Sino-Confucian background, are equally swayed by his thesis in spite of their long-standing association with Muslims and their religion.

It is argued here that there is a coincidence of interests between Muslims and non-Muslims in the context of Asian development. While the convergence is not necessarily pervasive, given existing differences, the appropriation and incorporation of Islamic values on both sides should enable them not only to co-exist peacefully but also to progress together. No doubt, the adoption of Islamic principles will find support among Muslims with a fundamentalist bent, but nevertheless it may still accord with the interests of non-Muslims, provided they understand Islam as a total system.

ISLAM AS A RELIGION FOR ALL

Contrary to popular non-Muslim beliefs, Islam is not an exclusive religion intended for followers of the faith alone. It is a religion that addresses Muslims and non-Muslims alike. In fact, beyond that, it is also a creed that is concerned with the welfare of animals and insects, the well being of the plant world, and the whole environment. The Quran in categorical terms refers to Prophet Muhammad as "a mercy for the whole universe" (21: 107). Adherents of the faith who understand its religious teachings abide by them, even though throughout Muslim history there have been aberrations and deviations which all in all have damaged Islam's reputation as a religion of peace.

Having subscribed to the faith, Muslims are obliged to remain Muslims, come rain or shine. As the Quran puts it: "If anyone desires a religion other than Islam (submission to God), never will it be accepted" (111: 85). In living out this life, they are also enjoined to manifest their Islamness under all circumstances. "Verily, my prayers and my sacrifices, and my life and my death are all for God" (6: 163). In other words, their beliefs and actions are governed and circumscribed by the dictates of their religion. Islam is meant to play a definitive role. But such exclusivism stops there. Islam is also a religion for all.

It is incumbent upon Muslims to lead a positive life, "to do good and avoid evil" [*amal makruf nahi munkar*]. While it is true that Islam is a missionary religion, it is not hell-bent on forcing others to adopt the faith. It is stipulated that Muslim preachers (*dai'*) should "invite (all) to the way of your Lord with wisdom and goodly exhortation and argue with them in the best possible manner" (XVI: 125). In another verse, the Quran commands that "there should be no coercion in religion". Prophet Muhammad, as an embodiment of Quranic principles, respected Jews and Christians in his midst in spite of religious differences. Their places of worship were considered sacred and were safeguarded under Islamic rule, in line with the Quranic exhortation: "Revile not ye those whom they call upon besides Allah, lest they out of spite revile Allah in their ignorance" (VI: 108). Even *jihad*, the much talked about holy war in Islam, is partly a defensive war. In this context, the Quran explains: "Fight in the cause of God those who fight you, but do not transgress limits; for God loveth not transgressors" (11: 190–93). But, more importantly, it is an inner struggle intended for the betterment of oneself, essentially for the purification of the soul.

Islam as a matter of course does not view differences arising from the multiplicity of racial, cultural and religious practices as something unnatural.

God in his wisdom has "formed you into nations and tribes so that ye may know and be good to one another" (XLIX: 13), and on the basis of this Quranic reference, Muslims should not perceive human variety as a problem, but rather as a means for the establishment of a better universal society. By virtue of its universality and by the fact that it is not meant for any particular people or chosen race, Islam therefore should be in a position to address itself to all Asians. This is made all the more easy by the fact that a substantial number of the populace has long embraced Islam. Following centuries of Islamic proselytization, or *dakwah*, there are now Malaysians, Indonesians, Filipinos, Thais and Chinese who profess the religion, and who have adopted Islamic values. Religion permeates all aspects of their life, and shapes their attitudes towards others. Even non-Muslims amongst them have been exposed to certain aspects of the tenet. Apart from normal cultural encounters associated with racial co-existence, either within Muslim societies or in non-Muslim ones, there have also been cross-border interactions between peoples of different religions who have come together for trade and the like. In short, Islam is not alien to the Asian scene, and significantly predates Western thinking in the region.

The preoccupation with Islam shown by Asian Muslims means that they have properly imbibed Islamic culture, and as such already accept Islamic values as expressed in the Quran and the Sunnah. Such a disposition does not necessarily run counter to local or indigenous traditions. In fact, cultural encounters have enriched the Islamic way of life itself, as evidenced in the lives of the Malay Muslims of Malaysia. Taken as a whole, the admixture of Islamic beliefs and practices, and indigenous traditions has constituted a support system for the developmental process in the areas concerned. However, Islam's overtures may not have touched the lives of the majority of non-Muslims Asians. Propaganda against Islam following 9/11 for example, and notably the age-old stereotyping of the religion as being against progress, have not only distanced many of them from Islam and the Muslims, but have probably caused many of them to team up with the West to wage an anti-Islamic campaign. Together, they see the religion and its followers in the light of the conflicts Christians have had in the past with Muslims, especially their bloody encounters with adherents of the faith in Europe and the Middle East. Nevertheless, those who interact with Muslims in the region have had the opportunity to observe the operation of the Islamic belief-system at close quarters. In some cases, the presence of Muslims has had such a strong impact on society at large that Islam is no longer seen as a religion that militates against societal life.

ISLAM AND DEVELOPMENT

Development, be it political, socio-economic or socio-cultural, necessarily falls within the purview of Islam. As an encompassing system that deals with all facets of human existence, Islam has established parameters of its own concerning man's societal relations and his place in the universe. Since the whole idea of progress is not unrelated to spiritual and moral considerations, multi-dimensional development has to take place within the framework of divine principles and prophetic traditions. In the Islamic scheme of things, as one scholar observes, "development has a religious significance and religion has a significance for development" (Hassan Askari, 1986: 78). As such, each one of man's pursuits is deemed as worship, and he is accountable for his actions and is responsible for their moral consequences.

In this regard, man is entrusted with the role of God's vicegerent on earth. He is not only endowed with mental capacity and physical capability, but is also given the responsibility to realize and harness the resources of the world for the benefit of others. The following Quranic verses are illustrative: "Allah has made everything in the heaven and the earth subservient to man" (45: 13); "explore it therefore and seek of his bounty in it" (67: 15). For him as God's trustee, there is no escape from his chosen role. "When prayer is over, disperse in the world and search for the bounty of Allah" (62: 10). He is not supposed to forget his "share of the world" (28: 77). At the centre of the Islamic conception of development is the improvement of the quality of life. Respect for human dignity, the development of the individual's personality, the advancement of his material life, and concern for the physical environment all entail, among others, the defence of personal freedom, the provision of modern amenities such as public health and medical care, the eradication of poverty and the prevention of crime and suicide. Islam's preoccupation with the health of its followers is a manifestation of its concern with the growth of individuals and society at large.

Likewise, Islam also puts great emphasis on the development of education. In this respect, the Prophet in one of his sayings noted: "To seek knowledge is a religious duty for every Muslim, male and female". In another utterance, he stressed that "he who leaves his home in search of knowledge walks in the path of God". The acquisition of technical skills and technological know-how therefore is very much in line with Islamic teachings. Islam too is equally preoccupied with the betterment of the family and society as a whole. Family cohesiveness and the promotion of good values among society's members are greatly stressed. Societal harmony and collective morality are to be cultivated and pursued. While the acquisition of wealth is allowed, Muslims also have to take into account the welfare of others, who might, for example, fall prey to the operation of market forces. In utilizing and harnessing God-endowed resources, they have to care for the sufferings of fellow men. Islam is against monopolistic practices and the exploitation of labor. Those in power especially are responsible for maintaining order and harmony in society and nation. "Those who, if we establish them in the land, establish regular prayer and give regular charity, and enjoin good, forbid evil. And Allah is the end of affairs" (22: 41).

THE ASIAN WAY

Talk of "The Asian way", whatever that means, has a long history, but with the Asian values debate arising from the so-called Asian economic miracle, it has assumed additional importance. Coincidentally, the globalization of Islamic values as a function of the religious revival of the seventies and eighties has also led to a further contextualization of the issue. Under the circumstances, Islam, which has increasingly been seen as militating against the West, is perceived as an antagonistic religion and an ideology which has the potential to undermine national security. There is also the belief that a triumphant Islam in Muslim-majority countries will work its way in a deterministic fashion to reshape the political and social order, and substitute the existing dominant culture with its own civilizational paradigm. In heated discussions, the Asian Islamic past, with its concomitant pluralistic features and its celebration of diversity, was drowned in the controversy or simply dissociated from present-day Islam. At the very least, the introduction of Islamic banks, *halal* food and *Shariah*-based insurance systems are seen as attempts to carve up a Muslim space at the expense of others.

"The Asian Way" crystallized quickly to mean, or was conflated to denote, hard work, discipline, and sacrifice, qualities which were seen as major contributing factors to the rapid growth of Asian economies. Some protagonists of the Asian Way, very much overwhelmed by the success story of Japan, Taiwan, Singapore and Malaysia, considered other "Asian values" to have been equally crucial in making the region economically buoyant and resilient. Other virtues that were paraded include the importance of the family with its patriarchal values, and the associated teamwork that provided stability and aided the development process. There were also references to communitarian concern at the societal level, with its emphasis on the welfare of the group and personal ties. *Gotong royong,* or mutual help, was often cited as a manifestation of a typical kind of cooperative effort and communal solidarity. Unsurprisingly, certain Asian leaders also adopted the idea of "Asian values" for rationalizing their rule and policy, and even for justifying authoritarianism. To them, their achievements were the result partly of state intervention and partly of the collective discipline subsumed in the Asian tradition.

At issue is the integration of global tendencies with Asian local values, and related to that, the possible conflict between these values and Islam. Islam here is both an external and an internal factor. Since countries in the Asia Pacific are in the main of Sino-Confucian background, Islam as such is pitted against Buddhism, Taoism, Shintoism or Confucianism. With the agitated West already consumed by its conflict with the "new communism", as the rising tide Islam has been dubbed, and in view of the Asian Tigers' economic relationship with Western nations, the two issues have come to be inter-related. While most if not all of the affected countries are comfortable with their relationship with the West, Islam and Muslim peoples have come under greater scrutiny than ever before. Islam, which had flourished in their midst, now acquires agitational value to the extent that its very presence has created renewed cohesion amongst them. With 9/11, there has been a further demonization of Islam, and several Muslim societies are seen as safe havens for terrorists.

The antagonistic cross-cultural context thus produced is a challenging spectre for those who champion civilizational dialogue as a solution for various conflicts of our time. In seeking common ground between all groups concerned, the past will continue to be invoked, for all of them are rooted in history and in ancient traditions. However, the problems they face and the challenges they have to surmount are all related to the present: how to keep pace with the fast development of the rest of the world, and how to translate that into progress. While Islamic and Asian values generally forbid denial of material life, they both abhor and deplore actions that dehumanize man as a creation of God, taken in the pursuance of growth. Should the people of Asia succumb to Western didacticism, or allow the mutual incomprehension between certain segments of the Western world and the Muslim people to dominate their thinking?

THE DEVELOPMENT OF ISLAM AND ASIAN DEVELOPMENT

With the worldwide campaign against terrorism, a large number of Muslims and non-Muslims in the Asia Pacific have come to view Islamic movements and Muslim organizations in the area as part of singular world terrorism.

Even groups fighting for autonomy or a separate state, such as the Moro National Liberation Front (MNLF) and the Patani United Liberation Organization (PULO), both of which predate al-Qaeda, are increasingly seen as part of the Muslim terrorist network bent on destroying the political order, the social fabric and the economic structure of the region. External events that play on the prejudices of the West *vis-a-vis* Islam and Muslims have also convulsed the Asia Pacific to the extent that the religion is now perceived to have destabilizing effects on the nations involved.

Islam has been part of the Asia Pacific scene since its advent in the thirteenth century, and it is going to remain embedded in the development of the region, with or without 9/11. Muslims groups, ranging from governments in power to civil society organizations, will respond differently to outside challenges and internal opportunities, in making adjustments to change. On the one hand, there will be those who will work for the realization of the *Shariah* [Islamic Law], who will express millennialist sentiments, and who will exhort others to their orthodoxy. In affirming their faith and identity, they will struggle for greater adoption of their religious prescription in the administration and reconstruction of society. On the other hand, there will be those who will settle for something far less religious, perhaps by virtue of their minority status or marginalized position in society. They may engage in good governance at the most, but beyond that their concern will be for better living standards. In between these two, there will be factions who will exhibit a large variety of Islamic sentiments.

There is therefore a need to understand these various forms of Islamic expressions. That is a basic requirement. Failure to contextualize the development of Islam in the Asia Pacific will deprive its people of the opportunity to cultivate positive relations with Islam and Muslim inhabitants, and the Islamic world in general. Asian development, including attempts by various governments in the area to protect strategic concerns, will otherwise be adversely affected, which is what is presently happening in several parts of the region. However, there is a risk that moves to rectify the grievances of the Muslim populace may backfire. Where government actions are construed as oppressive, those on the receiving end are prone to retaliate, and their reactions may be perceived as part of, or may in fact evolve into, international terrorism.

Islam has occupied centre stage in the modern development of some predominantly Muslim countries, such as Saudi Arabia and Pakistan. Of late, Malaysia too has been pursuing Islamic goals. The establishment of interest-free banking and Islamic insurance systems, the incorporation of Islamic values in the administrative service, and the introduction of *halal* food and the like, are moves to restructure the national economy. It is all part of an Islamic path to development. Attempts have also been made by certain sectors to turn Islam into a source of modern culture. Not all of these measures have met with opposition from non-Muslims. In the case of Islamic banks, with its profit-sharing and loss-sharing arrangement, non-Muslims are able to utilize their facilities for their own benefit. Many amongst them have already subscribed to the innovations.

The presence of non-Muslims in Muslim-majority countries is not an impediment. The Islamic idea of progress with its emphasis on social justice, natural harmony and overall prosperity is a welcome feature by them. With the decline in morals, drug addiction, environmental degradation and the violation of human rights, any system of ethics compatible with the values of all those concerned, will not be directly rejected. Even non-Muslim practices such as the rearing of pigs and the acquisitive drive normally associated with them are not incompatible with the Islamic idea of statehood and governance. Islam does not prohibit religious activities. It allows private property and market competition. Now with the threat of SARS and bird flu affecting everyone in the Asia-Pacific region, cooperation between those concerned becomes all the more necessary.

ISLAM IN ASIA: THE WAY AHEAD

Islam is here to stay. With its commitment to development, it will remain a directing force and a major influence in the lives of many. While Islam as a religion operates within a certain set of rules, it is also open to change. The Islamic art of improvization not only allows accommodation but also the adoption of new strategies. Islam in this context is dynamic and yet conservative. Muslims therefore have to continuously design ways to adjust to the development around them. Otherwise, their presence as an instrument of moral authority will become irrelevant.

Since Muslims and non-Muslims share certain common values, a convergence of cultures is not impossible. With or without the adoption of Western-style democracy and the operation of a market economy, moral principles governing human relations in Asia must remain in place. Respect for authority, the promotion of civil society, and the importance of the family, are some of the perennial concerns of all Asians. At present, due to the lack of nuanced information about Islam, many non-Muslims have become uncomfortable with the Muslims in their midst. The commonalities that should bond them are being forgotten, while their differences are been exploited as never before.

References

Aidit Ghazali. *Development, An Islamic Perspective*, Subang Jaya: Pelanduk Publications, 1990.

John Esposito, ed. *Islam and Development*: Syracuse University Press, 1980.

Hassan Askari. Religion and Development: Search for Conceptual Clarity and New Methodology — The Special Case of Islam *The Islamic Quarterly* 30, no. 2 (1986).

Hashim Makaruddin, ed. *Democracy, Human Rights, EAEC and Asian Values* (selected speeches by Dr Mahathir Mohamad). Vol. 1, Subang Jaya: Pelanduk Publications, 1995.

Steven J. Hood. "The Myth of Asian-Style Democracy". *Asian Survey* 38, no. 9 (1998).

Inamul Haq. "Islam, Modernism and Development". *Journal of the Research Society of Pakistan* 37, no. 3 (2000).

Huntington, Samuel P. *The Clash of Civilizations. The Remarking of World Orders.* New York: Simon & Schuster, 1996.

Mohamad Abu Bakar. "Islam, Civil Society and Ethnic Relations in Malaysia". In *Islam and Civil Society*, edited by Nakamura Mitsuo et al. Singapore: ISEAS, 2001.

———. "Islam, Malaysia and Europe: Perceiving The Past, Perfecting The Future". In *The Islamic World and Europe*, edited by Ismail Hj. Ibrahim and Abu Bakar A. Majeed. Kuala Lumpur: IKIM, 1998.

Muddathir Abd al-Rahim. *Islam and Non-Muslim Minorities. Just World Trust*, Penang, 1997.

Muhammad Umar Chapra. Objectives of the Islamic Economic Order. In *Islam Its Meaning and Message*, edited by Kurshid Ahmad. London: Islamic Council of Europe, 1975.

Neher, Clark D. Asian Style Democracy. *Asian Survey* 34, no. 2 (1994).

Sheridan, Greg. *Asian Values Western Dreams*. Sydney: Allen & Unwin, 1999.

Lily Zubaidah Rahim. "In Search of the 'Asian Way': Cultural Nationalism in Singapore and Malaysia". *Commonwealth and Comparative Politics* 36, no. 3 (1998).

INDEX